Extreme Preemption

Extreme Preemption

Ignite Your Safety

Peter E. Schultz

Old Julian Press

RAMONA, CALIFORNIA

Extreme Preemption by Peter E. Schultz

Old Julian Press
PO Box 2269
Ramona, CA 92065

Website: ExtremePreemption.com
E-mail: Contact@OldJulianPress.com

Copyright © 2017 by Peter E. Schultz

All rights reserved. This book or parts thereof may not be reproduced in any form, stored in any retrieval system, or transmitted in any form by any means — electronic, mechanical, photocopy, recording, otherwise — without permission from the publisher, except as permitted by U.S. copyright law.

ISBN: 978-1-946366-01-6 (Paperback)

Library of Congress Control Number: 2017916927

Printed in the United States of America

To book Peter Schultz for a speaking engagement,
email him at Contact@OldJulianPress.com.

This book is dedicated to all Defenders who protect Innocents and our self-defense rights.

Love to my wife who cheers my ideas with great affirmation.

Many thanks to my students who re-enroll in new training, as we learn from each other.

Contents

Introduction 13
Chapter 1 — Fundamental X-Pree
Nuggets, Obliviolence 17
Ground Rules 19
What is X-Pree? 20
Preemption in History 23
Lessons for Today 35
X-Pree for Tomorrow 36
ITOTR 38
X-Pree Framework 40
Topic Discussion 1 43

Chapter 2 — Your Mission: Train
Weapon 46
Awareness 47
Avoidance, Breath 49
De-Escalation 50
Bare Hands 51
Legs & Feet 53
Adopted Tools 54
Bat 55
Cane 56
Communication Guards 57
Firearm 60
Fire Extinguisher & Hose 69
Flashlight 70
Knife 72
Kubotan 73
Marshmallows 74
Pepper Spray 74
Security Systems 76
Tactical Pen 77
Vehicle 78
Summary 78
Topic Discussion 2 81

Chapter 3 — Your Mission: Detect
Is Detection Possible? 83
Detection Basics 85
Personal Goals 86
"What?" Not, "Why?" 88
Flavors of Villain 89
Breadcrumbs 97

Chapter 3 (continued)
Slave Trader 99
Terror Villain 102
Active Shooter 106
Child Slayer 108
Rapist 111
Intimate Demon 113
Elder Abuser 116
Internet Thief 119
Cyber Bully 123
Bushwhacker 126
Housebreaker 127
Summary 128
Topic Discussion 3 131

Chapter 4 — Your Mission: Preempt
Safety Bubbles 133
One-Second Law 136
Preemption Basics 136
Summary 139
Topic Discussion 4 141

Chapter 5 — Scenarios 1 to 10
1 - Rape, Home 143
2 - Espionage, Corporate 145
3 - Accidental Shooting, Inner City 146
4 - Bushwhackery, Street 148
5 - Abduction, Park 150
6 - Rape, Nightclub 151
7 - Mass Murder, School 153
8 - Carjacking, Mall 156
9 - Robbery, Parking Lot 157
10 - Burglary, Home 158
Topic Discussion 5 161

Chapter 6 — Scenarios 11 to 20
11 - Verbal Abuse, Home 163
12 - Mass Murder, Church 164
13 - Bullying, School 167
14 - Robbery, Mall 168
15 - Vishing, Home 170
16 - Cyberbullying, Home 170
17 - Attack, Golf Course 171

Contents

Chapter 6 (continued)
18 - Phishing, Online **172**
19 - Burglary, Home **173**
20 - Abuse, Parking Lot **174**
Topic Discussion 6 **177**

Chapter 7 — Scenarios 21 to 30
21 - Groping, Parking Lot **179**
22 - Cyberbullying, School **180**
23 - Physical Abuse, Home **181**
24 - Burglary, Home **182**
25 - Bushwhackery, Street **183**
26 - Robbery/Knife, Street **184**
27 - Credit Card Fraud, Home **184**
28 - Robbery, Store **185**
29 - Confrontation, Street **186**
30 - Robbery/Knife, Park **187**
Topic Discussion 7 **189**

Chapter 8 — Scenarios 31 to 40
31 - Carjacking, Street **191**
32 - Robbery Error, ATM **192**
33 - Confrontation, Parking Lot **193**
34 - Rape, Home **194**
35 - Slavery, Apartment **195**
36 - Attack/Knife, Street **196**
37 - Carjacking, Parking Lot **197**
38 - Carjacking Error, Parking Lot **199**
39 - Robbery/Knife, Parking Lot **200**
40 - Slavery, Church **201**
Topic Discussion 8 **203**

Chapter 9 — Scenarios 41 to 50
41 - Molestigation, Gas Station **205**
42 - Mass Murder, Mall **206**
43 - Road Rage, City **207**
44 - Employee Termination, Office **208**
45 - Confrontation, Club **209**
46 - Low Fuel, City **210**
47 - Mass Murder, Restaurant **211**
48 - Abduction, Street **212**
49 - Confrontation, Party **213**

Chapter 9 (continued)
50 - Bare Hand Attack, Park'g Lot **214**
Topic Discussion 9 **217**

Chapter 10 — Scenarios 51 to 60
51 - Elder Abuse, Care Facility **219**
52 - Slavery, Junior High **220**
53 - Attack/Knife, Gas Station **221**
54 - Active Shooter, Office **222**
55 - Carjacking, Home Garage **224**
56 - Adultery, Anywhere **225**
57 - Bullying, School **226**
58 - Verbal Abuse, Office **227**
59 - Low Fuel, Rural **228**
60 - Theft, Gas Station **229**
Topic Discussion 10 **231**

Chapter 11 — Scenarios 61 to 70
61 - Confrontation, Parking Lot **233**
62 - Elder Abuse, Home **233**
63 - Child Slaying, Home **235**
64 - Bushwhackery, Home **236**
65 - Bushwhackery, Park **237**
66 - Sexual Harassment, Office **238**
67 - Attack, Park **240**
68 - Mass Murder, Office **241**
69 - Bushwhackery, Parking Lot **243**
70 - Sextortion, Online **244**
Topic Discussion 11 **247**

Chapter 12 — Scenarios 71 to 80
71 - Child Abuse, Store **249**
72 - Child Slaying, Junior High **250**
73 - Abduction, Park **251**
74 - Gun Storage, Home **253**
75 - Auto Fire, Highway **253**
76 - Bushwhackery, Home **255**
77 - Grab & Grope, Club **256**
78 - Slavery, College **257**
79 - Attack, Wheelchair **258**
80 - Attack, Parking Lot **259**
Topic Discussion 12 **261**

Chapter 13 — Scenarios 81 to 90
81 - Rape, Anywhere **263**
82 - Attack, Laundry Room **264**
83 - Bushwhackery, Alley **265**
84 - Elder Abuse, Home **266**
85 - Phishing, Online **267**
86 - Terrorism, Market **268**
87 - Vishing, Home **270**
88 - Bushwhackery, Sidewalk **270**
89 - CC Skimming, Gas Station **271**
90 - Attack/Knife, Anywhere **272**
Topic Discussion 13 **273**

Chapter 14 — Scenarios 91 to 100
91 - Attack/Handgun, Anywhere **275**
92 - 911 Call **276**
93 - Burglary, Toolshed **277**
94 - CC Skimming, Store **277**
95 - Snakebite, Garden **278**
96 - Robbery, Vacation **279**
97 - Vehicle Attack, Vacation **280**
98 - Drugs, Teenage Overnight **282**
99 - Trespassing, Rural Property **283**
100 - Attack Error, City Street **284**
Topic Discussion 14 **287**

Concluding Remarks **289**
About Defenders **293**
About the Author **295**
Endnotes **297**

Introduction

Defender,

Envision your private security force. You get up in the morning and greet personal guards who have been at their posts all night. Then, you leave home for an active day, knowing that a well-trained team is ready to defeat any threat to your safety. Return home relaxed and refreshed, expecting another great sleep, confident that your security heroes will deal with any danger which occurs during the night.

Not everyone has a personal protection unit of former Green Beret, Raider, or SEAL team members. So, for the rest of us, what can we do to really be safe? Everyday safety is not exclusively available to a special class of people. You can learn protection practices used by America's elite Defenders.

Be your own personal security force.
Self-reliance is the heart of present-day safety.

You're about to discover simple methods to radically dominate everyday safety. Learn to defend yourself using *Extreme Preemption*. Your self-sufficient self-defense is not only possible, not only a nice option; it's required in today's world. Response time for sheriff's deputies might be twenty minutes, or more, where you live. Even if your urban home is only two minutes from the local police station, self-reliance is still a necessity.

In his speech on December 18, 1963, Martin Luther King Jr. gave us this famous counsel,
> "...while it may be true that morality cannot be legislated, behavior can be regulated. It may be true that the law cannot change the heart but it can restrain the heartless." [1]

Unfortunately, we are now living in an era when attempts to curb crime are falling short of legislators' well-intended objectives. In many jurisdictions law enforcement resources are meager, and the current number of laws in place are choking our criminal justice system with complexity.

Introduction

Though his overture was made at a time when laws and norms were deeply mired in racial discrimination, Dr. King's consistent plea for justice through nonviolence is still valuable for us today, with just one twist. Regardless of the volume of legislative actions, we can live safe individual lives simply by making it more difficult for criminals to victimize us.

As we advance from being easy targets to becoming challenging targets, perhaps the criminal mindset will also advance. For example, as we make stealing for a living more troublesome for the thief, he might supplement his lifestyle of thievery with some honest work. Or, he might decide to find easier prey by moving to a more socially tolerant environment — maybe Antarctica! Let's remain hopeful.

This book is about your safety solutions. It presents *Extreme Preemption*, a.k.a. *X-Pree*. You and I will explore what it is, how it's legal in today's world, and why it ignites all elements in your safety plan.

Then, we'll carefully construct a framework which you can use in any situation where your safety might be threatened. Is there a one-size-fits-all safety solution for everyone? If so, is it difficult? How do we implement it? Answers to these important questions are straight ahead. Along the way we'll examine a variety of self-defense tools and how you can use each one.

Finally, we will explore 100 scenarios based on real events. Our examination of effective *X-Pree* solutions, versus what doesn't work well in real life, opens up safety options for you which you might not believe are achievable. These opportunities are not only possible for you right now, they're begging for you to claim them.

My company's mission is to "Improve Your Safety by Self-Defense Education." My mission in this book is to show you that *Extreme Preemption* radically enhances personal, corporate, and even national security!

It's not complicated. Your life and the lives of people near you are sacred. You have the right and the responsibility to defend those lives by basic self-defense. It's unalienable, built into you naturally.

I don't train citizens to be murderers. I train ordinary Defenders to be safer while they do ordinary things in their everyday lives. My students know they can defend themselves if they are forced into a fight. They live more peaceful lives than people who live in fear.

Your ability to defend lives by *Extreme Preemption* begins with one thing — your decision to use the framework in this book. Your age, fitness level, and stature are not as important as your inflexible decision to never become a victim. That determination is the foundation of your safety. Then, watch *X-Pree* quickly become the igniting force in all of your safety plans.

You are the wave of a much safer future. By choosing to study this book you are a Defender, perhaps with some room to grow. You are a Defender because you have the heart to defend yourself and other innocent people who are close to you. Ignite your safety now!

P. E. Schultz

Chapter 1 - Fundamental X-Pree

Nuggets

Extreme Preemption is the result of ten years of intense research, training, and teaching by me. Along the way I have become acquainted with and studied other professionals' work. They have expertise in the nugget principles which meld together to form the refined golden crown, *Extreme Preemption*. Their permission to freely share copyrighted content in this book is truly a privilege. Your support of their work is well-deserved.

Normally, the probability of your actual study of sources in a bibliography is lower than waking up tomorrow and finding an adult Woolly Mammoth sipping coffee on your patio. In light of this, I strongly encourage you to invest in the resources which are cited in my "Endnotes," you guessed it, at the end of this book. As your *X-Pree* lead instructor, I want you to always have the best learning implements. As of this writing, the nuggets here are worthy of your time and supporting money when it's appropriate.

Obliviolence

There is a reckless perspective which needs to be corrected. Many people falsely assume that studying self-defense is synonymous with training in neanderthal head-bashing or the uncontrolled spraying of neighborhoods with bullets. Sadly, these misconceptions are certainly pushing many thoughtful people away from learning true personal protection. Those who resist addressing real threats to their safety can move so far away emotionally, that the mere mention of "defense" is both frightening and disgusting to them. Our modern culture is demanding much more from all of us, students as well as instructors. Unwarranted knuckle-dragging stereotypes need to be replaced, because they help precipitate at least one dangerous condition in the general population — obliviolence.

CHAPTER 1 - FUNDAMENTAL X-PREE

Obliviolence is our term for the common human condition of being oblivious to violence (pronounced oh-BLI-vee-oh-lents). One of the world's loveliest places is obliviolence. In fact, it's a wonderful spot where most people prefer to be. Let's all live out our days without a whisper of violence, without reports of even the threat of violence! I sincerely want to be there, and you probably do also. But, how does obliviolence measure against the real world? Not too well.

What is most challenging about obliviolence is its one-sided nature. As potential civilian recipients of violence, most of us don't want to hear about it, ever. Violence hurts and kills, so discussing it can be as distasteful as gulping down a big mug of used motor oil.

Our problem arises from the presence of folks who are willing to deliver violence to us — Villains. They are comfortable with performing acts which hurt and kill other people. We have Villains scattered on the planet who are ready to deliver violence to us without prior notice. So, chronic cases of obliviolence by innocent folks (Innocents) are attractive opportunities for victimization by Villains.

Only one instance of violence for an Innocent can be life-changing, and not for the better. It is best for Innocents to follow these general steps:
1. Become aware that violence is real; not necessarily commonplace, but it is real.
2. Prepare to meet violence with an effective self-defense.
3. Live confidently, knowing that if violence is delivered they can preempt it.

Widespread inoculation with these three vaccines is our medicine to eradicate obliviolence. Truly balanced living is blending our knowledge of the possibility of violence, coupled with our knowledge of sure defenses against violence. Then we can replace worry with peace of mind, because we're ready to meet violence instantly, head-on. At that point, our desire to live in oblivion about violence becomes silly and undesirable.

Humans are different from other earthly species. We need to learn to defend ourselves — we aren't born with self-defense skills. No, dramatic crying to get your way doesn't count. To some extent, obliviolence goes along with our defenseless nature from birth.

Perhaps you are already free of obliviolence. Congratulations! You have a distinct advantage in pursuing a safer life. On the other hand, if you're harboring a strain of obliviolence, you should enjoy a perceptible recovery during your study here. You might not experience an immediate cure, but it will be a noticeable, solid progression as *Extreme Preemption* works healing in your life.

Ground Rules

Many dedicated, highly skilled people work in the field of security who are at their posts 24/7 in order to keep us safe. They deserve our continuous gratitude. At the same time, some professional security jargon has progressed to such a degree of imagination that we wonder about the inventive effort it took to get us here.

Today's security-gifted professional class makes its communication efficient by the artful use of acronyms — those pesky words made of letters, each representing a word. Here's a hypothetical statement, "Within NAEMS, we leveraged MAICS to help EACs run more efficiently." Translated, this might mean "Within the North American Event Management System, we leveraged all Multiagency Intelligence Coordination Systems to help the Emergency Action Centers run more efficiently."

In the heat of a critical event where emergency personnel are responding as fast as possible, those acronyms save precious seconds of communication time. For the rest of us, let's just leave them alone. In other words you are safe from them, for now. I give you just a few, as memory aids.

Keeping all content here in its simplest form is another strict regulation. Our next sacred rule in this book is the minimal use of **Tactical** terms. Your understanding of the everyday value of this content is vastly more important than washing over you with **Tactical** jargon. Forging ahead, we now look closely at *Extreme Preemption*. As we proceed, forgive any **Tactical** slip of the tongue.

CHAPTER 1 - FUNDAMENTAL X-PREE

What is *X-Pree*?

Many folks still remember one of the first encounters America had with "preemption." It was a disappointing experience. In front of the ancient black and white TV, we gathered to watch 1960's shows which we believed held immense cultural value. Ok, that's what we thought.

Settled in, with foil-cooked popcorn ready, and all commercials ended, we waited for the show theme song to start. If you lived in those years go ahead, hum one of them right now. Here we go... That's it! You remember! Don't worry, your ear worm will pass within a few hours.

Then... Oh no! Not tonight! That dreaded voice-over piped up, "Our regularly scheduled program will not be seen..." Because, it was P-R-E-E-M-P-T-E-D! Topping off an already intolerable situation, my family had a total of three TV channels from which we could pick a show; that is, if the aluminum antenna mounted on our roof still worked properly.

Fortunately, preemption is one of our best friends today. It is an indispensable element of our lives. In the context of self-defense, preemption is not only desirable, it is inseparable from our consistent ability to defend ourselves. *Extreme Preemption*, or *X-Pree*, brings us that sweet peace of knowing that we're safe, really safe.

You probably never wake up proclaiming, "What a beautiful morning! I think I'll learn more about preemption today!" It's a term which doesn't get nearly as much attention as other p-words, such as "passionate," "paintbrush," or "pistachios." So, let's take a close look at *preemption*.

We begin with a few basics about timing. Study of some relevant words gives us a clearer understanding of the essence of *preemption*. Here are a couple of formal definitions which are valuable:
1. *the act of purchasing [taking] before others* [2]
2. *a prior seizure or appropriation: a taking possession before others* [3]

Villains rarely set appointments with their intended victims. Street attacks are usually ambushes. Attackers don't organize flash mobs for group assaults, because no one would likely show up. They count on surprise and quick, heavy use of force to get control of their victims.

Ponder this scenario:
> Innocent is caught by Villain while she's taking a walk. Then he punches and stabs her. As soon as Villain gains control of Innocent, his next steps might include rape, kidnapping, robbery, or just a hearty chuckle about the dominance he has over Innocent.

Applying Definitions 1 and 2 to Innocent's safety, here's the principle we're looking for:
> Innocent claims her safety before Villain can get it. Before Villain works his plan to steal her safety, Innocent takes possession of it.

That's an excellent definition of *X-Pree*, giving us this much more refreshing scenario:
> Villain's intentions are discovered by Innocent before his attack. Then, Innocent launches some kind of protective counter action — her counter attack.

In this new scenario, there is a high probability that Villain will be slowed down and even defeated by Innocent.

Sudden disruption of Villain's hurtful plan is classic preemption!

What if Innocent is moderately skilled in the use of some kind of self-defense tool? Then Innocent will be able to preempt Villain's attack by putting a more potent legal attack on Villain. One classic idiom illustrating preemption is "beating someone to the punch." How appropriate! Please raise your hand if you like this one. Yes, a room full of hands! Thank you.

Common synonyms for *preempt* are *appropriate, commandeer, confiscate, seize,* and *take*. In every instance, the concept of preemption is accompanied by some version of positive action. It's fascinating to note our opposite terms for *preempt* are *fail, forfeit, lose, relinquish,* and *surrender*.[4] They all reflect inaction or submission.

As you read this book, innocent people are surrendering their safety for absolutely no worthwhile reason. This is very likely because they simply don't know how to preempt an attack. When we're confronted with danger, without a self-defense framework most of us don't know what to do. Our lack of understanding then leads to fear. In the state of fear, real danger resides. Unchecked fear brings us hesitation or freezing in the face of a threat to our safety. In this condition of waiting, we are truly inactive and vulnerable to injury.

Our lack of self-defense knowledge is not a crime. It's only a void. Our good news is this; all of us can individually fill that vacuum with a little skill in preemption. Knowing what to do, when to do it, and being committed to do the doing as needed — well, that is action!

When we add *SPEED* to our action, we get *Extreme Preemption*. You might be thinking, "Oh, I can never do that." Yes, you can. Absolutely, you can. In the face of a modern criminal attack, you must do that.

We will look very closely at the *X-Pree* framework throughout this text. Your ability to defend life by *Extreme Preemption* begins with one essential thing, your commitment to do it.

You must commit to actually defending yourself or someone near you.

Later in the book, I'll show you exactly how to employ *X-Pree* by offering a variety of precise defense tactics. As we progress through the text, I'm not withholding key info to tease you. There is a path of logic which we need to follow in order for *X-Pree* to make sense. Following this line of reasoning will enable you to understand its genuine value, making it your own.

Many folks are afraid of defending themselves. Even a little self-defense is terrifying to them. If you are one of those people, you're not alone! All seasoned Defenders in military and law enforcement roles also experience some degree of fear. In the face of radical danger, you will certainly be afraid. Rest easy. There are specific ways to not only manage your fear, but use it to your great advantage. You will read about these methods later.

Civilized people don't hunger for the sport of injuring others, even in self-defense. Your distaste for working an injury on someone else is the

trademark of those who are sane and humane. However, as you will see, there are circumstances in which you have only two choices:
1. Use every method at hand to defend yourself.
2. Do nothing and be injured or killed.

Prepare to experience an awakening which will give you confidence in all areas of your life. Your worry about safety will be replaced by a calm, strong self-assurance that you can navigate through everyday life with an inner peace which is unshakeable.

Preemption in History

Preemption is a critical concept in self-defense, but it's not new and can be traced far back in human history. There are actually innumerable occasions where preemptive use of force has saved human lives in both lesser known and high profile cases. Here are some milestone instances that deserve our attention. Some of these events illustrate employed preemption. Others show the consequences of the absence of preemption.

You might wonder why I point out events which are national and international in scope. How do they relate to preemption on a personal scale? Look closely at the principles entwined in each case, and you will have your answer. If you are a legal scholar, don't rush into a nervous breakdown yet. International law is not synonymous with individual rights. We are reviewing some events here as illustrations of the presence and absence of preemption. These few examples are listed in chronological order.

c.1420 BC

In the Bible, early Mosaic law gives us a glimpse of self-defense principles:
> "If the thief is found breaking in, and he is so struck that he dies, there shall be no guilt for his bloodshed. If the sun has risen, there shall be guilt for his bloodshed." [5]

Today's Castle Doctrine is founded on this ancient principle. It insulates a Defender from prosecution if that person believes the intruder presents an unknown danger to people who occupy the space that has been invaded. In this context, the resident of a home can use preemptive force, even deadly force, to defend the home at night: without a detailed analysis of the intruder's intent, without knowledge of thoughts in the intruder's mind, and without waiting for personal injury by the intruder.

When exercising self-defense, a measurable delay by the Defender can result in immediate injury or death of an Innocent. Castle Doctrine insulates the Defender from a large array of unknowns.

1651

Thomas Hobbes, an Englishman, published the book titled *Leviathan* (abbreviated). Hobbes finished his treatise during the English Civil War (1642-1651). He proposed the best solution for social unrest is a very strong, central government. Other legal scholars at the time probably threw a tantrum over Hobbes' infatuation with this system, but compared to the chaos of his day the potential stability offered by a well-anchored state authority was attractive to some people.

What is most significant for us today is that *Leviathan* includes the first formal use of the term "self-defense." Unrelated but coincidentally, in 1651, a Russian man charged with homicide reportedly made a plea for self-defense.[6] Although mention of this is a short excursion away from our primary topic, it's vital to understand that the legal roots of self-defense, including preemption, run deep in human history.

1770

Early in American history, preemption played a colorful role in the defense of nine British soldiers. They were surrounded by an angry, aggressive mob of over three hundred civilians in Boston. Verbal threats were shouted at the soldiers. Various objects were thrown at them. Shortly after one of their own was knocked down, the British guards fired into the crowd. Five civilians died and more were wounded. This event is known as the Boston Massacre on March 5, 1770.

Those British soldiers reluctantly preempted their own serious injury by firing into the mob. Remarkably, one of America's primary founders successfully defended the soldiers against the charge of murder, making a strong case for their self-defense rights. This might seem abominable to us today, but John Adams' passion for the rule of law was apparently more preferable to him than popularity with his fellow patriots.

Facts in the case proved Adams to be entirely correct. Seven out of nine of his British clients were acquitted, two found guilty of manslaughter. What about his damaged reputation? In an era when honor was paramount, public opinion of John Adams was sufficient to get him elected as the second U.S. President — as a man of solid integrity.

1837

An event occurred which cemented preemption, or "anticipatory self-defense," into the large forum of international law. People who occupied the area of present-day Ontario, Canada, revolted against the British government. While the U.S. did not openly take sides in the squabble, some Americans aided the revolt by moving supplies and troops on the Caroline, a steamboat navigating in the Great Lakes region.

After discovering what the Caroline's crew was up to, some members of the Royal Navy entered the U.S. waters and destroyed the Caroline on the Niagara River. All of the ship's cargo and an American were lost when the burning boat went over the Niagara Falls. Hostility boiled over in more skirmishes over the next few years.

In 1842 Daniel Webster, U.S. Secretary of State at the time, arranged a treaty with Britain's Lord Ashburton. In the proceedings, the 1837 incident known as the Caroline Affair was addressed. Britain argued that their preemptive attack on the Caroline was one of self-defense. Webster claimed that the British would have to cite the following proof in which the necessity of their self-defense was,
> "most urgent and extreme" and "leaving no choice of means and no moment of deliberation." [7]

It is a substantial stretch of imagination that the British attack actually met that requirement, but Webster's rules of justification for self-defense have evolved into the "Caroline Test," a component of our present day customary international law. As you will see later in this chapter, the same components cited by Daniel Webster are included in our argument for personal use of force today.

CHAPTER 1 - FUNDAMENTAL X-PREE

1939

One of history's extreme absences of preemption was Arthur Neville Chamberlain's diplomacy-based foreign policy. During his term as U.K.'s Prime Minister (1937-1940) Chamberlain acted to appease Germany with the expressed hope that the Nazis would find their place in a peaceful alliance with the rest of Europe. This collective stall of preemptive military action against Germany's aggression proved to be disastrous, costing over 60 million lives in World War II.

Legal scholars still debate the value which preemption would have brought to the world in that day. How would Britain have justified its attack on Germany without a long list of proven atrocities committed by Nazis throughout Europe? What other legal measures pursued by the international community might have reigned in Hitler's addiction to domination? Seeing obvious answers to both of these questions, what would have spurred the international community into action?

In the mid-twentieth century, as well as today, we see governments balk at their opportunities to take action against known threats. Germany's power had already been crippled in World War I. Employment of only moderate constraints on Germany could have legally stopped its remilitarization.

In retrospect Paul Joseph Geobbels, Adolf Hitler's Minister of Propaganda, gave us an honest but chilling metaphor in 1940. This statement from his journal has been quoted perhaps as many times as he whitewashed his atrocities:

> "They could have suppressed us. They could have arrested a couple of us in 1925 and that would have been that, the end. No, they let us through the danger zone... They let us alone and let us slip through the risky zone, and we were able to sail around all dangerous reefs. And when we were done, and well armed, better than they, then they started the war!"

Here we have one of history's most ruthless deceivers personally testify for the deadly consequences of a delayed defense. With innumerable factors to consider, it's no wonder that preemptive action by any nation might be delayed. It is the nature of civilized people to resist deadly counter attacks. On the international stage, there is usually much time for complex debate.

In the realm your personal self-defense, fractions of seconds are critical.

1944

Raphael Lemkin, a Polish attorney, is credited with early use of the word "genocide" — the intentional destruction of a homogeneous group of people. He was an early advocate for the prevention of genocide. As a result of passionate lobbying by Lemkin, in 1948 the newly formed United Nations agreed that genocide should be classed as an international crime.

In addition to the Holocaust started in 1933, the world has been horrified by attempted human extermination on at least twenty occasions in modern history. This unthinkable crime has resulted in millions of ruthless murders on six continents.

How is the mass killing of innocent civilians relevant to preemption and our individual self-defense? Answer: It's a blasting siren warning us about imminent danger — in this case, it's enormous in scope. We will cover this concept in great detail in the chapter *Your Mission: Detect*. For now, remember this: Whenever any entity (belligerent national leader or obnoxious neighborhood bully) spouts threats of radical dominance and control of a person or people, there is a high probability that bad things are coming to the targeted victim. Warning signs always exist.

On a national level or a personal level, we might wonder if these signs are difficult to detect. Their presence is often painful to accept by an observant Innocent. They are always easier to see if we are willing to look at them. Control of people is the most common harbinger.

Lemkin's definition of "genocide" and his persistent quest for justice are still sleepy concepts today. As you read this book, academic professionals are studying genocide to reach consensus on topics ranging from terminology to international law. Meanwhile, some fanatical leaders are using the strategy of genocide unreservedly.

Our stepping back, to give the full view of this large-scale absence of preemption, should give us a concussive jolt; a shocking reminder that inaction in the presence of a strong threat is a sure recipe for disaster, sometimes the size of genocide. Our pursuit of preemption hinges on recognizing the warning signs Villain spews just before the attack. His noxious omens are always there, observable by those who are willing to look for them.

1962

In October 1962, a season of posturing between the United States and the USSR (Union of Soviet Socialist Republics, 1922-1991) peaked out in what is called the "Cuban Missile Crisis." After discovering the Soviet installation of ballistic missiles in Cuba, U.S. President John Kennedy called for a blockade by ships to prevent the delivery of more missiles coming from the USSR to Cuba.

Clear evidence that those nuclear weapons could effectively strike many targets in the United States brought tensions among all nation players to the breaking point. With U.S. Navy ships in position and emotions running hot, the international audience was anxious about the high probability that what previously had been a dangerous cold war might quickly intensify to an all-out nuclear war.

After almost two weeks of sharp negotiations, President Kennedy and USSR Premier Khrushchev reached an agreement to remove the quarantine and respective missile installations, along with other conditions.

President Kennedy cited the importance of a preemptive national defense in his address on October 22, 1962:

> "Neither the United States of America nor the world community of nations can tolerate deliberate deception and offensive threats on the part of any nation, large or small. We no longer live in a world where only the actual firing of weapons represents a sufficient challenge to a nation's security to constitute maximum peril. Nuclear weapons are so destructive and ballistic missiles are so swift that any substantially increased possibility of their use or any sudden change in their deployment may well be regarded as a definite threat to peace... The 1930's taught us a clear lesson: Aggressive conduct, if allowed to grow unchecked and unchallenged, ultimately leads to war. This nation is opposed to war." [8]

This is just one instance when the existence of a fast, catastrophic missile-capable offense justified a significant preemptive counter offense (defense) which included, at that time, the possible U.S. invasion of Cuba. Was the threat of war substantial? Probably. Did preemptive action get high marks? Definitely.

1981

Iran launched an unsuccessful attack on an Iraqi nuclear reactor in September 1980. Describing its Osirak reactor in 1980 as "a grave danger" for Israel, Iraqi media reiterated that the reactor would not be used as an attack tool against Iran. Instead, its presence would aid in Iraq's certain future attack against Israel.

While closely following this event, Israel's security, military, and political leaders waged their own private skirmish, wrestling with the decision whether or not to destroy the nuclear reactor in a preemptive attack. Iraq had not entered any cease-fire agreements with Israel, reserving its right to renew attacks at any time, in any location — making the destruction of the reactor an attractive option. On the other hand, the reactor's site near Baghdad posed serious challenges.

If too much time elapsed in Iraq's nuclear development process, bombing the Osirak reactor would annihilate a huge civilian population in Baghdad by fallout. Left entirely unchecked, a nuclear bomb could wipe out millions of Israelis, while rendering large areas of Israel uninhabitable for many years.

As was widely reported, Israel's Prime Minister Menachem Begin emphasized the deadly consequences of bombing the target too late:
> "...if the reactor were activated and we were to bomb it,
> radioactivity would spread over Baghdad...
> The children of Baghdad are not our enemies."

Discussions reached a crescendo as the internal debate within Israeli command rolled on and on. Should they wait, risking huge casualties, or should they take out the reactor early, facing international hatred?

On June 7, 1981 Israel bombed the Osarik reactor in its Operation Opera.

This preemptive strike was simultaneously ridiculed and also praised by leaders from nearly every major country in the world. As a textbook surprise attack, the airstrike was seen by many nations as a clear violation of international law. As a necessary preemption with minimal civilian fatalities, the military operation saved thousands, perhaps millions, of lives that would have been lost in both countries.

In June 1991, U.S. Secretary of Defense Cheney gave a satellite photo of the destroyed reactor to Israel's general who commanded Operation Opera, captioned,
> "...with thanks and appreciation for the outstanding job he did on the Iraqi nuclear program in 1981 — which made our job much easier in Desert Storm." [9]

Here we have prime evidence that a shift in perspective can profoundly change our long-term evaluation of preemption.

2002

Terrorist attacks in the United States on September 11, 2001 killed 2,977 innocents and wounded over 6,000 others. Raising the eyebrows of many international players, President Bush's administration published the National Security Strategy in September 2002, a paper now called the *Bush Doctrine:* [10]
> "Given the goals of rogue states and terrorists, the United States can no longer solely rely on a reactive posture as we have in the past. The inability to deter a potential attacker, the immediacy of today's threats, and the magnitude of potential harm that could be caused by our adversaries' choice of weapons, do not permit that option."

Among other strategic goals it outlines a thread of preemption logic which can be summarized by this single sentence, *"We cannot let our enemies strike first."*

Looking at preemption with passion the paper states,
> "The United States has long maintained the option of preemptive actions to counter a sufficient threat to our national security. The greater the threat, the greater the risk of inaction — and the more

compelling the case for taking anticipatory action to defend ourselves, even if the uncertainty remains as to the time and place of the enemy's attack. To forestall or prevent such hostile acts by our adversaries, the United States will, if necessary, act preemptively."

Many counter terrorist actions have occurred around the world as a result of this policy. On November 3, 2002, six Islamic extremists were killed by a missile from a U.S. drone near a farm in Yemen. There was no prior attack on U.S. military personnel in the few days before the missile strike. None of the six occupants of the car shot at the Predator drone before it blew up their vehicle. Solid intelligence reports simply provided evidence that the men had engaged in and/or were planning to support attacks on Americans.

This event in Yemen is one of many counter attacks which are founded on the executive order issued in 2002, a critical turning point in America's overt national defense.

U.S. invasion and occupation of Iraq began on March 19, 2003. In the world's political arena an endless discussion about Operation(s) Desert Storm and Iraqi Freedom will continue with facts, fabrications, and high emotion clashing together in raucous disharmony. Did the United States' military find sufficient evidence of weapons of mass destruction? Did Saddam Hussein and his allies successfully dispose of WMDs before U.S. forces arrived? In a theater of actors screaming death threats to western nations is preemption a solution that will be adopted internationally? Is it the only rational solution? Is preemption a universal long-term future remedy, or is it an overbearing liability? There are many questions.

We now know that the wavelike flow of intense attacks and occupation of Iraq followed by a scheduled U.S. withdrawal from the region provided a garden for today's popular terrorist actors to grow their organizations. At the time of this writing, territory in the Middle East, Africa, and Indonesia is presently at risk with continued forms of terrorist occupation. Once again, our lesson is simple: Any murderous power which is left unrestrained in the present is a power that is free to injure and kill in the future, whether the setting is a continent, a huge battlefield, or someone's living room.

CHAPTER 1 - FUNDAMENTAL X-PREE

2015

On July 22, 2011 a lone terrorist made two attacks in Norway. Seventy-seven innocents were killed and over 319 wounded, most of them under the age of twenty. These were ranked as the deadliest attacks for Norway since World War II, and for western Europe since 2004. Other attacks occurred in Paris, France and Copenhagen, Denmark early in 2015.

Sweden released a document in August 2015 titled, *Prevent, Preempt, Protect - the Swedish Counter-Terrorism Strategy.* [11] It states,
> "The goal of all counter-terrorism activities is to keep terrorist attacks from being carried out. This work is divided into three areas - Prevent, Preempt, Protect... The Government particularly wished to focus on preventive measures in order to prevent more people developing an intent and capability to commit terrorist attacks in the longer term."

Why is their plan structured that way? They gave us the answer:
> "A fundamental premise underlying all work to counter terrorism is that human rights and the principles of the rule of law are respected. This also applies to protection of personal privacy."

They very clearly knew that their citizens' concocted visions of storm troopers smashing in Swedish front doors at 2 AM would not boost the government's popularity.

Increased national, regional, and local "collaboration" and "cohesion" among agencies were cited as key ingredients toward Sweden's gains in its counter terrorism efforts. This is similar to the spirit of the U.S. Department of Homeland Security which unified twenty-two departments and agencies in 2002.

There is an important universal principle in play here. For the sake of safety, agencies should communicate efficiently with each other. Likewise, individual citizens should communicate with citizens in their community and their government agencies. Of course, our apex of improved collective awareness is closer communication among average family members.

What deserves our special attention is Sweden's purposeful effort to get ahead of the terrorist killing process with tools which "Prevent, Preempt, Protect" the country against it, in contrast with an obsolete wait-and-see approach.

You might be wondering about the current success of Sweden's Counter-Terrorism Strategy. We must roll back a few years to get a good perspective. Europe's Schengen Area is a large territory of twenty-six countries which, by the Schengen Agreement (1995), doesn't require passports, visas, or border checks for travelers moving and living among those countries. Early in 2016 Sweden and a few other Schengen member nations began border checks because of an unexpectedly high number of refugees who emigrated from the Middle East. In spite of Sweden's highest-ever terror threat level, the country endured one additional attack in April 2017.

However, U.S. National Bureau of Economic Research (NBER) reported in June 2016 that Sweden ranked fourth place in the world for offering up foreign fighters for ISIS (Islamic State of Iraq and Syria). In other words, at that time when Sweden's own incidents of terror attacks were low, its production of young terrorist recruits was relatively high.

NBER explained it this way:
> "Building on previous research that suggests that recruitment is driven by religious and political ideology, the researchers find that the more homogeneous the host country is, the more difficulties Muslim immigrants experience in their process of assimilation. This social isolation seems to induce radicalization, increasing the supply of potential recruits."

> "Although the researchers are unable to determine precisely why people join ISIS, their results suggest this difficulty of assimilation into homogeneous Western countries and ISIS's appeal to impressionable youth through its sophisticated propaganda machine and social media are major contributors." [12]

As we'll discuss later in Chapter 3, isolation is generally and globally one of the prime fertilizers in the birth and development of today's criminal mindset. Few human conditions are more influential.

CHAPTER 1 - FUNDAMENTAL X-PREE

2016

On January 1, 2016 California Assembly Bill 1014 went into effect, enabling the creation of the Gun Violence Restraining Order (GVRO). Search of homes or businesses for potential seizure of firearms and ammunition is streamlined by a GVRO:

> *"18100. A gun violence restraining order is an order, in writing, signed by the court, prohibiting and enjoining a named person from having in his or her custody or control, owning, purchasing, possessing, or receiving any firearms or ammunition. This division establishes a civil restraining order process to accomplish that purpose.*
>
> *18125. (a) A temporary emergency gun violence restraining order may be issued on an ex parte basis only if a law enforcement officer asserts, and a judicial officer finds, that there is reasonable cause to believe…*
> *(1) The subject of the petition poses an immediate and present danger of causing personal injury to himself, herself, or another by having in his or her custody or control, owning, purchasing, possessing, or receiving a firearm."* [13]

In everyday English, a law enforcement officer who is armed with a GVRO may search the property of, and take firearms and ammo from, someone who poses a present or future danger of causing personal injury to himself, herself, or another person.

Possible consequences of AB-1014 are extensive. This law can be ultra useful, potentially life-saving, as an effective law enforcement tool in the preemption of mass murder. Similarly, someone might also cause misguided chaos in an innocent person's life by falsely initiating a GVRO. Many people are disturbed by the potential abuse of the GVRO, but it opens a significant door for progress in exercising lawful preemption by California's law enforcement personnel.

Other U.S. states are currently pursuing similar legislation. Civilian vigilance in the early detection of violence might find some healthy traction here. Government overreach might also find a dangerous foothold here. Will the GVRO be used responsibly and respectfully? Or, will the GVRO become the newest craft for enemies of America's Bill of Rights to trample its liberties? U.S. citizens will be watching this preemption tool closely.

2017

Preemption made a dramatic cameo appearance in London on June 3, 2017. Three terrorists drove a rented van into pedestrians on London Bridge. After exiting the vehicle, they randomly attacked people with knives in Borough Market. Eight victims died and forty-eight more were hospitalized. This was the fifth attack on British civilians in about six months.

Before responding police officers fatally shot the terrorists, several people in the restaurant and pub district fought back in self-defense. Amid the absence of civilian defensive handguns, they had limited choices — mostly glasses, tables, and chairs.

Instead of commonplace panic and fearful retreat, those few Innocents chose preemption. Solid resolve to raise an immediate, improvised defense saved them. Their speedy denial of access and spontaneous counter attack were effective in protecting many friends' lives by disrupting the horrific plan which had already snuffed out many others. Cheers to you, Brits!

Lessons for Today

Time will prove both the wisdom and the folly of our strategies against today's malicious actors. Specialists are calling for asymmetric counter terrorism; that is, fighting an unconventional enemy in unconventional ways. Active shooters and suicide bombers are penetrating otherwise sleepy, peaceful cities which have no prior quarrel with these killers. Mischievous cyber hackers are busy engineering digital destruction wherever possible in the world. As employees, private sector insiders are compromising the in-house systems and processes which they are entrusted to protect.

There are many unanswered questions about the application of preemption in global and local communities. Amid both government and private sector operations to preempt crime, there are always inherent limits on individual freedom. In order to root out potential attacks, close observation of citizens' behavior always carries with it an encroachment into the privacy of those citizens.

Much discussion about civilian privacy versus government snooping is ongoing. Over several years, we have hard evidence that high-tech watching and listening has thwarted hundreds of intended attacks on United States' civilian targets. Advances in government intelligence gathering and analysis have made this possible. So far, in our present state of national security, as it resides in today's global environment, U.S. defensive scouting into private sector activity is keeping us relatively safe. Right now, the respectful detection by loyal good guys in our agencies is weighing heavily in our favor.

In the future, will our culture choose apathy, tolerance, strict control, or some unknown combination? Who will decide? How will detection and enforcement be defined? To what degree of watching and listening will corporate security programs extend? There are many relevant legal and ethical questions which will undoubtedly receive answers.

International rulings related to preemption will inevitably be expanded in the behavior of nations — an arena where political, economic, and cultural forces can easily blur otherwise well-defined legal rules. Preemption is not a new concept, but its place in the order of governance demands refinement. For many more decades, precisely tuned definitions of acceptable "preemption" versus "prevention" will churn on in the legal universe, without the slightest help from you or me.

Regardless, preemption's application in our private lives deserves acute attention. *Extreme Preemption* is the practical, potent framework to accomplish individual self-defense. We can be sure of one thing: Every private citizen must awaken now, earnestly learning to protect what is close and precious.

X-Pree for Tomorrow

How can we summarize all of this? What good is the history of this wide range of large-scale to relatively small events? And, how do they relate to an individual's self-defense?

At the level of national security, there is enormous risk in hesitating when faced with an imminent attack on a civilian population. On a personal level, the same principle applies. We would not be thrilled with a government that, having thorough knowledge about a certain attack on civilians, did nothing in the defense of its people. Likewise, you should not be satisfied with your personal hesitation in self-defense when an imminent threat is standing in front of you.

There are fellow citizens who, right now, truly believe that Villain must attack Innocent before Innocent can legally raise a defense. This attitude is a deadly strain of obliviolence. If we collectively live by that principle, there will be an enormous surge in business for hospitals and mortuaries! First strikes on civilians without any risk of injury to Villain will give us brand new national crime waves!

In contrast, our sane response to Villain is *Extreme Preemption*. There is a staggering array of online videos which show one-strike bare hand attacks that are injurious and/or fatal to the hapless victims who receive those blows. X-Pree is the remedy for this misguided tolerance of personal brutality. Innocent victims are not required to receive personal injury which they know is coming. Villain must be stopped at the instant he is identified as a threat and before he hurts Innocent.

> **Innocent victims are not required to receive personal injury which they know is coming.**[14]

Obliviolence is so dangerous because preemption has no chance — it is crowded out by unawareness, then hesitation. Delay in necessary personal defense usually brings injury or death to the unsure victim. *Extreme Preemption* brings safety.

What about the complicated legal factors? Aren't there ambiguous ramifications in exercising self-defense against another person? Answer: Not necessarily. What if we could boil down much of the legal jargon to succinctly define civilian rules of engagement? Carrying around a short use-of-force checklist in our everyday lives would be a big help. Well, read on. Here it is...

CHAPTER 1 - FUNDAMENTAL X-PREE

ITOTR

Legal complexity is not easy to wade through, as evidenced by the number of active attorneys in the world. Apply this simple formula to determine if you can legally use force, even deadly force, when defending yourself or a person near you. I call it ITOTR (pronounced "eye-toter"). Yes, it's one of a few acronyms in this book. ITOTR is a generic formula to help you make a split-second decision. Here's what it means:

I — Represents four precepts:
1. **Innocence** — As an intended victim you need to be innocent of starting, continuing, or escalating a conflict by your actions or your speech. When using profanity or that all-powerful middle finger against someone's annoying behavior, you actually compromise your self-defense legal rights.
2. **Intent** — Villain has clear intent to inflict serious injury on you or a person near you. This is a judgment call by you. "Near" means very near, generally within a few feet.
3. **Immediacy** — Villain is an immediate threat to your safety. He is present to hurt you right now, not one hour from now or next week.
4. **Imminence** — Villain presents an imminent threat to your safety. You must be certain that you or someone near you will be hurt unless you raise a defense. Your honest perception of the event is a key to your legal success. Being unsure about this point can quickly bring undesirable results. It's another judgment call by you.

T — Tool

Villain has the tool to hurt you: bare hands, knife, gun, vehicle, etc. We use the term "disparity of force," meaning Villain has an attacking force (400 lb. boulder, for example) which is greater than the force you have to defend yourself (your phablet, for example). So, you are entitled to meet that force with the use of a self-defense tool — an equalizer. Villain's bare hands might be a less obvious attack tool than his knife, gun, or boulder. Your heightened awareness will help sort this one out.

O — Opportunity

Villain has the actual opportunity to do the hurting. He is not separated from you by a fence, river, building, etc., which can isolate him from you. He has the actual chance to injure you.

T — Trap
>You are trapped. You cannot escape from Villain. Limited egress from a room, alley, or hiking trail has blocked your escape.

R — Reasonable Person Standard
>You believe that, after the defensive encounter, when all of the emotion has faded away, a reasonable member of society will agree with your use of force in self-defense.

ITOTR is not universally perfect legal advice.

According to many criminal justice experts, ITOTR is a valid formula to quickly define your civilian rules of engagement. Use of force law in your locale might vary slightly. Conditions in violent encounters will certainly differ from case to case. Do your homework! Confirm with your local police, your attorney, or your District Attorney that ITOTR fits their view of your decision-making process to use force in self-defense.

ITOTR does not guarantee your freedom from arrest or prosecution.

Today's jurisprudence is complicated and subjective in most cases. Even if you've defended yourself legally, responding law enforcement officers might still choose to detain or arrest you. Your best defense is nearly fanatical overemphasis to always stay clear of conflict, using force as an absolutely last resort.

Learn the ITOTR. It's not complicated. Your safety depends on it when faced with an attack, because you have no time to waste deciding whether or not to use force. Your quick ITOTR analysis needs to be complete in about HALF of 1 second. Yes, 0.5 second — you can do it!

Start thinking about your ITOTR now. Look closely at your daily activities. Start playing "What if…?" Visualize possible encounters with Villain in your everyday life, and determine if your planned use of force is justified in each fictional situation. You'll be surprised at how quickly you can dial in ITOTR. It's your antidote to the otherwise fatal seconds of indecision which can steal your life. Own your ITOTR!

CHAPTER 1 - FUNDAMENTAL X-PREE

X-Pree Framework

In review, preemption is the action of forestalling. Preemption is an action that dominates another future action by stalling, stopping, or replacing it.

Your personal decision to act in a preemptive manner might someday be a saving solution with huge consequences — big enough, in fact, to help national security. We will explore that later. For now, let's focus on the core of your personal safety strategy.

We need a guide to be able to put *X-Pree* to work. *X-Pree* is your superior action to stop an attack before you or a person near you is injured. But, how do you actually get it done? Answer: By acting within this 3-step framework:

Your *X-Pree* Mission: Train, Detect, Preempt

1. **Train** - Learn the essential skills for your chosen defense tools.
2. **Detect** - Learn to instantly identify potential threats to your safety.
3. **Preempt** - Learn to stop an attack before you are injured.

Here's the logic:
1. First, you must *Train* to be able to use the defense tools that you choose. Otherwise, you can't defend anything. Simply keeping happy thoughts in a violent situation is not a reliable defense, sorry.
2. Then, you must have a reason to defend someone. You have that reason when you *Detect* some hurtful behavior or the intent to hurt somebody.
3. Finally, you stop the injury to yourself or someone nearby when you actually *Preempt* it.

Your SPEED puts the *Extreme* in *X-Pree* — Extreme Preemption.

In almost all cases, *X-Pree* is *FAST*. From the moment you identify a threat, you might have only one second to preempt it. We've heard a thousand times in the driving world, "Speed kills!" Well, in the realm of your security, *SPEED* Saves!

Here comes another acronym. Show restraint; no eye rolling, thank you. I give you this memory aid to store in your long-term cranial database.

SAFE = Speed Always Foils 'Em

For more than 30 years, the interpolation of statistics in the FBI's Uniform Crime Report[15] and first-hand accounts have shown that violent encounters are usually finished within 3 to 5 seconds. This means you must launch *X-Pree* within 1 to 2 seconds. Yes, that is fast. You can be that fast. You need to be that fast. I'll show you how to be that fast.

Applications of *Extreme Preemption* are infinite. *X-Pree* may have many different varieties:
- One instance of *X-Pree* could involve an extended period of detection where your skill in identifying pre-incident indicators of an attack is the winning remedy.
- On another occasion, just your simple call or report of suspicious activity to law enforcement might be the key to a saving response.
- Or, *X-Pree* could be your ultra-creative use of an adopted defense tool that stretches even the wildest imagination.

Crime trends require speedy, precise action against today's Villains. You will see that your self-defense framework to *Train, Detect, Preempt — FAST* is simple and attainable by any stable member of society. That's you!

Summary

Your Mission: Train, Detect, Preempt — FAST. Your intense, off-the-charts-fast, effective response in the face of a threat to your safety is *X-Pree*. Whether it's an attack by a transnational terrorist organization or one ugly personal encounter with Villain, your application of *X-Pree* is necessary and historically grounded. Standing by, wallowing in indecision, being fearful about taking charge of your safety, and wondering if it's right to fight your way out of trouble are all very bad choices. You are smarter than that. You can take charge of your safety right now. How can you actually do that? Learn to *Train, Detect, and Preempt*.

Embrace *X-Pree* as part of your everyday life. Strap in and prepare to

Chapter 1 - Fundamental X-Pree

explore your role in owning true security for yourself personally, for your group corporately, and for your country nationally. You're on an adventure that will radically change your life.

Complete Topic Discussion 1,
then go to Chapter 2 — Your Mission: Train.

Topic Discussion 1 — Fundamental *X-Pree*

What is the element of *X-Pree* which makes it *Extreme Preemption*? How often is this element applicable in your self-defense?

What are the considerations in balancing civilian privacy and national security?

If you could have solely made the decision, would you have given the order to bomb the Osarik reactor in 1981? Why or why not?

After a threat is identified, how is the role of hesitation different for a nation, compared to an individual?

What four attributes are represented by the "I" in ITOTR? Give an example of each one.

What does the first "T" represent in ITOTR? Give three examples.

TOPIC DISCUSSION 1

What does the "O" represent in ITOTR? Give three examples.

What does the second "T" represent in ITOTR? Give three examples.

What does the "R" represent in ITOTR? Give three examples.

What are the three elements of the *X-Pree* framework?

What is the minimum time you should allow to launch your *X-Pree* defense?

What is the significance of SAFE in your self-defense?

Notes:

CHAPTER 2 - YOUR MISSION: TRAIN

In this chapter we identify a variety of self-defense tools and give you tips for learning how to use them proficiently, along with a few specific training resources.

Humans are an odd group. We're born without a natural ability to protect ourselves. Our defensive craving might be extremely intense, but our defensive skills need to be nurtured and developed. We don't have massive teeth and the knack to lock our jaws on the underside of Villain's neck. That's the natural skill of a leopard trying to procure a tasty zebra dinner. Unfortunately, we humans would need to study and practice that technique — but not at home, or with friends.

Imagine that Sheze Innocent is out for a walk and her instinct says, "Danger ahead, high alert!" She might have the desire to defend herself, and she might be highly motivated to do so. But, if she doesn't have a clue about how to actually do the defending part by *X-Pree*, then Sheze Innocent might quickly become Sheze Hurting.

Coming up next, we have an overview of many self-defense tools and ideas about how to train for each one. Depending on your selections and your location, a variety of training opportunities are available. This chapter is not an ad for any particular training. As with other skills, your commitment to truly learning some defense tools is necessary for your success.

Pursue in-depth training for every defense tool you choose.

Your successful training can be at home by a variety of media, or in a formal classroom environment. Choose your self-defense education with great care, so that whatever resources you spend will improve your safety.

Weapon

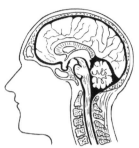

If everyone could select only one weapon to have ready, without any fuss, at all times, what would that be? You might say, "Military platoon!" That's a good choice, but one of our qualifiers is "without any fuss."

Our fundamental weapon is the human mind. Without getting extremely heady about this, think carefully for a moment. No matter what self-defense tool you have in your hands, your success in using the tool is driven by clear, precise instructions given to your body by your mind. Judgment about when to use defense tools also resides only in your mind. Your resolve to win a violent conflict is born and sustained only by your mind.

Consider how some of your valuable mechanical devices work. If you bake things, you know all about relying on your mixer and its various attachable tools: wire whip, dough hook, or food grinder. Likewise, your favorite yard trimmer has its different tools: string trimmer, blower, or edger. As the mixer and trimmer are your machines around the house, your mind is your primary machine (weapon) to which you can attach a variety of self-defense tools.

Our minds are truly amazing little mechanisms, but they need to be managed. We have a built-in defense system in our bodies which revs to high speed when our senses detect a serious threat to our safety. Neuro-Chemical-Cardio-Muscular-and-otherwise-weird functions go berserk inside us! (Pause here to appreciate this ultra-technical pseudo biology term.) Bottom line, our ability to do precise things with hands and feet is seriously limited. Experts call it "loss of fine motor skills" (unrelated to auto repair).

In self-defense, your mind must be controlled by two decisions:
1. **Keep all of your training simple.** Why? Because we drop down to our lowest level of mastered training when we're faced with violence. Decide now to keep your self-defense stuff really simple.

2. **Be willing to counter attack.** In a violent attack against you, most often the only defense that will work is your violent counter attack against your attacker. Let's examine this. If you spend precious seconds just blocking punches or thrusts with a knife, you're going to eventually get tired. At that moment you will get hurt or killed.

If your defense is actually a fast counter attack, the results will likely be much better for you. Why? Your attacker will be surprised, maybe shocked and confused. And, if you are even a little skilled, you can stop the attack by disabling your attacker.

Your mind is your weapon. Keep your training simple. Decide NOW to injure your attacker if necessary. If you engage in complicated self-defense training techniques or are unsure if you can really counter attack against your attacker, then your *FAST X-Pree* component will be annihilated by indecision or hesitation. Your *X-Pree* will turn into Lame-Pree in a big hurry. During the fight, portions of seconds matter. Get your mind clear right now.

Let's take a look at some available self-defense tools. Make sure you thoroughly research each tool you select, and get professional training whenever possible. Your instructor should be able to explain not only the use of a particular tool, but also how to practice your skill development with that tool.

Awareness

Several years ago, I was driving to a nearby town. On the road near the village a young woman was jogging. Not being a gifted multi-tasker myself, I watched in total amazement as she simultaneously,
- Jogged along the road
- Managed her small dog on a leash
- Read a book
- Ate an energy bar
- Listened to whatever played through her earbuds

Chapter 2 - Your Mission: Train

This jogger's fitness level was great, but her score as a potential kidnap victim was perfect!

Awareness, often referred to as "situational awareness," is a foundational safety tool. Sleepwalking is the near absence of awareness. We frequently see people who are preoccupied with texting on a smart phone or tablet, consumed by a relationship crisis, or brain-pickled by drugs or alcohol. Villains also see these people, waiting for the best time to attack an especially vulnerable, easy victim.

Your training in awareness can be boiled down to learning the traditional Safety Color Codes[16] and how they apply to your life — White, Yellow, Orange, Red.
- Condition White = Unaware. You are vegging at home with a book, music, or TV.
- Condition Yellow = Aware. You are driving or shopping with your focus on surroundings.
- Condition Orange = Alert. You observe someone in a hotel lobby who doesn't look right to you.
- Condition Red = Alarm. You realize that you must stop that person if necessary.

Live in condition Yellow or above when you're away from home. Always know what's going on around you without diving into a self-concocted high level of stress. Remember, your ultimate safety is peaceful, not tense.

Practice awareness. While driving, notice other cars in all directions. Every few seconds, test yourself to see if you remember who's there. This is also a great exercise when you're in a restaurant or walking through a crowded store. Watch others to see where they are, what they're doing, and if they are watching you! There is an extremely low possibility that Villain can ambush you if you see an attack coming early.

Your everyday awareness is a critical element in *X-Pree*, because it unlocks the discovery process. Without it, your self-defense readiness is handicapped. With it, you have an essential tool equipping you to preempt Villain's harm.

Avoidance

Famous parental advice: "You shouldn't be there!" We all remember that one, reiterated one thousand times or more. Maybe it's our sense of pioneering spirit or common ignorance that magnetizes unsafe locations which must be explored, drawing us into trouble as moths are attracted to bug zappers.

Your choice to avoid locations which are not safe is always simple, but it might not be easy. Think safety first. Plan your work, play, free time, and veg time to include avoidance of unsafe conditions. There are few peace-time places where the risk of personal injury is worth entering voluntarily.

Breath

We need to air to stay alive. Breathing is the result of an involuntary body system that usually works easily and efficiently. When our intake and exhaust of air is disrupted, our bodies don't react well. Go ahead, just stop breathing right now, and come back when your body starts rebelling...

Hey, good to see you! Back already! When stressed or threatened, your body's respiratory system responds to some temporary chemical changes by demanding more air — a.k.a. oxygen. When it doesn't receive the required additional dose of air, some odd reactions can occur, including heavy sweating and/or fainting.

Tactical Breathing is an excellent respiratory weirdness suppressor. It's simple.

Just inhale to a slow count of four, then exhale to a slow count of four. Each round should take about eight seconds.

Let's try it right now. Here we go… Inhale, two, three, four. Exhale, two, three, four. Again… Inhale, two, three, four. Exhale, two, three, four. If you were obedient, joining tens of millions of *X-Pree* students, you should already feel some refreshing re-oxygenation.

Train yourself to immediately begin your **Tactical Breathing** at the first hint of danger. Will this help you in the face of an annoying manager, obnoxious co-worker, profoundly attractive date, or even an audience you are about to address? Absolutely, yes!

De-Escalation

We have inconsistent estimates of the value of diplomacy. Modern thinkers differ in their appraisal of its effectiveness. On the personal protection front, you will likely never have time to discuss terms with Villain. Silence is often your most powerful de-escalator. Diplomacy is an art, certainly not to be mistaken for inaction. If you plan to use de-escalation as a defense tool learn to be good at it.

Develop your balanced diplomacy skills to the best of your ability. Constant rude or offensive behavior toward other people might backfire one day if you meet someone who is more rude or more offensive than you are. Likewise, continuously portraying yourself as a fragile, vulnerable target might invite an attack by the Villain who is looking for easy prey.

If Villain crosses your safety threshold as defined by your ITOTR then you absolutely must fight your way out. There is no time and no opportunity for discussion. Your fight is on at that point. You will either dominate Villain or be dominated by him. Successful negotiations are not possible then.

Bare Hands

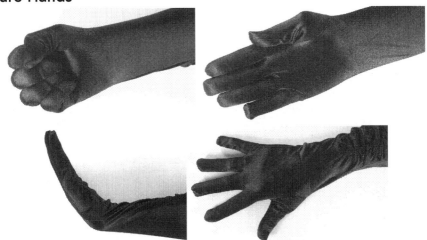

Your best versions of bare hand defense are,
- Hammer Hand (closed fist)
- Hand Chop
- Palm Strike (heel of hand) with fingers up and out of the way
- Finger Flail to the eyes

There is nearly every imaginable martial arts discipline in the world taught within every major U.S. town or city. However, they all have one major handicap. They are at least a little complex.

Street fighters hit hard and fast. We discussed *SPEED* already. All competitive martial arts include rules defining which areas of the body can't be struck and/or the force an opponent may use when striking. These rules help martial arts students avoid killing and maiming each other in their respective sports. This is certainly a good idea!

Here's the difficulty: If we repeatedly avoid hitting a particularly vulnerable spot on the body in training, then we will surely miss or hesitate hitting that spot in a street fight. If we train to hit at half speed, then that's likely to be our fight speed when defending ourselves.

Every responsible martial arts school deserves endless kudos for the training offered. My responsibility is to give you the shortest path to effective self-defense success. Damian Ross offers a disc media and online street-fighting training series called *The Self Defense Training System*.[17] This training fits any schedule, in any location. It teaches street fighting in an easy-to-understand, at-home format. Martial arts regimens are great, but they require regular attendance at a training facility, generally over a long period of time.

Using a training dummy is absolutely necessary. Commercial models are worth the expense, because you can adjust the dummy's height and hit him with full-power strikes. He doesn't complain, bleed, or run away to phone an attorney. If that's too pricey for you, then stuff some old clothes with rags for your indoor dummy. It is not necessary to be able to break boards with your bare hands.

Study and practice striking with a closed hand (fist) as a hammer, chopping with the edge of your open hand, thrusting the heel of your hand, and flailing your spread fingers. Except for shots to the torso, abandon old fashioned punches which are delivered with knuckles as your strike surface. They will probably break when your hand impacts Villain's head or another boney part of his body.

Finger flail to the eyes also works very well. It requires no special style. Quickly flail your hand so that when it extends your fingers do also, jabbing into Villain's eyes. What if he's quick enough to close his eyes? No worries. Try this: With your eyes closed, very gently tap on one of your eyelids with increasing force, until it's uncomfortable. Go for it. I'll wait... That didn't take long, did it? Unlike fictitious action heroes in the movies, our bodies are remarkably fragile.

You might be wondering if the finger flail works on someone wearing glasses. Answer is "Yes!" With a little practice, you can learn to strike very fast and very hard. Odds are excellent that your striking fingers will slip under prescription glasses or sunglasses and get the job done.

Observe a snake strike to see how fast it occurs. If you have not personally seen a snake strike, then find a video on the Internet. Our local California rattlesnakes don't strike then lay there fully extended. They quickly strike and then instantly recoil. That's how fast your bare hand strikes need to be.

Practice bone-breaking strikes on a home-made or formal training dummy. Hits with half speed or half force will embed a weak defense in your muscle memory system. Train to strike as fast and as hard as you can. These defenses require study and practice.

Legs & Feet

Except for rescuing someone else, the best way to win a physical conflict with Villain is to **run away**. Among all of my students, the most difficult notion to dispel is their resistance to get out of there. Some of the most physically fit Defenders want to hang around to see if they can really prevail in the fight — not the safest and brightest plan.

If you can escape to safety without fighting Villain, you are absolutely guaranteed to win the conflict! Attaining the perfect role as an untouched, retreating person is a brilliant defense. Despicable names hurled toward you are irrelevant when compared to the wholesome victory of returning home uninjured. Are you a coward? No one cares! If you are defending only yourself, it's always better to be a smart untouched coward than a foolish beaten hero.

When escape isn't possible, your best alternative is to run directly toward your attacker. If you're trapped, with no escape route, then run over your attacker — breaking him on the way. Too short, you say? Your smaller size can be a huge advantage. For example, a much taller, stockier Villain is going to be astonished if you step on his leading foot (trapping it) and lunge forward using your forearms as rams to help him fall backwards. Your success with this technique is literally running over him on your way to safety.

Practice those running skills! You don't need to run the 100 meters in less than 10 seconds. Having the stamina to run 100 meters will probably suffice. If you can't run at all, then you need to fight in place.

If your running ability is good, but you can't outrun the predator, here's an excellent strategy. Make your dash away from Villain. As he closes in on you, turn and charge him. He probably won't believe what's happening, and you'll have a great opportunity to run him over.

In addition to running, learn to stomp and kick. From the front, stomping an attacker's knee cap or instep, or both, is a really effective start in your defense, especially if your hands are trapped. If he gets turned to one side, then crushing his ankle works well. If he gets turned around, smashing his heal to rupture the Achilles tendon is another winning strategy. One-legged predators won't chase you very far on foot. When you're out and about, wear shoes with soles that might snag Villain's knee cap or hurt his instep. Flip flops and ballet slippers won't get the job done.

You can always invest in long-term training enabling you to execute Spinning Roundhouse Kicks, or Wheel Kicks which are part of the formal martial arts world. These are motion picture winners, but they probably won't work in a street fight unless you spend hundreds of hours and dollars in training.

By the way, tall heels and restrictive clothes are not going to allow you to run. Leave them home except when dressed for a special occasion, when you have other defense tools with you. Search for your dream mate without setting yourself up as a victim. Some legs out there, by beautiful appearance, are at this moment reducing grown men to whimpering fools. However, that's another tactic for another book.

Adopted Tools

Extreme Preemption

In the absence of traditional self-defense tools, you might need to adopt one or more common physical items to use against Villain. They range from remarkable to ridiculous, outstanding to outrageous. These are a few of many adopted defense tools which might be available to you in an office:

> attache, backpack, book, broom, chair, fire extinguisher, knickknack, mug, desk organizer, stack of paper, handfuls of pens or pencils, picture, potted plant, plate, paper punch, scissors, stapler, small table, wall plaque, and waste basket

Your actual list of optional items to throw at Villain is probably much longer, limited only by your imagination. He will be disoriented, possibly incapacitated, when receiving any of these to his upper body, head, or face. Adopted tools don't need to be instantly lethal; they need to simply force Villain to deviate from his plan by distracting him. Villain's hesitation creates your opportunity to launch a more forceful *X-Pree* defense.

Practice finding adopted defense tools wherever you are at that moment. In a safe area, train to hurl them by hanging one or more old blankets or sheets on a horizontal rope. Throw your tools at the sheet to gain experience in how far you can launch them. Heaving a bulky chair gets a little tricky when you must avoid hitting yourself or an innocent person nearby. Get a little know-how ahead of time. Crack the classic boredom of your next office party. It could be truly exciting!

Bat

Truckers use a short bat to quickly check the air pressure of their tires. One quick thump resonates to an experienced driver whether the tire pressure is within a desirable range. This tool is called a tire thumper or truncheon (pronounced "TRUN-shin").

From circa 1400 A.D. until about 20 years ago, constables carried them as reliable pieces of equipment. Related tools such as "billy club," "bludgeon," and cousin "nightstick" are seldom used for civilian self-defense today, because they cannot be legally concealed.

CHAPTER 2 - YOUR MISSION: TRAIN

Batons and expandable batons are the modern replacements for law enforcement officers. These are regulated in most U.S. states. However, the short baseball bat or truncheon is still a potent, inexpensive self-defense tool at your home or place of business.

Hardwood truncheons vary in length from under 12 inches to about 19 inches. Used with one hand or two, the strikes and practice are the same as those for your walking cane. Standard baseball bats are usually longer, up to 42 inches. They require moderate skill to be able to hold onto them in a fight.

Practice the four strikes used for Cane in the next section. Remember *SPEED*.

Cane

If only as a conversation starter, everyone should own a shillelagh (pronounced she-LAY-lee). Traditionally, it's a stick of blackthorn or oak wood in various lengths from short walking canes to long staffs. Irish history is filled with applications of the shillelagh. Used for self-defense, sparring, old-fashioned discipline, and help on a peaceful stroll, it has survived hundreds of years without any improvements. In fact, the Shillelagh has been so dominant in Irish folklore that when Ford won the contract for a fearsome anti-tank missile in 1958, the company chose the name "MGM-51 Shillelagh."

There is no venue where a walking cane is not allowed. Classified as a "mobility-assistance device," you can take one with you on a commercial airplane, train, or ship. Please note that creative modifications such as a lead-filled knob at the top, concealed sword, or a cane gun will definitely cause a delay in your travel schedule. Accessorizing your cane in these ways can get you a room at the local gray-bar building. No, that is not a pub.

How is it used for self-defense? Grasp both hands tightly on the cane, about shoulder-width apart. In this position you can use it to thrust forward making contact with the bottom tip. You can also raise or lower it to strike Villain in the neck, face, or head. Finally, your stick can block one of Villain's blows while on it's way toward his incredibly thick skull. This tool is simple and versatile.

What is the best size? You can determine the correct length of your cane by standing up straight, with your arm bent slightly at the elbow. Measure the distance from the heel of your hand to the floor. That's the proper length of your walking cane.

Practice on your training dummy. Rehearse these strikes:
- Thrust shaft end to torso
- Sweep crooked end across head/face
- Bar coming up under chin/nose
- Bar coming down forehead/face

Your *X-Pree* defense is your counter attack while going through Villain. Merely blocking his hit should always be your last resort.

Communication Guards

This is a huge book-size topic, so let's cover some highlights. Identity theft is a great moneymaker for Villain. He can get info about you to put together a "profile." This is a collection of your most important information, such as birthdate, social security number, home address, driver license number, and parents' names. Experts call this "incremental information gathering," because your profile is pieced together bit by bit.

At some point in Villain's plan, he will try to get a credit card or borrow money using your identity. If he's successful in the impersonation, your finances can get very ugly very quickly. You can be made responsible for the money Villain borrows. Once the lender or credit card company believes your story about the identity theft and fraudulent loan, you might still spend a lot of time and effort to get your credit report corrected.

Social Media — If you're a messaging or tweeting pro, I applaud your desire to share your world with others. Be aware that Villain and his allies are out there in cyber space trying to piece together a profile about you, while you might have no idea who they really are. That yummy picture of your "friend" with an attractive personal profile info might be as accurate as the performance of a drunken bowler in the dark.

Fraud Control — Know your enemy. "Phishing" is the tricky misuse of email to get your info. For example, you receive an email that says your checking account pin has expired, and you're required to contact your bank immediately. Just "click the link below." Let's say you do that. Most often you will then see a window where you can fill in a variety of personal info. And, there goes your identity!

"Vishing" is the telephone version of phishing. "Pharming" is another trendy activity where Villain drops harmful code onto your computer which guides you to a fraudulent website, instead of one you intended to visit. "Smishing" is a scam using text messages to your cell phone. If you respond to the message, there is usually an imperative request for your personal info.

Your real bank will NEVER ask for private info by email or phone.

Parental Control Software — As you would never let a child wander alone onto a busy highway, you should never allow children to explore the universe of Internet traffic without supervision. Social media is overflowing with explicit pornography. In today's culture, there is no part of the human anatomy that is sacred enough to prevent it from being displayed in a high definition photo or video.

You might be thinking, "How prudish! It's a free society after all!" Not for some people. Minors who are exploring sex for fun can easily be lured to web pages that are run by human traffickers looking for new slaves. Pedophiles often begin their online relationship with minors who are fooled by their ploys.

Extreme Preemption

What about privacy? What about parent-teenager relations at home? There is a high probability that your child will be solicited for sex and you will never find out. Include in the facts-of-life talk not only the physiology of sex but also Villain's possible online scams. It's a jungle out there.

Parental limits on your home computer and tracking software for a child's phone (logs of locations, calls, emails, messages) are available and effective. Worried about intrusion? Let's go back to the highway traffic illustration. Letting your minor run wild on the Internet is as dangerous as jogging blindfolded into traffic on a four-lane highway.

There are many things you can do to prevent your identity from being stolen. One easy approach is to get a membership with an identity theft protection service. Which one? Your best protection is from a company that actively tries to find Villain's misuse of your personal ID info out there in cyber space.

Take time to learn some of the names for Villain's dirty cyber tricks. Get protective software that matches your lifestyle; something that fits your computer(s), your work, and your budget. Lots of packages are available. See how they're rated, then find the best one for you.

When you're ready to turn off your computer, tablet, or phone, clear the internet browser's history. Various species of cyber garbage will be removed. Limit or block the use of "cookies" on your device. They're tiny cyber gremlins that love to share info about you and your Internet travels. Marketing specialists use cookies to determine, among many things, your buying history and what products you might buy next!

Finally, rejection is a beautiful thing for some people. If you receive any phone call, text message, or email that you don't feel comfortable with, hang up or delete it immediately. Your gracious, heartwarming explanation is not necessary. Sales folks are trained to handle your silent end to their solicitations. You won't break their hearts. Above all, keeping your blood pressure within a healthy range is good.

Firearm

Guns are handy because we can defend ourselves with them at a moderate distance. I teach defensive handgun and concealed carry courses because I believe in the value of the handgun as an extraordinarily effective self-defense tool. We'll spend more time on handguns here than other self-defense tools because there are more intricacies associated with their use.

What is so special about guns, anyway? What's the big deal? As any Defender might throw an available object at an attacker in self-defense, guns throw bullets. Primitive self-defense methods included the option of throwing a stone at the attacker. Modern defense gives us the option of throwing a bullet at an attacker. Stones are big, slow, and moderately accurate. Bullets are small, fast, and very accurate. Everyone knows that it's much easier to carry a personal self-defense handgun than a pail of stones!

What would America look like without guns? This regressive step in self-defense would, of course, leave us with swords and spears. We know this because thousands of years of history reveal this fact. Archeological evidence says that common spears were generally 6 feet to 8 feet long. Today's sub-compact cars radically reduce our potential success in lugging around a six-foot spear.

Consider the obvious liability. How would you feel about unintentionally skewering a pedestrian with the spear protruding out of your car's window? Add to that embarrassing blunder the unavoidable contempt expressed by the world's jousting community, and you could be in a serious legal predicament!

Logically, "Spear Control" lobbies would immediately spring into action, forcing us to resort to the much shorter knife for self-defense. But wait, knives are already wildly popular attack tools in Asia and Europe. So, after knives are banned, then what? How will we cut our food?

Let's note that every regressive notion about reducing the number of firearms in America, under the mask of increasing overall public safety, is based on ignorance, fear, or blatant deception. Your responsible ownership and educated use of firearms will work better support for the USA's Second Amendment than thundering political debate.

If you live in a region where self-defense handguns are not allowed, my heart aches for you. Considering the advanced technology of modern handguns, with their inherent safety, a truly progressive culture embraces effective modern self-defense by firearms. It's bona fide sanity at work.

There is a myth associated with shotguns for home defense which is, "We don't need to aim with a shotgun. Just point and fire. Shotguns are much easier to shoot than handguns." In the real world, at about 15 feet, the pattern of the shot coming out of the average shotgun will fit in a 6 inch circle. In the home environment, there is obviously an acute need to aim any defensive firearm when using it — including shotguns. Also, shotguns are relatively long. Go ahead, try to quickly turn around in a small space with one, or attempt to carry a concealed shotgun around town. Your success is unlikely.

I prefer a handgun over a shotgun or rifle when potentially used against a Villain who is closer than 100 feet. Handguns are small and mobile, so they can be concealed easily. CCW means "carry concealed weapon." Most areas of the USA allow some form of CCW licensing. Let's remain hopeful that, in regions where heavy restrictions on legal gun ownership are strangling modern self-defense, the leadership will awaken from the Stone Age very soon!

Chapter 2 - Your Mission: Train

Master your gun skills by initially practicing with only one gun. There are differences between various handguns. If you frequently switch guns, you will probably handicap yourself. Those quirky variations, no matter how minute, will slow you down in your gun handling and degrade your defense — carrying, drawing, aiming, and firing the gun. Anything which inhibits your *SPEED* also limits your safety. It is best to select one handgun and become extremely proficient with it before moving into a collection of them for self-defense.

Selecting Your Perfect Handgun

As with the purchase of shoes, you probably would not send a family member or friend out to shop for you. So it is with your handgun purchase. When choosing the gun that is best for you, make your selection according to these attributes, in this order:

1. **Grip** — Most important among a handgun's features is its grip. In a defensive encounter you must have absolute control of the gun. With excellent control of the gun your speed and confidence will naturally develop with practice. If the fit of the gun, for you, is awkward and uncomfortable, every subsequent step in your skill development will be a discouraging struggle. Some pistols are made with interchangeable backstraps. These are handy in changing the overall circumference of the grip to fit your hand. Many revolvers and semi-auto pistols have aftermarket grips available which are inexpensive and easily installed. Likewise, many handguns have grips which are not alterable. What's the test? You should be able to operate the trigger and magazine release (or cylinder release) without substantially changing the position of your shooting hand.

2. **Trigger Squeeze** — Your trigger finger should land on the trigger somewhere between the pad of your index finger and the first joint. If the trigger is exceptionally heavy for you, then your accuracy will likely be difficult to perfect. If the trigger is exceptionally light, then your risk of an accidental discharge is high. Each modern handgun has a trigger which is carefully engineered for that gun. Most extremely heavy triggers are perfected with your safety in mind. Be very reluctant to change the trigger weight that is designed for the gun at the factory. You can test the trigger squeeze by borrowing a dummy (inert) round at the gun store.

3. **Sight Alignment** — Your preference about how the sights align is as personal as your preference for color. Some sights are very easy to acquire with your eye. Other sights are more difficult to "find" quickly. You should be able to bring the gun up and very quickly align the sights. Have I mentioned *SPEED* yet? Try to stay with the sights that come from the manufacturer. If the sights are hard to align or they look ugly to you, the gun dealer can help you change them. Alternatively, select a different gun.

   Fuzzy Eyesight — No, we're not talking about geezer eyebrows bushy enough to shade a person's face. Age brings a widening array of body parts that no longer work well. You might have considerable trouble getting your eyes to focus with standard handgun sights. Quickly drawing a pair of bifocals during a fight is not realistic. Instead, try a laser grip or a holographic sight. Both of these place the point of focus at the target, not at arm's length on the gun's standard sights.

Revolver or Semi-Auto Pistol?

Buy a revolver if you —
- Can't easily cycle the slide on a semi-automatic pistol
- Are overwhelmed by the complexity of features on a semi-auto
- Don't want to take meticulous care of the semi-auto and its ammunition
- Want a gun that is very simple to operate overall

Buy a semi-auto pistol if you want —
- A compact gun in a larger caliber
- More shots per load
- Fast loading
- Fast shooting

What Caliber?

Defensive firepower must be balanced with safety. Select the largest caliber that you can safely control. If the recoil of your gun always scares you and/or hurts your hand, then shooting it with total confidence and proficiency will be almost impossible.

Chapter 2 - Your Mission: Train

Deep in the bowels of gun lore, the debate over optimum self-defense caliber will continue to rage for many more decades. Most of our students are buying 9mm semi-auto pistols and .357 Magnum revolvers. Recoil from the 9mm is very manageable, and cartridges are economical. Revolvers which are built for the staggering .357 Magnum are also able to shoot gentler .38 Special and mid-range .38 Special +P cartridges. In my humble opinion, .22 caliber is not adequate for self-defense against Villain; for rodents the caliber is wonderful, but not for violent human pests.

What Brand?

"You get what you pay for" is very likely true with new guns and ammunition. Most manufacturers offer limited lifetime warranties with their handguns. If you theoretically do a quick internet search for the "best six-shot intergalactic phasonator," you might find innumerable reviews, blog posts, and comments with many contradictions, pontifications, and baseless factoids all mixed together.

Do some intelligent homework. There are many excellent handguns which will give you good service for many years. No handgun is perfect. Narrow your choices by Grip, Trigger Squeeze, and Sight Alignment. Take your time. Make your best choice. Adapt to the gun, and don't look back.

Selecting Your Firearm Training

All legitimate, certified firearm training is about safety. There are thousands of qualified firearm instructors in the United States. These dedicated safety pros offer a wide variety of courses.

How do you select one? Referrals from friends are always helpful. However, make sure your instructor focuses on defensive use of the handgun. Target shooting and defensive shooting begin with some common points. However, beyond only a few fundamentals, the two training disciplines differ a lot.

For example, when target shooting, the proper breathing method is to take a moderate breath, exhale to some comfortable point, then smoothly press the trigger to fire the shot. Defensive shooting demands constant breathing at a somewhat managed rate.

Aiming methods are also very different. Target shooting is best accomplished by focusing on the front sight of the handgun. In contrast, defensive handgun shooting requires your continuous focus on the predator. In a violent encounter, it is necessary to monitor Villain's every motion. This can't be done if you are only focused on the front sight of the gun. Fractions of a second are crucial. There is no time to waste by switching your focus from gun to Villain, then back to gun.

An easy way to determine if your instructor teaches defensive handgun shooting is, you guessed it, just ask! It might go like this, "Hello, I would like to enroll in one of your handgun courses. Do you offer defensive handgun training?" These are possible responses:
- "What do you mean, defensive?"
- "Well, there really is no difference."
- "If you're a beginner, you don't need that right now."

If you are blessed with any of the above answers, then graciously move along to consider another instructor. Get the best instruction that's available. Lives might depend on it!

Carrying Your Concealed Gun

We have as many holsters and variations of holsters in the marketplace as there are tennis shoes. So, what's the concern? Actually, it's a huge factor. Where and how you carry your handgun is crucial in defending yourself with the gun. In the next section we'll explore the One-Second Law. To meet the requirements of the One-Second Law, you must have a concealed carry method that supports *SPEED*.

There are four key considerations in deciding your carry technique: Concealment, Access, Retention, and Comfort. Our National Rifle Association's course handbooks and the U.S. Concealed Carry Association's *Concealed Carry and Home Defense Fundamentals*[18] are excellent resources on this topic.

Concealment — If you have a CCW license or permit, your gun is normally required to be concealed completely. This is easy if you always wear a jacket, but not so easy if you live in a hot climate with only a light-weight shirt to cover your pistol.

Access — Your gun must be concealed so you can get to it quickly. Safety is compromised if you need to wade through layers of clothing, zippers, buttons, even velcro closures.

Retention — No matter how you carry the gun, it needs to stay put; so it doesn't fall out if you get knocked down or forced into some position other than standing erect.

Comfort — Few things will discourage you more than trying to carry a handgun that's uncomfortable. Your combination of gun and holster must be comfortable for year-round, all-day wear.

Here are some common terms: "IWB," "Pancake," "Horsehide," "Level I," "SOB," "Condition 1," "Strong Side," etc. You're probably thinking, "Why did I buy this book?" Relax. Gun-lore terminology is not vast in scope, but it's too much to dive into in this book. Most important are the four factors cited above and making sure that your carry system matches your gun. Be certain that the holster you use is made specifically for your exact model of gun, and that you can carry it all day. Some astute shopping will bring you success.

One-Second Law

I teach a regimen to my concealed carry students, based on what we call the "One-Second Law." Again, *SPEED* is an essential part of our *X-Pree* framework. Anyone who is lawfully carrying a concealed handgun for self-defense should be able to draw from concealment and fire the first accurate shot at close range (up to 6 feet) in less than one second.

Here's the *X-Pree* logic behind the One-Second Law:
- In the U.S., violent encounters are generally finished in 3 to 5 seconds. To be safe, let's assume a worst-case time of 3 seconds.
- Villain can draw from a waistband and fire at close range in about 1.3 seconds.
- Trained Defenders need to deliver a reliable firearm defense in less than 1 second.
- Your One-Second Law is an essential training standard.

Train for the One-Second Law according to the following steps:

1. Begin by selecting your concealed carry method. Will you carry your gun "on-body"; that is, will it be in a holster which is attached directly to you? Or, will the gun be concealed in a purse or daypack? We call this "off-body." Inside-the-waistband (IWB) or ankle holsters might not allow a fast enough draw. However, if you can consistently keep your overall speed under 1 second with one of them, then my awestruck compliments to you!
2. After you figure out your carry method and its position — right or left, near front or at your back — you can determine how the gun is to be concealed. Will you wear a loose-fitting shirt over it? Will it be on your thigh under a skirt? Is a Hawaiian shirt going to work best, or a sport jacket?
3. Next, select a holster which fits your gun precisely. It should not allow the gun to flail around and fall out, but it should not slow down your draw either.
4. When all of the previous pieces are in order, begin practicing your draw using dummy rounds for at least the first 45 days of practice. Plant your non-shooting hand on your chest.
5. You will be able to perfect the draw by conducting your practice very slowly, first reaching your holstered gun, then grasping it with your shooting grip. This step is critical. Your hand must land on the gun with something close to your exact shooting grip, less your thumb and trigger finger which must be fully extended. Work out this step ultra-slowly, paying attention to every detail.
6. Practice drawing the gun and immediately rotating it toward the target at close range. For this step, use an assistant, a laser, or a light to determine the angle to hold your gun. At no more than 6 feet from a human silhouette target, learn the correct angle to point the gun when it's just outside your holster or purse.
7. Be certain that you angle the gun slightly so the slide on a semi-automatic pistol does not hit your ribs when it operates. Position your revolver so the front of the cylinder is forward of a vertical plane at your chin — to reduce the effects of muzzle blast.
8. Verify that your shooting hand is aligned straight with your arm, so your wrist is not bent. This will enable your hand, wrist, and arm to work together in absorbing the recoil.
9. Don't rush to attain speed. Your *SPEED* will improve naturally as you practice your draw/fire form the same way every time.

10. Practice your optimum draw and dry-fire shot for 10 to 15 minutes per day over 45 days without using live ammunition.
11. Complete at least 1,500 repetitions, making sure that you can squeeze off the first dry-fire shot in less than 1 second before you begin to practice with live ammunition.
12. It's most important to learn your precise draw method very slowly at first, paying close attention to your safe, perfect form! Your speed will improve naturally when your technique is identical with every draw. If you rush the process by jumping into live fire, the noise and recoil from the gun will be a major distraction, delaying your attainment of *SPEED*.

Do NOT begin practicing the One-Second Law with live ammunition. Your One-Second Law applies to any self-defense tool, not just a firearm.

Continuing Education

There are five other relevant points related to your self-defense firearm training. Your safety will be improved by the following:
1. Stay current in your knowledge of laws and proposed legislation related to firearm ownership and use in your jurisdiction.
2. Learn to accurately shoot while you are moving, and learn to shoot moving targets. Exquisite stationary target shooting is valuable and necessary at the beginning of everyone's defensive firearm training. However, real world gunfights rarely occur in restricted spaces where two combatants stay in place. Classic dueling expired centuries ago.
3. Consider training with non-lethal cartridges. Availability and cost are improving for this ammo which enables you to safely practice in many creative environments — including your house, garage, or yard.
4. Investigate laser training systems. Sophisticated, yet simplified, indoor/outdoor equipment enables you to develop nearly all gun handling and marksmanship skills in almost any environment. These systems are either low-noise or silent.
5. Continue honing skills such as threat assessment, gun handling, and mid-range handgun shooting (i.e., target at 75 feet).

In-person courses which are certified by the National Rifle Association

(NRA)[19] or the United States Concealed Carry Association (USCCA)[20] are excellent, affordable, and widely available. You will receive a handbook and a course completion certificate as evidence that you are prepared to contribute to a safer world of gun ownership.

If learning exclusively in your pajamas more closely fits your lifestyle, at-home training media are available from Concealed Carry University,[21] I.C.E. Training,[22] and USCCA. There is heavy emphasis on safety throughout these training programs. In fact, safety is the core of the course offerings.

Active Shooter Training

Referring to the need for civilian training in the complex, violent dynamic of active shooter defense, a pivotal 2016 study cites the following:

> "The 'active' aspect of the definition inherently implies that both law enforcement personnel and citizens have the potential to affect the outcome of the event based upon their responses to the situation. The consistency of these incidents supports the paramount need for training and exercises for law enforcement, other first responders, and citizens alike." [23]

Out of 200 active shooter events studied from the year 2000 to 2015, twenty-seven of those incidents were stopped by citizen intervention.[24] Is this a blanket endorsement to launch your second career packing heat and hunting down active shooters? No. On the contrary, it's a wake up call to all American civilians about the need to obtain specialized training devoted to active shooter defenses. There is much to do in this arena. Fortunately, as Americans, there is much we are able to do!

Fire Extinguisher & Hose

With an average weight of 4 to 20 pounds, dry chemical fire extinguishers are superb defense tools. Creating a thick powdery fog will buy you seconds to counter attack and disable Villain. If spraying his face is not a viable solution, built-in solid handles give you a sure grip to swing these oversized red clubs.

To train for use of the fire extinguisher, simply sacrifice the dry agent in one of them by test spraying a trash can outdoors. You might be surprised at the range and thick coverage just one unit provides.

Another close relative of the fire extinguisher is the fire hose. Many commercial buildings still have standpipes and working hoses. In addition to providing a defensive blast of water, the nozzle can double as a heavy club. Strewn in a hallway or stairwell, hoses and wet surfaces can slow Villain down. Yes, tripping works well.

If your building still has a fire hose system, get trained in its use. However, target practice using a charged hose is not recommended.

Flashlight

Have you ever looked straight into a camera as the flash goes off? Then you know how disorienting it can be. Likewise, your self-defense flashlight can be exceptionally useful. There are hundreds available today, in all sizes and power levels.

Many defense lights are under 6 inches long and about 1 inch in diameter. This compact size works nicely for most people. Many of them are water- and impact-resistant. Batteries are easy to find in a variety of stores. Some flashlights are rechargeable, even by USB port.

Older lights with the classic breakable switch along the side of the flashlight have been replaced by a sturdy push-button control at the tail end of the body. Modern lights are often selectable with high, low, and strobe beams.

"Lumens" are the units that measure the amount of light coming from your light. How many lumens should your self-defense flashlight have? Well, 150 lumens is a good minimum. Some larger, high-output lights are rated for 2,000 lumens or more. Peak output of the left flashlight in the photo is 850 lumens. Theorists estimate that Villain will be momentarily blinded at night with 150 lumens, in the daylight with 300 lumens.

Here's a crude example: If we directed all the light from a standard 60 watt incandescent light bulb into a small beam, that would be the brightness of a 800 lumen flashlight. Imagine the predator who is skulking around in the dark, with eyes conditioned to very dim light. Then, at 15 feet or less, you flash your 800 lumens into Villain's eyes. It is extremely bright! Temporarily blinded, he will be vulnerable to your escape or your counter attack.

Another handy feature on modern flashlights is a defensive bezel. What? That rim around the front end of the flashlight is called the "bezel." If it's notched (faceted or crenellated) it will deliver a lot of pain when impacting Villain's face or head.

High intensity flashlights don't require any type of permit. They can be carried nearly everywhere. Their value is extremely high because of their ability to temporarily disable Villain's vision. After the 2012 theater shooting in Aurora, CO, several experienced specialists agreed that the use of only one defensive flashlight by one movie-goer would have probably blinded the mass murderer for several seconds, enabling a possible counter attack.

In addition to all of the above, today's compact flashlights can illuminate objects that are several hundred feet away.

Your *X-Pree* self-defense flashlight needs to fit your hand securely and be located where you can use it in One Second!

CHAPTER 2 - YOUR MISSION: TRAIN

Knife

There are hundreds of knives in today's marketplace. However, you can quickly narrow your choices by considering two factors — legality and grip. Your defensive knife must be legal, and it must fit you.

U.S. states and many smaller jurisdictions have laws about what types and sizes of knives can be carried concealed or in plain view. Pay close attention to variations in these rules and act in compliance. Know the law!

If the knife handle is too large, you cannot get a tight enough grip on it. If it's too small you will never get a tight grip, boosting the likelihood that your hand will slip down the handle, past the guard, and get severely cut by the blade.

There are only two major categories of knives: Fixed Blade and Folding Blade — pretty simple. Fixed blade knives have a blade sticking out of the handle all the time. They require a sheath to protect the person carrying it and the blade. Folding knives (jack knives) have a blade that pivots on one end, either out to a locked open position or folded closed inside the handle.

Today's knife handles are made of a wide variety of materials: steel, aluminum, wood, high-tech plastics, bone, etc. Knife blades built for professional use are made of hardened steel with either smooth or serrated edges. For under $100 you can buy an excellent knife with a razor-sharp blade.

Stabbing is the traditional self-defense knife technique. For this one you'll need a rock-solid grip. Repeated stabs with a narrow blade are usually necessary to incapacitate your predator. As usual, *SPEED* is the winning element, partnered with accuracy. Major arteries and components of Villain's circulatory system are your targets.

Slashing is the alternate method for your knife defense. You'll need a very firm grip on the handle. Slash Villain with your arms close to your body; either upward, downward, diagonally, or from side-to-side. If you slash with majestic sweeping arcs, your performance might look good in a movie, but on the street your act (and your life) will be short. Ruining Villain's arteries and key muscles will stop him. *SPEED* is king, not your award-winning musketeer reenactment.

You must have a training dummy for practice. Human skin is somewhat tough. To simulate it, gather a bundle of rags into a pillow case or old clothes, then wrap your dummy in two or three heavy trash bags. Practice stabbing and slashing your dummy in his neck, upper shoulder, inside upper arm, center of chest, abdomen, groin, and inner thigh.

Use extreme caution with any knife. Begin with slow and light strikes, increasing your speed and power gradually. You will develop a precise grip that works for you. Stick to it, with only a few refinements as needed.

That One-Second Law applies here, too. You will likely have one second to counter attack Villain on the street. Identify your knife and your carry style accordingly.

Kubotan

It's one of the most useful defense tools around (pronounced "KYOO-bu-tan"). Contemporary kubotans come in a few shapes and colors. My students sometimes forget the name, describing it as "that clever pointy thing." Most kubotans are about 6" long with a built-in key ring. Good ones are made of strong aluminum.

Gripping the kubotan with your hammer fist, its pointed end can be directed at Villain's exposed body regions. His eyes, neck, solar plexus, and groin are favorites, but driving the point into many other spots will give him intense pain.

Your training here is simple:
1. Practice a solid grip.
2. Be ready to get your kubotan into the fight in one second.

Marshmallows

There is a pervasive attitude among millions of sweet, kindhearted, civilized people that Innocents are obligated to treat Villain nicely. They want to avoid striking him at any cost. They desire to fire warning shots near Villain with the hope that he will have a miraculous change of heart. They want to merely scare him away. Envisioning a perfect environment, they will do anything to entirely avoid hurting Villain.

> **Attention:** Thrown marshmallows are not reliable defense tools, unless they are launched by the bushel.

Pepper Spray

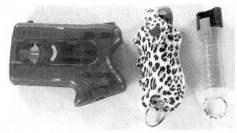

Also known as "OC Spray" (oleoresin capsicum), Pepper Spray is named for the hot component in chilis or peppers. Manufacturers use chemicals to extract the OC, then add a liquid solution, and finally load it into a small pressurized canister.

Extreme Preemption

Defense by Pepper Spray can be an extraordinary success. It can also be a deplorable failure. It does a few things to the person receiving a dose of the spray. First, if it gets into the eyes it will cause intense pain and heavy tearing; usually, this radically limits or shuts down Villain's vision. Second, any skin that is exposed to OC immediately will have an excruciating burning sensation.

It's important to remember that any skin which is touched by Pepper Spray will suffer the intense burning sensation, including yours. If you get caught in the spray mist or breathe it, your body will react just like Villain's.

Can it be wiped off? Not easily. Any wiping of the oily OC spreads the oil and the pain. Thoroughly washing the sprayed area somewhat reduces the effects. Time is the most common remedy, and not a happy one to endure.

Buying a canister with a concentration of about 2% gives you a potent defense tool. Useful range of most sprays is less than 10 feet. If Villain has been juiced up with alcohol or drugs, beware that he might not be affected as much, possibly not at all.

Effects of OC spray usually last 30 minutes or more, giving you time to get to safety. OC spray is designed for use as a distraction so you can escape the area. Immediately sending your predator into a helpless fetal bundle on the ground is not a guaranteed outcome.

Pepper Spray is far superior to Mace, because it works on **any** skin, not only the eyes. On social media, you might see some old posts encouraging the use of bug or wasp spray for self-defense. Do not use one of those. There are notices on the spray canisters forbidding their use for anything but insects. It's in fact a violation of federal law.

"Bear Attack" OC versions are available, but the large size of the canisters makes them difficult to carry in a concealed manner.

Some fundamental training is a good idea. I highly recommend buying an inert training canister to experiment with it. Pepper Spray is readily available and legal for self-defense use in most U.S. states. Verify this with your local law enforcement agency, asking about subtleties in the law. In some rare cases there have been minor long-term side effects on predators. Villain's breathing can become very difficult with coughing and/or asthmatic reactions.

Many canisters have key rings built into them, but your attached keys can easily get tangled with the small canister and trigger an accidental discharge in your pocket or purse. You'll be safe keeping a canister very handy and thoughtfully stored. Remember, you have One Second to get your Pepper Spray canister into the fight.

Security Systems

Right before our eyes, Burglar Alarms (an ancient 20th century name) have now morphed into "Security Systems" which can work wirelessly, see everything in a designated space, control traditional electric fixtures, and install without a building contractor's help.

Along with nearly every tech advancement in phones and cameras, our contemporary security systems are sleek, slick, and simple. You can install the components almost anywhere if you have a basic plug-in ability. Smartphone and mobile applications enable you to control the system from any location where your phone works.

Because the entire system is cellular-based, you can get the following:
- Immediate notifications and alerts
- Live video feeds
- Automation of your home
- Fire alerts
- Carbon monoxide alerts
- Health and life alerts
- System tampering alerts

In the huge security marketplace there are also alarms which use land lines, a.k.a. corded phone lines. But, they're being overrun by new technology that makes security systems more reliable and less expensive.

Someone right now is saying, "Whoa, buddy! Those cellular systems can be hacked!" This is true, but system manufacturers are also aware of that challenge. Software updates can easily be added as the defensive improvements are made available. Alternatively, one snip of a phone line running an older corded system will disable it.

Many good security systems are available. Do some thorough homework, then choose one which you can afford.

Tactical Pen

Defensive pens are becoming popular among many of our safety students. These pens have a durable body, are easy to carry almost anywhere, and pack some nasty impact or puncture wounds when used properly.

Unlike a standard pen, the tactical version has a graspable body which is made to withstand a strike to Villain's targeted regions — eyes, head, throat, neck, solar plexus, groin, and thigh.

Your strike with the tactical pen is simple. Use a very tight grip, coupled with fast, targeted stabs. As always, do some respectable homework to determine if the pen's grip and cartridge replacement are easy to manage. Prepare to also deploy this tool in One Second.

Yes, I have breached my "Ground Rules" by not sparing you from all things **Tactical**. But, if you purchase one of these pens, you will likely honor my transgression with warm appreciation of another effective self-defense tool. And, yes, you can write with it too.

Vehicle

Your car, truck, even motorcycle, is a lethal tool when used to hit or run over Villain. Be aware that your apparent insulation inside a vehicle can be compromised. Windows can be quickly broken. Bullets can travel through glass and doors. So again, when driving, always be aware of what's happening around you. Keep vehicle doors locked at all times.

You cannot engage in any form of road rage and call it legal defensive driving. Your vehicle is a deadly weapon. Your ITOTR rules apply here.

In traffic, always have an escape route. Practice allowing enough distance in front of your vehicle to get free of the congestion by driving right, left, over a curb, or making a u-turn. No matter what you're in or on, **never** get boxed in with no escape route!

Summary

Perfecting the world's greatest arsenal of personal defense tools is an admirable goal. Our readiness to use those defense tools is enough reason to have them. Still, they are inanimate objects. Our training must progress beyond simple defense tool handling and play simulations.

For example, if you choose pepper spray as a defense tool, make an investment to strategize your carry method, research the effectiveness of the canister you own, understand the relevant laws in your jurisdiction, and properly maintain your spray unit. Don't make a purchase, then throw the canister in the bottom of a purse or briefcase feeling confident in your ability to use it defensively. Villain is betting that you cling to this illusory view of your defensive ability.

In his *Self-Defense Training System*, Damian Ross boils it down:
> "No matter how deadly a weapon is, it can do nothing by itself. A weapon is a tool, it needs someone with intent to pick it up and use it. So the faster you can attack, injure and disable your assailant, the greater are your chances of surviving and winning an assault...Your ability to defend yourself is directly related to how much you can injure your target, period." [25]

Choose defense tools which match your lifestyle and your resources. Some people enjoy training with media-based systems because the curriculum can be followed at home, any hour of the day. Other folks prefer the in-person, classroom environment. Pursue whatever training enables you to learn your defense tools well. Also, train as you live — in your business suit, bathing suit, or birthday suit. Train in the manner you live everyday life.

Watching a few random online videos is not real training!

Many students repeatedly attend courses, but never practice the skills introduced in those sessions until their next formal training. This habit is a hindrance to safety. Commencement will occur at the end of your course, but it signifies a "beginning." Content from any superb training session can quickly fade from your memory unless you **practice** the skills which are presented by the instructor. Graduating from a formal course is not the end of your learning experience on that subject; it's the beginning.

Remember our *X-Pree* framework: *Train, Detect, Preempt — FAST*. If you never have a criminal encounter ever in your life, but you are ready to respond anyway, you will probably have decades of peace-filled days.

Next, we move to the *Detect* phase of *X-Pree*. Villain's attacks can take many dangerous forms. Early discovery of his plan to attack you is an essential component in *Extreme Preemption*.

Complete Topic Discussion 2,
then go to Chapter 3 — Your Mission: Detect.

Topic Discussion 2 — *Train*

In your own words, why is your mind the core weapon in your self-defense?

What are the differences between Awareness and Avoidance?

How is training for street fighting different from training for competitive martial arts?

Is running away from a violent encounter a good defense? Why or why not?

Does your state allow carrying a tire thumper or bat in your car for self-defense?

What is a shillelagh?

How would you use a bat and a cane similarly in self-defense?

TOPIC DISCUSSION 2

What is the One-Second Law? Why is it critical in self-defense?

What are the attributes of a high quality self-defense flashlight?

Do adopted defense tools require practice? Why or why not?

What knives can be legally concealed in your jurisdiction?

What are the advantages and disadvantages of pepper spray?

Notes:

CHAPTER 3 - YOUR MISSION: DETECT

By this time you should have at least a sprouting confidence in your ability to acquire and become proficient in some self-defense tools. Detection is the next critical building block in the construction of our *X-Pree* framework. This section is devoted to the fine art of detection in its many forms.

If we are never able to detect criminal action before we get hurt, there is little value in learning about defense tools. We can wear bright targets on our shirts with the lure "Attack Me First." What a nice service this is for people around us who are genuinely concerned about their safety. Volunteering as live bait for Villain will be thoroughly appreciated by everyone nearby! And, it will make crime very profitable. With many "Attack Me First" folks present, predators will always have a juicy assortment of easy victims.

Contrastingly, if we are always, or nearly always, able to detect criminal action before we get hurt, our training to use defense tools has great value. We can see danger coming and we're ready to handle it before we are injured. All the readiness in the universe to avoid an oncoming freight train is worthless if we don't see that train coming. But, if we know what to look for, if we know how to spot a dangerous freight train, and if we see the actual train coming — then, a simple hop to the side of the tracks will keep us safe.

Is Detection Possible?

Imagine Villain standing next to you poised with an overhead strike to smash you with a baseball bat. Woe to you if you never see the bat before it lands. Somewhat better is your spotting the bat as it's falling; you might be able to block the strike. Still better is your identifying signs given by Villain that he's going to raise the bat to hit you. Finally, a perfect solution is your extra-sensory perception that he intends to hurt you. That would give you plenty of warning, plenty of time to not go near Villain in the first place.

You might be wondering, "Are you saying that I need to be clairvoyant to be safe?" No. As with all things *X-Pree*, we will explore some ideas that stretch you. Whoa! Before you light your barbecue with this book, let me explain.

We've all heard the expression, "Well, I sure didn't see that one coming!" We have a wide range of popular apologetic expressions: "It was impossible to predict!"; "Absolutely no warning signs!"; and "Wow, it came out of nowhere!" Everyone has likely experienced something bad which was also a complete surprise. Can we do better? Yes. Can we see the danger ahead of time? Yes.

There are federal agencies with lots of employees with lots of equipment who are watching and listening. No worries. They do it to keep us safe. Let's be serious. Average citizens don't have those kinds of resources. So, we give the government considerable slack. If we're going to have either pure privacy or radically enhanced safety, let's vote for safety.

Here are the big questions: In our everyday lives is detection of bad guys by ordinary citizens possible? Yes, it is. How often is it possible? Very often. Does it require clairvoyance? No. Does it take some clear-headed thinking? Absolutely yes! What is the importance of detection in today's culture? Extreme.

In 2014, Patrick Van Horne and Jason A. Riley brought us significant refinement in the detection process with their systematic approach presented in *Left of Bang*.[26] They point out a key advantage for all Defenders is the abundance of pre-incident indicators displayed by Villains. This premise is not new. Over twenty years ago, experts rattled the civilian safety world with the declaration that warning signs are always present.[27] Villain's decision to harm others is not the result of an instantaneously snapped mind.

By the end of this study, you should be able to detect a variety of criminal behaviors and preempt them. There are no special talents required. No special education is needed, only your sincere desire to *Train, Detect, and Preempt — FAST*.

Detection Basics

Our adopted dog Oreo is usually a mellow and gentle guy. He spends his happy days playing, eating, and sleeping indoors. But the sight of a lizard outside in the yard works an instantaneous transformation in our little buddy. He launches a wigged out pacing-strutting-let's-go-attack persona that always gets our immediate attention, and it also tires him out. My wife and I are thankful that he hasn't yet run over or through anything of high value in the house. If you continuously live in a mode similar to Oreo's hyper-vigilance, your life expectancy is going to be reduced.

Here's a tiny neuroscience summary: We accept information through the brain's section called the Thalamus, which takes an initial look at what it receives through our senses. If the incoming info is non-critical (non-emergency), the Sensory Cortex processes and then messages the Motor Cortex which tells muscle groups to stand up, sit down, lift a towel, turn a door handle, etc. At this point in the body's operation we experience normal activities.

If there are signs of a crisis (emergency) received by the Thalamus, the brain's Amygdala jumps into gear and triggers some special glands into action. In particular, the pituitary gland jumps up, then the adrenal glands release adrenaline and cortisol into the blood. Instantly, our heart and breathing rates skyrocket causing the Motor Cortex to work muscle groups at reflexive speed.

Together with this high stimulation, we experience the loss of some motor skills. These are tasks in which we use delicate finger movement. In crisis mode, we inherently lose the ability to complete those finely tuned motions; such as, screwing a small lid onto a bottle, dialing numbers on a tiny keypad, painting accurately with a brush, and writing gracefully.

Some ugly physical and psychological problems occur if we operate in this critical mode for indefinite periods of time. These include the negative affects of stress on our bodies and minds from our own chemicals, which are designed for short-term emergencies, not for long-term use.

When we voluntarily dwell in crisis mode more than we should, the toll on us is genuine. It's important to grow into a detection attitude that is balanced, calm, and wise — not frenzied. All of us must give attention to the healthy balance of work and rest. We must also maintain a safe balance of awareness and relaxation.

How do we remain vigilant, but not to the degree that it destroys us? How is that accomplished? We get there primarily through our preparedness. Our overall readiness to defend against Villain's plans helps all of us remain calm. Learning *Extreme Preemption* will give you a substantial boost in this process.

Is there an element of detection that is entirely natural, in other words built into us? Is there an easy piece of this whole safety puzzle that doesn't require intense study or sweat? There is! Your gut feeling, instinct, intuition, whatever you want to call it, is your best companion. It's powerful. It's an easy and potent defense mechanism.

Now, you might be confused. So, let's get unconfused. In the vast spectrum of safety, your intuition is your best ally. When confronted by danger, your instinct will ring your alarm bell as discomfort or fear. Fear is good. Fear is an easy, natural response to danger, enabling you to detect and do amazing things. But, too much time in fear is not good. We'll give you examples to clarify all of this in the *Preemption* portion of the book.

Personal Goals

In the introduction I proposed this:
> *"Envision your private security force. You get up in the morning and greet personal guards who have been at their posts all night. Then, leave home with a day plan filled with action, knowing that a well-trained force is ready to defeat any threat to your safety. Return home relaxed and refreshed, expecting another great sleep, confident that your security team will deal with any danger which occurs during the night."*

Safety's best result is a soothing peace. Tense, fearful days filled with frightening unknowns are not healthy days. Terrorism, by definition, is the production of intense fear. That's what folks acting as terrorists hope for us. Their ambition is to give us unlimited days soaked with the dark stench of worry about unknown future catastrophes. What's most healthful for us is the calm, always-ready condition which comes by *X-Pree*.

Caution: Do not travel down the Law Enforcement Look-Alike Road. Currently, there are over one million law enforcement officers serving in the United States.[28] In most cases, their training is extensive. They have equipment and skills for enforcement which the majority of us don't have. Plus, average citizens are not normally authorized to detain or arrest a suspected criminal. Do not fall for the notion that by self-appointment you can run around acting as a sworn officer, spy, or other government agent.

However, the U.S. government is emphatically asking for your help as a citizen observer. On September 11, 2001 the shock of death, injury, and property damage from a terrorist attack was perhaps seconded only by the revelation of existing barriers in inter-agency communications. After President Bush appointed the first Director of Department of Homeland Security (DHS) on September 22, 2001,[29] twenty-two federal agencies allied their efforts to radically enhance U.S. national security.

On September 12, 2001 a New York ad agency offered the Metropolitan Transit Authority its slogan, "If you see something, say something." By July 2010, DHS launched a nationwide campaign asking for U.S. citizens to report suspicious activity we might detect in our everyday lives:
> *"Because only you know what's supposed to be in your everyday. Informed, alert communities play a critical role in keeping our nation safe. 'If You See Something, Say Something™' engages the public in protecting our homeland through awareness–building, partnerships, and other outreach."* [30]

We all have opportunities to observe and report many types of crime, including terrorism. Our warnings, which are propelled by ill feelings, should motivate our actions without incapacitating us.

Are we really a bunch of semi-conscious blobs of protoplasm waiting to be annihilated in ambushes with no choice in the matter? No, we're not. Are there always signs that trouble is ahead for us? Yes, and we need to recognize them.

Are there changes we need to make? Certainly. *X-Pree* is the framework within which you can live a safe, peaceable life. Can trouble still approach to smack you in the face? Yes, but you will have clues, and you can be ready to stop Villain's strike.

"What?" Not, "Why?"

Turn back the clock to around 1870 in Verona, Italy. We find Cesare Lombroso, a pioneer criminologist, hard at work on his anthropological criminology theory — associating someone's physical features with that person's probable criminal behavior. According to Lombroso, if you have enlarged lips and oversized jaw, for example, you will be more likely to commit a serious crime. His theory was later discarded, but his analytical approach was an early version of profiling, which has been used by law enforcement departments for many decades.

Since Lombroso's time, criminal psychologists have been trying to figure out why people do bad things; that is, why do some people commit crimes? Here is a partial array of influences that might cause someone to choose criminal activity: social status, heredity, economic status, political preference, age, education, free choice, emotions, biochemistry, loneliness, addiction, boredom, psychological defect, class label, physical defect, disease, illness, and on and on.

What is the conclusion reached by today's best criminologists? Answer: They agree that no single factor is responsible for crime more than another:
> "No single theory has gained ascendance as an explanatory model for all types of violence. Perhaps the diversity in behaviors regarded as violent poses an inherent barrier to such a global theory." [31]

Well, whoopdy-doo! That's hardly any help for the rest of us! Fine, let's dig a little deeper and turn our effort away from the "Why?" of criminal thinking and toward the "What?" of criminal behavior. What is it that criminals do which we might detect early in their process of committing a crime?

Discerning any feature of criminal behavior is a priceless advantage in preempting the completion of a criminal act. For example, the Swedes remind us,

> "No one is born a terrorist. The aim must be to identify radicalisation processes as early as possible in order to counteract further radicalisation of these groups or individuals and prevent them from ultimately committing terrorist acts." [32]

There it is! As we focus on the "What?" of Villain's actions instead of the "Why?", we learn there are many sturdy stepping stones for us to cross the muddy river of criminal behavior detection. This principle holds true with all varieties of crime.

Flavors of Villain

People are individuals with different souls, physical features, and experiences. There are no two criminal profiles that match in all categories. However, we can confidently group Villains into a few common flavors: Psychopath, Sociopath, Narcissist, and Machiavellian. We see these qualities acted out by the Cash Villain, the Control Villain, and sometimes the Terror Villain.

Professionals in the psych fields generally gather their information then publish findings based on empirical data and clinical case studies. Empirical data is information we can gather using our senses, by observing and/or experimenting. Clinical case studies usually take considerable time to build, because a person needs to be studied over time.

Since the probability of recruiting a criminal volunteer prior to his commission of a crime is very low, there were only a few formal studies focused on the pre-incident indicators. Hence, there is a growing consensus among criminal psychologists that such studies must get much more attention and funding than they are currently receiving.

In the year 2000 Professor Andrew Silke reiterated this about research on terrorism:

> *"Our knowledge of terrorism most certainly is deficient but the field shows no clear ability to improve this situation. After 30 years of study, we simply should know more about terrorism than we currently do. That we continue to languish at this level of ignorance on such a serious subject is a cause of grave concern."* [33]

Fortunes can be spent globally on psychological inquiries, while at the same time, elite professionals in the field still have plenty of unanswered questions. Given the scope of such a to-do list, falling back to reliance on our own empirical data doesn't sound so far-fetched. In fact, it is our best plan when we need answers right away. As ordinary citizens, we can rely on ourselves to detect the signals, odors, and alarms of criminal behavior before someone gets hurt.

These "pre-incident indicators," "precursors," or "behavioral indicators," as professionals call them, are detectable by all of us. There are some naming conventions associated with Villain's many varieties. Not all versions are universally accepted by all psych practitioners. So, we'll proceed here with the most common forms.

Oh, just one more thing. Before we dive in, let's remember that no one is perfect. If you see some sprinkles of the following deviant behaviors in people you know — or even more frightening, in yourself — no worries! Everyone is flawed, regardless of how angelic he or she might appear. Yes, even you and I.

We probably would not take a car with a speck of rust to the junk yard and abandon it. Likewise, we should not be too hasty in discarding friends or family members over a few tiny behavioral blemishes. When I'm tempted to do so, I consult my mirror. My anxiety is usually relieved in seconds.

Among the human population, we all express a blend of qualities which are, at the same time, both unique and common. Let's investigate some of Villain's common flavors to see what they are like.

Psychopath

Our classic psychopath is a person who is void of conscience and empathy.

He selfishly takes whatever he wants without feeling any regret or guilt. His actions are impulsive and erratic, freely taking on high-risk conduct. Incapable of nurturing normal relationships, the psychopath turns his victims' emotional weaknesses into his opportunities for ruthless physical or monetary control. He is volatile with a high propensity for violence.

Sociopath

With more control than a psychopath, our sociopath is a schemer and calculator. Suffering from antisocial personality disorder, he can appear normal in a shallow relationship, while designing a plan to prey on his selected partner by manipulation. His control extends through his own behavior by taking calculated risks, but lacking empathy and remorse. Dangerous, frightening circumstances don't upset him. Social norms, including friends, have little value for him. He thoughtfully pursues crimes of opportunity with an inconsistent willingness to use violence.

Narcissist

This one is frequently an attractive, flamboyant type. Personal vanity, a hunger for admiration, and an entitlement attitude are dominant traits of the narcissist. He is named after a young Greek mythological hunter (Narcissus) who was enraptured by his own reflection in a pool of water. He must be in control as a manipulator or as an idol with people who are near him. He can fall into rage if he's not in control or he perceives that his image is tarnished by criticism.

Machiavellian

Here we have an elegant name for entirely despicable behavior. Machiavelli was a politician (c.1500) who chose to turn deception into an art form. He demonstrated that trickery without limits was the core principle in his successful politics. Our machiavellian takes craftiness to levels which are shameless, and dishonesty to levels which are ruthless. Needless to say, he is incompetent in perceiving the sentimental needs of others. Why bother? He frequently dabbles in two sports: white-collar crime and the annihilation of his victims' feelings. While he will likely avoid violence, he will trample the hearts of those who get in his way.

CHAPTER 3 - YOUR MISSION: DETECT

Dr. Wendy Patrick's book *RED FLAGS* is an excellent study in which she reveals the essence of the "Dark Triad Personality" — narcissist, psychopath, and machiavellian combined.[34] Her tag for this Villain is merciful, considering his perverse neapolitan ice cream nature which often looks delicious on the outside while it is fundamentally as black and poisonous as tar.

Those four popular flavors of Villain, in turn, drive his criminal behavior. In our present world culture we have three classes of dangerous actors. Our Cash Villain, Control Villain, and the most recent Terror Villain all exhibit some of the classic flavors. However, they do so in varying degrees. After all, no two people are the same.

Cash Villain

Our Villain in this class is simply a person who wants your stuff. He will rob you and burglarize your home or business to steal personal property. His reasons vary. Most often he wants to sell what he steals to generate cash to support his drug or alcohol addiction. He is certainly a criminal, but not necessarily an ignorant one, learning and refining his skills with every crime.

Control Villain

As a particularly twisted character, the Control Villain wants the exhilaration which accompanies acts of violence. Our rapists and serial murderers typically commit acts in order to satisfy their desire to cause and control physical and emotional pain in their victims.

Terror Villain

Last and perhaps most popular on our list is the Terror Villain. Humanity's least humane behavior is currently falling under this heading. In 2007 the U.S. Department of State defined terrorism as,

> "premeditated, politically motivated violence perpetrated against noncombatant targets by subnational groups or clandestine agents, usually intended to influence an audience."

The Federal Bureau of Investigation (FBI, USA) defined terrorism as,

> "the unlawful use of force or violence against persons or property to intimidate or coerce a government, the civilian population, or any segment thereof, in furtherance of political or social objectives."

Professor Silke cites this dominant strategy by today's Terror Villain:
> "Fundamentally, terrorist campaigns are about breaking the will of the enemy. ...To do this, one does not need to kill all of the enemy's personnel or destroy all of its resources. One simply has to destroy the idea that ultimate victory is possible." [35]

Sadly, recent terrorist acts include murder by public beheadings, torture, excruciating rape, mutilation, drowning, burning, bombing, acid sprays, and running down pedestrians. Murder of women and children, and murder by women and children are now part of an international terrorist standard. Unthinkable brutalities which used to be classed as preposterous even by violent criminals are now trendy tactics meted out by today's Terror Villains.

Over several decades, psych professionals have looked closely at terrorist violence. There is an elusive nature about terrorism which defies simple categorization and conventional problem-solving. When a terrorist act is committed, government officials normally piece together the steps that the terrorists followed in their cycle of planning to completion of a plot. This would ordinarily be invaluable in the suppression of future terrorist acts except for one thing. Terrorists are adapting and modifying their strategies as they are discovered.

We are left with a bundle of observations:
- Terrorist attacks are being committed by "lone wolves" as well as teams.
- Their targets are increasing in size, from small to larger groups of Innocents.
- Terror Villains continue to refine their tactics.
- Their international reach continues to expand wherever their presence is tolerated by the indigenous population.

In a comprehensive study published in 2004, Randy Borum cites Walter Laqueur's conclusion based on more than twenty years of personal research on the topic:

> "Many terrorisms exist, and their character has changed over time and from country to country. The endeavor to find a 'general theory' of terrorism, one overall explanation of its roots, is a futile and misguided enterprise. ...Terrorism has changed over time and so have the terrorists, their motives, and the causes of terrorism." [36]

So, what is today's Terror Villain? When we consider the common flavors of Villain, there is a strong tendency to label the terrorist under one or more of our common varieties — perhaps psychopath or sociopath. There is robust logic in doing this because of the horrific nature of his actions. In fact, a few contemporary violent actors show clear symptoms of psychoses and/or personality disorders.[37]

Alternatively, we might consider another attractive theory which asserts,
> "the root cause of the threat we face is the extremist ideology itself." [38]

> "Terrorist violence most often is deliberate (not impulsive), strategic, and instrumental; it is linked to and justified by ideological (e.g., political, religious) objectives and almost always involves a group or multiple actors/supporters." [39]

This means the core beliefs of terrorists are a creed by which they grow from novice, non-violent volunteers in a terrorist group to skilled, committed murderers performing heinous acts on behalf of the group. Is his extremist ideology really the essence Terror Villain's behavior?

To round out our analysis, we should consider a third view. There is sizable research which shows that people are drawn to terrorism more because of identity issues than ideology. Professor Silke and Dr. Rick O'Gormon offer us this perspective:
> "We contend that recognising the altruistic dimension to terrorism is essential to fully understanding terrorism and, ultimately, moderating it."

> "The key message is that you have got to see the terrorists as they see themselves if you genuinely want to understand why people are getting involved. If you talk to terrorists themselves, they portray

> themselves as altruists — they see themselves as fighting on behalf of others..."
>
> "This theme of fighting on behalf of others and in reaction to the suffering of others... recurs frequently in accounts of the personal motivation of individual terrorists."
>
> "So you need to see it more in terms of how they see themselves and how they see the world. Then you can see the incentives to join and realistic obstacles to them doing it." [40]

After considering all of the above, our decoded conclusions about present-day Terror Villains are these:
- They are not, psychologically, fitting the classic flavors of Villain.
- They often see themselves as benefactors and political activists.
- They view themselves as heroes in a global struggle to free their people from oppression, using violence whenever necessary.
- Their logic is most often not aligned with brainwashing.

In his book *Terrorism: All That Matters*, Silke emphasizes,
> "Mental illness is not a factor in explaining terrorist behavior. Also, most terrorists are not 'psychopaths.'" [41]
>
> "Psychologists and psychiatrists who have met and assessed terrorists face-to-face have nearly always concluded that these people were in no way abnormal and instead have surprisingly stable and rational personalities." [42]

Nonetheless, thousands of innocent people in many countries are dying at the hands of terrorists. Most of us don't understand or even care about "Why?" Instead, we are concerned with "What?" the terrorist does to reveal his agenda before the killing begins. This enables us to preempt the murders.

Dr. Borum reached a similar conclusion, and he recommended the following:
> "When exploring the realm of terrorism, or other violent behavior, it may seem intriguing or even tempting to speculate about the

personality or internal dynamics of the actors. These questions may have some theoretical or even scientific merit, but they are unlikely to produce operationally-relevant findings."

"Operational research should set aside preconceptions about what 'causes' the behavior, and redirect interest to what behaviors precede the outcome." [43]

That is, regarding the Terror Villain and other types as well, let's focus on the "What?" of Villain's early behavior which will enable detection and, in turn, preemption! We citizens should not be as troubled about Villain's latest methods and injurious antics as we are intent on watching out for how he does not blend in with other people — how he or she displays early signs of the resolve to hurt and kill.

As we dissect the fine definitions of intra-national, international, and perhaps someday interneuronal[44] terrorists, our civilian focus needs to remain on "What?" these individuals are doing in everyday life. For example, trends of the "lone wolf" Terror Villain show his frequent use of social media to openly broadcast his plans before an attack. He commonly shares both his personal grievances and his desire to seek revenge.[45] What a thoughtful thing to do for those of us who are watching for such behavior!

Our challenge in this detection phase of *X-Pree* is figuring out what Villain looks like in his various flavors. Truthfully, in everyday life, he often looks like the rest of us. Here are some examples:

- That sociopath at work might dress very neatly, keeping to himself in a nearby cubicle, while he plots the murder of his dependent step-father.
- That narcissist who is a handsome top sales producer also has a booming illegal drug network.
- That machiavellian in your engineering department who has brilliantly developed a brand new application for nano technology is also busy laying the groundwork to sell his discovery through overseas corporate spies.

We can positively leave our outdated criminal stereotypes on the sidelines. In today's Villain world, cloaking is a widespread tactic used by a broad spectrum of nasty players. Some wealthy, well-dressed socialites are also engaged in the most deplorable treatment of people — forced labor. That rugged, disheveled brute who wreaks of alcohol is still in our cast of bad guys. However, he is being upstaged by the soft-spoken Villain who teaches history in a junior high school, while she secretly enjoys ongoing sex with the teenage boys.

On the other hand, there is cloaking on the victim side. Our computer programming student is quietly searching for identity theft victims at her community college. She has been warned that if her quota isn't met, her sister will be injured or killed. Likewise, the part-time helper at a small restaurant will be beaten and deported if he doesn't clock in on time. In both cases, these victims nearly act like average people, and they are controlled by Villains who also nearly act like average people.

Villain's flavors are present in every community whether its residents are rich or poor, well-educated or illiterate, young or old. Where does that leave us? It leaves us with plenty of helpful insight. Either by Villain's signs or by the signs of the victims, we can surely detect him or her.

No matter how normal he or she might appear, there are always signals of Villain's intent to injure someone.

Remember, sooner or later, Villain's cloaked, inward flavor will be reflected in highly visible outward behavior. He will surely unmask himself. She will unavoidably set aside her disguise, perhaps for only a moment. Our job as Defenders is to detect Villain's core nature when it's revealed, and as soon as possible.

Breadcrumbs

Villain always drops breadcrumbs. Trails of indicators, small and large, give us signs of his presence. Several lists and guides are coming up next to help you see warning signs in your everyday encounters with people. These lists are not absolutely complete, nor are they one-size-fits-all formulas in the detection process. They will give you a solid launching point to get started as a personal detection practitioner.

CHAPTER 3 - YOUR MISSION: DETECT

Preemption is possible because we can definitely see trouble coming. We can confidently abandon the old idiom, "You can't judge a book by its cover." Your *X-Pree* directive is to very effectively take a look at Villain's cover, and then make your best judgment call — making that call **FAST**.

One additional tool for you is this simple memory aid:

COVER = Character OVER everything else.

COVER reminds us that the character of that potential date, employee, neighbor, teacher, student, coworker, or acquaintance is your point of focus. It's here, with the individual's character, that we take our sharpest look to discover signals telling us whether or not to proceed with that person.

Character plays a major role in the manner people react to how their basic needs are being met. In 1943 psychologist Abraham Maslow published a paper introducing his "hierarchy of needs," a pyramid-shaped chart depicting the order of basic human needs. As a result of his study of exceptional contemporaries, Maslow concluded that human needs can be summarized by the following (the most essential listed first):
- Physiological — Air, water, food, sleep, basic bodily functions
- Safety — Protection from physical and financial harm
- Love / Belonging — Inclusive relationships such as family and close friendships
- Esteem — Confidence by meeting goals and earning admiration from others
- Self-Actualization — Individual freedom to experience well-developed individuality[46]

Significant focus of Maslow's work was on the positive, happy lives of his participants. It's important to note that in his chart "Love / Belonging" has priority immediately after the most fundamental human requirements. Maslow cited "belongingness" as a key ingredient in the successful, happy lives he studied. We can rightly conclude that, even today, isolation is not the most desirable or healthy attribute of a satisfying human life.

Sometimes, another person, circumstance, or event blocks our path to basic satisfaction. Depending on our mental fitness, we will likely react well to getting our way, and we might react poorly to not getting our way. No matter what, we all want to belong, to fit in somewhere with something.

Many of today's violent offenders are from 18 to 25 years old. They act out criminally because of some void in relationships — the absence of loving care, poor parental involvement, or weak social connections. Whether or not a young adult's needs were met in childhood can be a driving element in that person's reaction to unfulfilled needs in later years.

Other profiteering Villains can be over 50 or 60 years old. Their motivation is simply monetary gain. Somewhere along the way their sense of respectful behavior took the back seat to piling up wealth. For them it's just dollars instead of decency.

Your mission is not to be a self-appointed psychologist. Your mission is to simply step back a little while observing a person's character as much as you can. Your window to detect criminal intent might be months or weeks in the long term and only fractions of a second in the short term. Let's explore some breadcrumbs to pick out Villain's useful identifiers.

Slave Trader (a.k.a. Human Trafficker)

During a human trafficking seminar, former slavery victims related their stories. At many points in the day, the room packed with attendees was freakishly silent with everyone in amazement at the horrific challenges faced by the women. Some of the former slaves had healed considerably from their experiences, others were still in the restoration process.

What was the one factor which caused them to drift into the trafficking quagmire more than any other? Without hesitation and with quick consensus they responded "isolation" was the biggest factor. As teenagers, they needed a place where they belonged with people who genuinely cared about them. Each one thought her best choice for a good home life was going to be in the home of a slave trader. For every girl in the group, it was all a temporary illusion.

Even though real life as a human slave becomes unimaginably painful, it is often the victim's most attractive choice several years earlier. What grows into an unbearable conflict is the slave's hopeful desire to belong to a family, at the same time she is shackled to the impossibility of any real freedom in the slave trader's family. It is a battle which the slave cannot win. Current life expectancy of today's sex slave is only seven years from the time she is recruited.

For many other victims, their trafficked lives are involuntary from the start. They are snatched up and bound as forced laborers, often for an endless term which is riddled with torment.

One of the world's leading resources in combatting modern slavery is Polaris Project.[47] This valuable checklist from their website gives common indicators of victims. Identification of a slave trader's victims is often a sure path to Villain himself.

> Recognizing potential red flags and knowing the indicators of human trafficking is a key step in identifying more victims and helping them find the assistance they need. To request help or report suspected human trafficking, call the National Human Trafficking Resource Center hotline at 1-888-373-7888. Or text HELP to: BeFree (233733).
>
> COMMON WORK AND LIVING CONDITIONS: The individual(s) in question,
> Is not free to leave or come and go as he/she wishes
> Is under 18 and is providing commercial sex acts
> Is in the commercial sex industry and has a pimp / manager
> Is unpaid, paid very little, or paid only through tips
> Works excessively long and/or unusual hours
> Is not allowed breaks or suffers under unusual restrictions at work
> Owes a large debt and is unable to pay it off
> Was recruited through false promises concerning the nature and conditions of his/her work
> High security measures exist in the work and/or living locations (e.g., opaque windows, boarded up windows, bars on windows, barbed wire, security cameras, etc.)
> Poor Mental Health or Abnormal Behavior
> Is fearful, anxious, depressed, submissive, tense, or nervous/paranoid

Exhibits unusually fearful or anxious behavior after bringing up law enforcement
Avoids eye contact

POOR PHYSICAL HEALTH
Lacks health care
Appears malnourished
Shows signs of physical and/or sexual abuse, physical restraint, confinement, or torture

LACK OF CONTROL
Has few or no personal possessions
Is not in control of his/her own money, no financial records, or bank account
Is not in control of his/her own identification documents (ID or passport)
Is not allowed or able to speak for themselves (a third party may insist on being present and/or translating)

OTHER
Claims of just visiting and inability to clarify where he/she is staying/address
Lack of knowledge of whereabouts and/or do not know what city he/she is in
Loss of sense of time
Has numerous inconsistencies in his/her story

This list is not exhaustive and represents only a selection of possible indicators. Also, the red flags in this list may not be present in all trafficking cases and are not cumulative.[48]

In its March 2017 report, *The Typology of Modern Slavery*,[49] Polaris presents 25 versions of human trafficking occurring within the United States — today! Right now, this multi-billion dollar, global crime is likely enslaving more than 20 million innocent victims.

One California study, released in 2016, calculates the value of sex slavery in San Diego County alone was $810 million in 2013.[50] U.S. trafficking enterprises are so lucrative that some veteran drug barons are giving up their coveted territorial boundaries in order to cooperate with other trafficking criminals to build sex slave networks.

Major U.S. metropolitan areas are not the only centers for the trafficking business. All of the tranquility and isolation which rural getaways offer are ideal conditions for the private management of slave trade operations. There is a high probability you have already personally encountered at least one trafficked victim without realizing it.

As with other heartrending crimes, you're probably distressed upon learning about the success of today's slave traders. Unfortunately, when emotions get out of control, well-meaning citizens sometimes try to rescue trafficked victims by themselves. Usually the results are catastrophic for the victims as well as their wannabe liberators.

Law enforcement agencies are rapidly progressing in their detection and safe extraction skills in this arena. They need your help only in reporting possible incidents which you discover. Complex trafficking networks require professional, high-tech analysis and strategic capture by enforcement officers. Vigilante-style citizen actions against traffickers are illegal and potentially deadly. You will be most helpful by providing an accurate report.

Terror Villain (a.k.a. Terrorist)

While the results of terrorist actions are death and destruction in nearly every case, individuals' characteristics are difficult to define. In 2004, Dr. Borum of University of South Florida observed,

> "There is no terrorist personality, nor is there any accurate profile — psychologically or otherwise of the terrorist. Moreover, personality traits alone tend not to be very good predictors of behavior." [51]

But, he also pointed to a finding by Dr. Martha Crenshaw which confirms this Villain's passionate quest for socialization,

> ..."shared ideological commitment and group solidarity are much more important determinants of terrorist behavior than individual characteristics." [52]

As we cited earlier, the June 2016 issue of The NBR Digest (U.S. National Bureau of Economic Research, *"Where Are ISIS's Foreign Fighters Coming From?"*) offers us this insight:

> *"Foreign recruits into terror organizations come largely from prosperous, ethnically and linguistically homogeneous countries."*
>
> *"Building on previous research that suggests that recruitment is driven by religious and political ideology, the researchers find that the more homogeneous the host country is, the more difficulties Muslim immigrants experience in their process of assimilation. This social isolation seems to induce radicalization, increasing the supply of potential recruits."*
>
> *"Although the researchers are unable to determine precisely why people join ISIS, their results suggest this difficulty of assimilation into homogeneous Western countries and ISIS's appeal to impressionable youth through its sophisticated propaganda machine and social media are major contributors."* [53]

Aha! Here we are again with a group of people who want to belong! Fundamental human needs must be met. We can view the potential terrorist as a human magnet searching to bond with something. If he is unable to find social connections elsewhere, he will possibly be attracted to, and form an inseparable link with a terrorist organization.

So, what are the Terror Villain's pre-incident indicators? There are many sources. Here is a supplemented list of the widely publicized *Eight Signs of Terrorism*:

- **Financing** — movement of large amounts of cash by deposits, withdrawals, payments, donations, solicitations, money laundering, and illegal sales
- **Surveillance** — Villain's visits to the attack site multiple times at different hours to assess and study security, ingress, egress, and response times for first responders
- **Elicitation** — gathering info from site personnel about the target's security and operations by phone, mail, email, in-person visits, or obtaining a job at the target
- **Security Probe** — gathering info about security at the site by

testing or creating a fake breach
- **Supplies** — accumulating bomb materials by unusual quantities of common household items; purchasing/stockpiling weapons and ammunition; acquiring uniforms, badges, credentials, and maps
- **Suspicious Presence** — bombers' out-of-place appearance by their candor and clothing; phony impersonations of police, emergency personnel, military, employees, or delivery drivers
- **Dry Runs** — Villain's multiple practice trials prior to the event; rehearsals to confirm timing, traffic flow, and responses by police and emergency personnel
- **Deploying** — Terrorists' final staging of people, equipment, and supplies before the attack[54]

There are always unusual actions by Terror Villains immediately before an attack which are related to a vehicle, clothing, or behavior. Something is out of place.

In tune with our DHS "if you see something, say something™" program, SecureTransit.org offers this assurance and its own checklist:

"It can be difficult to know what 'something suspicious' looks like — but trust yourself when something doesn't feel quite right."

SUSPICIOUS BEHAVIOR
Race, gender or religious affiliations are not indicators of suspicious behavior.
Look for signs of reconnaissance or equipment tampering.
Don't be afraid to report any of the following:
Placing a package or luggage in a different compartment than the one being occupied.
People who stay at bus or train stations for long periods without getting on.
Anyone tampering with surveillance cameras, safety systems, machinery or other sensitive equipment.
People videotaping, sketching or taking notes on transit equipment and facilities or security equipment.
People entering unauthorized areas at train or bus stations.
People carrying aerosol containers or anything omitting a strange smell or gas.

Evasive answers to common questions regarding destinations; deliberate attempts to avoid contact with others or to draw attention.
Loose fitting clothing, large sweatshirt, vest or jacket in hot weather conditions. Clothing that is disproportionate to the body type of the person.
Attempts to abandon a vehicle in or near a transit parking facility, or cars in the parking lot without proper tags and license plates.
An individual who is fixated only on a particular object or location.
Suspicious activity or loitering around transportation facilities.
Consecutive round trips on the same transit route.

SUSPICIOUS OBJECTS
Unattended briefcases or bags may simply be forgotten or discarded items — but it's better to be safe than sorry.
Don't be afraid to report any of the following:
Bags, boxes or other packages left unattended on buses and trains, in stations, on platforms or on train tracks—especially if partially hidden or in unusual locations.
Exposed wiring, leaks, strange smells or other signs of potential tampering on buses and trains.
Suspicious carry-on items such as large backpacks, gym bags and luggage weighing more than normal.[55]

Terrorists strike close to home. Historically, up to 50% of attacks occur within 30 miles of the terrorist's U.S. home. They usually think globally, but act locally. Coupled with the fact that Terror Villains generally take awhile to plan their attacks, sometimes more than two months, this gives us more opportunities to detect their planned assaults.[56]

Contemporary terrorism is an especially deadly trend that's both domestic and global in scope. Unlike the Cash Villain or Control Villain who don't like getting hurt, today's Terror Villain is unusually comfortable dying for his cause when he attacks. Your personal civilian vigilance and your ability to detect are critical elements in defeating future terrorist actions, wherever you are on the planet.

CHAPTER 3 - YOUR MISSION: DETECT

Active Shooter (a.k.a. Mass Murderer)

Our FBI definition of "Active Shooter" is, "an individual engaged in killing or attempting to kill people in a populated area."[57] Our widely accepted term "Mass Killings" means, "3 or more killings in a single incident."[58] To avoid the strain of excessive detail, we are bundling "Active Shooter" and "Mass Murderer." You might be thinking, "But, wait, there are exceptions!" Yes, there are... Slow, deep breathing will help you feel better. That's it. There you go.

On April 20, 1999, two students launched a 45+ minute shooting spree at their high school in Columbine, Colorado. In total, fifteen people died and twenty-four were injured. This mass murder became a benchmark event from which a number of others have been inspired. Over many years other teenagers have mimicked this carnage, celebrating (posthumously) similar degrees of infamy.

In contrast, many positive results have also occurred. Tactics and training for police officers responding to active shooters have dramatically improved. School administrators and teachers are on a path toward implementing better safety solutions. Above all, there is a much greater effort to detect the pre-incident indicators of active shooters, then share that information with entities responsible for public safety.

Parental challenges are substantial in every household, because adults and their children change constantly. It's the nature of personal growth. Some changes are tiny, others are huge. Today, as armchair professionals with flawless hindsight, we are tempted to conclude that one of the Columbine students' behavioral shift was as ominous as a Category 5 hurricane. How easy it is for us to make that declaration.

Millions of households at this moment are struggling with the delicate balance of supervision and freedom. As our culture spins along, immersed in high-tech transmissions, our overall anonymity and personal isolation continue to grow. Someday, we might turn a corner and discover renewed value in face-to-face connections. If a picture is worth a thousand words, then a direct personal conversation must be worth so much more.

EXTREME PREEMPTION

One Columbine shooter laid bare his emotional health in this journal entry made on March 31, 1997:

> *"OOOh god i HATE my life, i want to die really bad right now — let's see what i have that's good: A nice family, a good house, food, a couple good friends, & possessions. What's bad: no girls (friends or girlfriends), no other friends except a few, nobody accepting me even though i want to be accepted, me doing badly & being intimidated in any & all sports, me looking wierd & acting shy - BIG problem, me getting bad grades, having no ambition of life, ..."* [59]

In 1996 the two friends began writing blog posts[60] which clearly illustrate their frustration with other students, teachers, and parents. Prior to the murders on April 20 they posted tips for building homemade bombs. Social media posts also included their estimate of the mayhem they would be creating.

In the realm of detection, their journal statements and their blog posts were beacons of blinding light, ear-splitting sirens of warning signs. In the end, no one treated these alarms seriously enough to report them to any person with authority. There is no secret vacuum where violence grows prolifically in the mind of a murderer; yet, it often remains unnoticed.

Since the Columbine murders, active shooters have killed innocent people at schools, churches, businesses, and in open areas. We have another list here which is a blended version with common characteristics of mass murderers in different venues. Mass murderers often,

- Act by themselves
- Shoot more than one target
- Shoot either specific targets, or as many as possible by going to venues with high numbers of people
- Use the massacre as an expression of hatred or rage (no monetary goals)
- Display suicidal or homicidal thoughts
- Don't attempt to hide their identity
- Give out details of their plans before the event
- Arm themselves better than police (multiple guns, many rounds of ammo)
- Know the target location very well

Chapter 3 - Your Mission: Detect

- Plan diversions at the target location
- Rehearse their plan at the site
- Choose location for tactical advantage (rooftop), or remain mobile
- Commit unrelated acts of violence ahead of the massacre
- Make threats to associates
- Harass, intimidate, or stalk associates
- Sabotage or destroy property
- Display erratic or bizarre behavior that makes others afraid
- Plan so that escape is not a high priority
- Prepare mentally for an intense fight[61]

Fortunately for the rest of us, the mass murderer is not concerned about hiding in the shadows of obscurity, because in many cases he's trying to escape from his self-imposed isolation.[62]

Future mass murderer detection will likely be accomplished over time, possibly long periods, by people closest to the murderer. There is a lengthy cycle of heating up the murderer's rage. It is not instantaneous. This is one element of the intricate quilt of human behavior for which we can be truly grateful. Our window for detection is usually large.

Remember that in every case, no matter how deep in the black hole of Internet, or other secrecy in which each mass murderer is living, every one of them at least momentarily peeks out to check on his popularity. Every one of them leaves a trail of breadcrumbs prior to the active shooting.

Child Slayer (a.k.a. Pedophile)

Our pedophile is an especially repulsive category of criminal, because he chooses to dominate the most innocent, naturally trusting person on earth — a child. Then, by an array of skillful, perverted techniques he methodically gains ownership of his victim. Finally, when his child property becomes useless and needs to be replaced, his method of disposal can be as heartless as cold-blooded murder. By the way, today's active pedophiles are both male and female.

Children who become the prey of these Control Villains truly end up as slain victims. In extreme cases they are physically mauled or tortured to maintain their submission to the Child Slayer. In cases where their bodies are injured to a lesser extent, the Slayers rob their purity and dignity. Young victims who survive Child Slayers most often are scarred for life.

Pedophiles have many combinations of the Villain flavors described earlier. As society's most artful chameleons, they look and act much like the rest of us. They slither among today's teachers, clerks, police officers, lifeguards, preachers, scientists, coaches, librarians, craftsmen, social leaders, counselors, and others. Their superb skill in hiding enables them to glide through background checks undiscovered. They try to satisfy their basic human needs as we all do, blending into their environment perfectly.

However, the pedophile is a deadly fraud. He believes that intimacy with children is healthy and normal, that most of today's world is deceived in its objection to his lifestyle. He wants his child partner for a long time. What has become known as the Slayer's "grooming" process can often extend for years. He is persistent and patient. Fortunately for our children, the Child Slayer's finely tuned strategies are the exact means by which we can detect him.

Child Slayer early stage strategies:
- Finds a child who lacks social skills, who is not popular (who wants to belong)
- Observes the child often, or regularly, or over a moderate period of time
- Gathers information about the child and family incrementally — piece by piece
- Asks probing questions of the child which are focused on feelings
- Presents an event or circumstance that prompts sympathy for the Slayer by the child
- Explores topics with the child that promote a bond
- Seeks an extremely private relationship with the child
- Exhibits an unusually kind, passive personality toward children

Child Slayer middle stage strategies:
- Emphasizes how the child is special to him
- Introduces a sexual reference (picture, provocative clothing) that appears unintended

- Cleverly orchestrates a first touch
- Explains that a special relationship like his with the child is genuine, true love
- Follows with more intimate touching
- Gives assurances that he will never hurt the child
- Reiterates the secrecy of their relationship
- Socializes primarily with the child, not adults; plays some important role in the child's life

Child Slayer late stage strategies:
- Threatens to expose their relationship
- Threatens harm to the child's family or pet
- Causes the child to be afraid of being arrested instead of or along with the Slayer
- Blames the child for starting the intimacy
- Orchestrates extended private time with the child
- Possibly shares a drug to reduce child's resistance
- Manipulates the child to believe that isolation with the Slayer is the safest place
- If there is a high risk of discovery, plans to end the relationship by any means necessary

Children who are sexually abused may exhibit behavioral changes based on their age —

Children up to age 3 may exhibit:
- Fear or excessive crying
- Vomiting
- Feeding problems
- Bowel problems
- Sleep disturbances
- Failure to thrive

Children ages 3 to 9 may exhibit:
- Fear of particular people, places or activities
- Regression to earlier behaviors such as bed wetting or stranger anxiety
- Victimization of others

- Feelings of shame or guilt
- Nightmares or sleep disturbances
- Withdrawal from family or friends
- Fear of attack recurring
- Eating disturbances

Symptoms of sexual abuse in older children and adolescents include:
- Depression
- Nightmares or sleep disturbances
- Poor school performance
- Promiscuity
- Excessive masturbation
- Substance abuse
- Aggression
- Running away from home
- Fear of attack recurring
- Eating disturbances
- Early pregnancy or marriage
- Suicidal gestures
- Anger about being forced into a situation beyond one's control
- Pseudo-mature behaviors

All adults have the responsibility to closely observe the relationships young children have with older children and adults. You have a mandate to inquire to any legal extent about anyone who supervises and interacts with children. They depend on you for their safety. You may be the one who sees danger that the child does not see. One out of every five girls, and one out of every twenty boys is experiencing sexual assault. Over half of abused children, receive their mistreatment from family members. Over 75% are assaulted by someone they know very well.

Rapist (a.k.a. Sexual Predator)

Running a close second in horror from being violated as a child is enduring rape as an adult. Today, one American is sexually assaulted approximately every 98 seconds.[63] Prosecution of rapists is a difficult task. Only 34% of rape victims report the crime. Out of that group of alleged rapists, only 18% are arrested. Among those arrested, only 21% are prosecuted. Among those prosecuted, only 50% are convicted.[64] Translation = Out of 1,000 women who are raped, only 6 rapists are convicted. Be aware that about 78% of rape victims personally know their attacker beforehand.[65]

Our checklist to detect a rapist is not complicated. What is challenging is the window of opportunity for detection. There is generally not much time.

Here are some other behavioral warning signals of male rapists:
- Phony charm, with a high degree of "nice"
- Deceitful assurance that his intentions are good
- Acute narcissism — fascination with himself and sharing info about himself
- Won't accept "NO"
- Obvious lack of patience with others
- Short temper — quickly gets loud and aggressive
- Machismo mentality that is attractively virile, but also inconsiderate of you
- Signs that women are lower-class people
- Refusal to accept responsibility for mistakes
- Unbalanced focus on alcohol or drugs

Our planet has many honest, compassionate people living on it. Sometimes it seems difficult to separate Villain from the good guys. Especially when first meeting someone, feelings and emotions can replace good judgment with brain fog. Whenever in doubt, always proceed slowly, with eyes open wide. Remember COVER. Always choose safety.

Your super detection tool is your feeling that you are at risk!

Coming up there are some examples of social events which illustrate the need for solid *X-Pree* self-defense. In the meantime, be certain to respond if your inner high-tech alarm system is telling you to slow down. Only then can it give you an analysis of the present, so you can decide about your future. When in doubt, do the safe thing. Sometimes that means putting everything on hold in a relationship. Sometimes that means just walking or running away. Good people will still be around for you tomorrow.

Intimate Demon (a.k.a. Domestic Abuser)

"Intimate partner violence" is physical, sexual, or psychological harm by a current or former partner or spouse, among heterosexual or same-sex couples and does not require sexual intimacy.[66] It is the spontaneous attack on an unsuspecting spouse or the calculated habitual mistreatment of a lover over time, and every version in-between. "Domestic Abuser" and "Intimate Partner Offender" are common designators for the men and women who prey on their mates. We'll go with "Intimate Demon."

Civilized folks are tempted to plunk this Villain into civilized categories which include people who occasionally vent anger or frustration, who belong to a particular race or nationality, or who are part of a particular age group. On the contrary,
> "Physical abuse is a tool of control and oppression and is a choice made by one person in a relationship to control another." [67]

On average, one American is the victim of an intimate demon every three seconds.[68] Is that a lot? Yes! Our Center for Disease Control's July 2017 report shows 55% of ALL murdered women in the U.S. are the victims of intimate demons.[69]

Intimate Demons have a ton of warning signs. Our biggest challenge is not identifying these signs; it's adequately heeding the warning signs after we detect them. Escape from the relationship is the best safety strategy, but it is often the most difficult. Human emotions, mixed with sex, results in a cocktail which can be absolutely blinding. We know this,

Human Emotions + Sex = Dangerous Cocktail

Dr. Wendy Patrick gives a detailed analysis of this social dynamic. She shows us that,
> "Bad people can look good because they are: Attractive, Powerful, Credible, Attentive, Affirming, Similar, Familiar, Exciting, Forbidden, Dangerous." [70]

Are all intimate relationships just floating mines in a harbor war zone? No. Do we need to jump into isolation to avoid heartbreaking disaster or sudden death? No, not at all. Escape from an Intimate Demon is much more difficult when the victim clings to heavily invested emotions. On the other hand, as we would not likely sleep with a cobra, our escape from a venomous partner can be sufficiently energized by the basic need to be genuinely loved and respected. Live your balanced love life with eyes wide open. Isolation is never a healthy strategy; neither is blind acceptance.

The National Domestic Violence HOTLINE (800.799.7233) is a resource. HOTLINE offers guidelines such as the following:

It's not always easy to tell at the beginning of a relationship if it will become abusive. In fact, many abusive partners may seem absolutely perfect in the early stages of a relationship. Possessive and controlling behaviors don't always appear overnight, but rather emerge and intensify as the relationship grows.

Domestic violence doesn't look the same in every relationship because every relationship is different. But, one thing most abusive relationships have in common is that the abusive partner does many different things to have more power and control over their partners.

If you're beginning to feel as if your partner or a loved one's partner is becoming abusive, there are a few behaviors that you can look out for. Watch out for these red flags and if you're experiencing one or more of them in your relationship, call or chat online with an advocate to talk about what's going on:
Telling you that you can never do anything right
Showing jealousy of your friends and time spent away
Keeping you or discouraging you from seeing friends or family members
Embarrassing or shaming you with put-downs
Controlling every penny spent in the household
Taking your money or refusing to give you money for expenses
Looking at you or acting in ways that scare you
Controlling who you see, where you go, or what you do
Preventing you from making your own decisions
Telling you that you are a bad parent or threatening to harm or take away your children
Preventing you from working or attending school

Destroying your property or threatening to hurt or kill your pets
Intimidating you with guns, knives or other weapons
Pressuring you to have sex when you don't want to
Pressuring you to do things sexually you're not comfortable with
Pressuring you to use drugs or alcohol [71]

Additionally, take action if your intimate demon does or has done any of the following:
Hurried the pace of the relationship at the start
Battered women in previous relationships
Uses alcohol or drugs as an excuse for violent behavior
Has a history of police encounters
Refuses to accept rejection
Minimizes incidents of abuse
Resists change — is inflexible, unwilling to compromise
Compares himself to violent characters in movies
Suffers radical mood swings
Experienced or witnessed violence as a child

By far, the most dangerous element of a harmful relationship is secrecy. In case after case, where domestic violence ended with murder, the early warning signs of violence were kept secret.

In a culture that thrives on personal isolation with smart phones, phablets, and tablets, we must recognize that the world community is not enormous. Remember, people still need to feel that they belong to something. Perhaps you can make a difference by including an Intimate Demon's victim under your watchful eye. Yes, it is your business. If you're seeing the situation accurately, it's everyone's business because of the far-reaching effects on many people. Consider this assertion by the Office on Violence Against Women:

> *"Domestic violence not only affects those who are abused, but also has a substantial effect on family members, friends, co-workers, other witnesses, and the community at large. Children, who grow up witnessing domestic violence, are among those seriously affected by this crime. Frequent exposure to violence in the home not only predisposes children to numerous social and physical problems, but also teaches them that violence is a normal way of life — therefore,*

increasing their risk of becoming society's next generation of victims and abusers." [72]

Elder Abuser

As senior citizens progress into their late years, they might become extremely dependent on family members or professional caregivers. There are innumerable opportunities to victimize a senior either by physical abuse or emotional abuse. Signs of abuse by Villain can easily be cloaked by the aging process, and poor mental or physical fitness.

Cases of victimization of elders occur at home, by family members, and in care facilities. Injury takes many different forms, some involving intimidation or threats against the elderly, some involving neglect, and others involving financial trickery.

HelpGuide.ORG is another invaluable educational resource. It has up-to-date, insightful articles on a wide variety of health issues. Following are website selections devoted to signs of elder victimization. Most common are the ones defined below:

"Physical elder abuse is non-accidental use of force against an elderly person that results in physical pain, injury, or impairment. Such abuse includes not only physical assaults such as hitting or shoving but the inappropriate use of drugs, restraints, or confinement.

In emotional or psychological abuse, people speak to or treat elderly persons in ways that cause emotional pain or distress.

Emotional elder abuse:
Intimidation through yelling or threats
Humiliation and ridicule
Habitual blaming or scapegoating
Ignoring the elderly person
Isolating an elder from friends or activities
Terrorizing or menacing the elderly person

Sexual elder abuse is contact with an elderly person without the elder's consent. Such contact can involve physical sex acts, but activities such as showing an elderly person pornographic material, forcing the person to watch sex acts, or forcing the elder to undress are also considered sexual elder abuse.

Elder neglect—failure to fulfill a care-taking obligation—constitutes more than half of all reported cases of elder abuse. It can be intentional or unintentional, based on factors such as ignorance or denial that an elderly charge needs as much care as he or she does.

Financial exploitation involves unauthorized use of an elderly person's funds or property, either by a caregiver or an outside scam artist:
Misuse an elder's personal checks, credit cards, or accounts
Steal cash, income checks, or household goods
Forge the elder's signature
Engage in identity theft
Announce a "prize" that the elderly person has won but must pay money to claim
Phony charities
Investment fraud

Healthcare fraud and abuse is carried out by unethical doctors, nurses, hospital personnel, and other professional care providers, examples of healthcare fraud and abuse regarding elders include:
Not providing healthcare, but charging for it
Overcharging or double-billing for medical care or services
Getting kickbacks for referrals to other providers or for prescribing certain drugs
Overmedicating or under-medicating
Recommending fraudulent remedies for illnesses or other medical conditions
Medicaid fraud

General warning signs of elder abuse:
Frequent arguments or tension between the caregiver and the elderly person
Changes in personality or behavior in the elder

Physical abuse warning signs:
Unexplained signs of injury, such as bruises, welts, or scars, especially if they appear symmetrically on two side of the body
Broken bones, sprains, or dislocations
Report of drug overdose or apparent failure to take medication regularly (a prescription has more remaining than it should)
Broken eyeglasses or frames
Signs of being restrained, such as rope marks on wrists
Caregiver's refusal to allow you to see the elder alone

Emotional abuse warning signs:
Threatening, belittling, or controlling caregiver behavior that you witness
Behavior from the elder that mimics dementia, such as rocking, sucking, or mumbling

Sexual abuse warning signs:
Bruises around breasts or genitals
Unexplained venereal disease or genital infections
Unexplained vaginal or anal bleeding
Torn, stained, or bloody underclothing

Neglect by caregivers or self-neglect warning signs:
Unusual weight loss, malnutrition, dehydration
Untreated physical problems, such as bed sores
Unsanitary living conditions: dirt, bugs, soiled bedding and clothes
Being left dirty or unbathed
Unsuitable clothing or covering for the weather
Unsafe living conditions (no heat or running water; faulty electrical wiring, fire hazards)
Desertion of the elder at a public place

Financial exploitation warning signs:
Significant withdrawals from the elder's accounts
Sudden changes in the elder's financial condition
Items or cash missing from the senior's household
Suspicious changes in wills, power of attorney, titles, and policies
Addition of names to the senior's signature card

Unpaid bills or lack of medical care, although the elder has enough money to pay for them
Financial activity the senior couldn't have done, such as an ATM withdrawal when the account holder is bedridden
Unnecessary services, goods, or subscriptions

Healthcare fraud and abuse warning signs:
Duplicate billings for the same medical service or device
Evidence of overmedication or under-medication
Evidence of inadequate care when bills are paid in full
Problems with the care facility: poorly trained, poorly paid, or insufficient staff; crowding; inadequate responses to questions about care

Among caregivers, significant risk factors for elder abuse are:
Inability to cope with stress (lack of resilience)
Depression, which is common among caregivers
Lack of support from other potential caregivers
Caregiver's perception care of the elder is burdensome, without psychological reward
Substance abuse" [73]

Proper care of seniors can be both heartwarming and satisfying, demanding and exhausting. It is a sad commentary about our contemporary culture to acknowledge that Villain will knowingly injure those who need and deserve our respect and care. Your watchfulness for signs of this crime, at any age, is extremely useful. Coupled with timely reporting, your detection of elder victimization can be a life-saving contribution.

Internet Thief

At some point in time Villain realized that physical confrontation, in the form of robbery, is a lot of trouble. Many easier possibilities for crime exist using the Internet and other high-speed technology. Impersonal, long distance stealing is relatively safe, and there's a low probability of being shot at or arrested. Compared to the old days when a neighborhood, town, or region was targeted, today's target is the entire Earth! Well, most of it anyway.

Chapter 3 - Your Mission: Detect

Identity theft is a popular crime trend where the thief gathers enough of your personal info to access your bank account and withdraw funds. Or, he can imitate you sufficiently to apply for a new credit card. Let's take a look at some popular cons to see what they're about.

Phishing is Villain's work to get your personal information about credit cards, user names, passwords, birthdate, medical records, etc. Emails are the tip of Villain's spear. Here is a phishing email I recently received:

> Dear Card Holder,
>
> This is an automated notice that your checking account has been deactivated due to large deposits of funds from unknown sources.
>
> You have received funds in the amount of $25,192.20 and $41,205.81 in the last 12 hours
>
> If these are indeed your funds, please login immediately to confirm and deactivate your account.
>
> \>> Go here | Verify fund transfer here
>
> (WARNING - if you do not deactivate within 24 hours we will be rejecting these deposits)
>
> Always at your service,
>
> Card Notice Department

Notice how the thief uses an attractive lure of "$25,192.20 and $41,205.81." An unsuspecting victim will follow the link (>> Go here...) and get asked to log into his bank account. Villain is waiting on the other end to capture his user name, password, date of birth, social security number, and any other personal information that can be stolen from Innocent.

"Spear Phishing" is focused, two-fold assault on a person or organization — stealing info and also leaving behind malware on the target's computer.

Vishing is like phishing, except the thief uses the telephone and cleverly worded language to gather your personal information:
>[Phone Rings]
>Innocent — "Hello"
>Thief — "Hello, this is Mr. Cash. I'm with New Money Services. Is this Innocent?"
>Innocent — "Yes"
>Thief — "We have an approved line of credit for you. We just need to confirm some information in order to release the funds."
>If Innocent is fooled, the thief will gather as much personal info as possible.

Pharming is the technique of rerouting the user of a website to a fake one where the thief gathers the user's personal info:
- Victim types in "Home Cownty Bank," for example, in the search bar.
- One of the website choices that appears is https://www.safe.homecowntybank.com"
- This might be a working link to an actual website, but it's a fake one. All of the graphics and labels look like Home Cownty Bank's real page. The "s" at the end of "https" signifies that it's a secure website. But, there is no padlock next to the address in the title bar.
- If the victim is fooled and proceeds to log on, the thief will gather the user ID and password, possibly additional personal info to be used to duplicate the identity of the victim.
- Thief is then able to log on Home Cownty Bank's real website and transfer funds out of victim's bank account.

Smishing is an abbreviated form of "SMS Phishing." SMS stands for "Short Message Service." The messaging system on your cell phone, for example, is its SMS. This scam is designed to trick the user into downloading some form of malware onto the victim's computer, tablet, or phone (device). One common smishing text message looks something like this:

>*Urgent: Enter 848484 to avoid late charges*

Malware is a general description of software that damages a device or its programs — a short name for "malicious software." Common malware

Chapter 3 - Your Mission: Detect

types are *Trojan Horse, Virus, Worm, Adware, Ransomware*, and others. Malware can collect information stored on the victim's device that is governmental, personal, financial, or business related. When loaded into a network server, malware can enable a thief to control all the computers in the network, that is, remotely operating as a *Botnet*.

Let's take a closer look at the common versions of malware:
- *Trojan Horse* is software that lures an unsuspecting user to give up information. For example, an email which asks the user to fill in blanks with personal info is one that can contain a trojan horse in the background.
- *Virus* is a program which embeds or attaches itself onto other programs to steal files, change them, or destroy them.
- *Worm* is a program that most often operates secretly in a network. Worms don't infect other software, per se, but they can carry a payload which is capable of damage, such as a virus payload. Worms can also create a backdoor in a targeted computer, which gives thieves remote access to the computer or network.
- *Adware* (short for "advertising-supported software") is probably the most common and annoying form of malware. Adware brings us those frequent pop-up windows which are difficult to close.
- *Ransomware* is software that infects a computer with locks called encryption. Once the thief encrypts files on a victim's computer, he will only release those files back to the victim after a monetary ransom has been paid.

Cyber crime waves are popular in many countries. Cyber scams have become an expensive security challenge for our entire technical world. Our FBI Cyber Division is now running IC4 (International Cyber Crime Coordination Cell) in response to the transnational cyber crime threat. FBI's IC3 is the U.S. domestic Internet Crime Complaint Center, with almost 300,000 complaints per year. In June 2016, FBI reported a combined $3.1 Billion loss from only one scam known as the "Business E-Mail Compromise."[74]

As Internet use expands, there will be more sophisticated flavors of cyber crime. Hackers are busy right now dreaming up new ways to steal your personal info by intruding into cell phone calls and Wi-Fi systems to obtain

your credit card numbers, passwords, photos, and conversations. Here are some tips to shield yourself:
- Only access websites with "https" and the small padlock.
- Avoid Internet access in public, unsecured Wi-Fi locations.
- Obtain identity theft insurance which includes automatic searches for misuse of your personal info.

Your individual mission to detect and report internet crime will potentially help hundreds, maybe thousands, of people even though you never meet them. If you see the breadcrumbs, say something.

Cyber Bully

Bullies never offer us anything except annoyance and potential injury. In the cyber world they can be deadly. Classic bullying is typically a power play by a stronger person against someone who appears to be weaker. Reasons for this Control Villain behavior range from violence and abuse in the bully's home to genuine sociopathic disorders.

Children who have quiet, shy personalities are often targeted on the Internet through social media. These children often choose to avoid the epicenter of social activity with their peers. Their retreat to social media can give them a safe haven. They might have thousands of good "friends" without the challenges of face-to-face failure in their social skills. Their fragile self-esteem is protected. At least, they perceive they are safe.

How does a bully generally operate? His goal is the isolation of the intended victim. If the bully can exclude another child from a conversation, a game, or a party, then his mission is accomplished! Calling the child victim insulting names, especially ones that become popular with the victim's peers, is another control technique. Finally, in-person pushing, hitting, and other physical intimidations are also very effective bullying crafts. In response to these bullying strategies the victimized child might withdraw to genuine seclusion with shattered self-confidence.

Cyberbullying can be different from in-person bullying, because cyber media allow for anonymity. In other words, we might read deplorable posts on a social media site, and never know who the bully is! For example, a blog

Chapter 3 - Your Mission: Detect

poll to determine "Who's a 10?" ("Who is very attractive?") might morph into a heartless discussion about "Who's a 10-4?" ("Who is a 10 at a distance, but a 4 up close?"). As a joke among good friends, this might begin as an innocent prank. Trouble can start when an outsider observes, misunderstands, then seeks to defend someone. One honorable online defense can escalate to bullying by teens and even parents who pile on with more barrages of insults. Combatants in the online war might never know who they are actually fighting!

When a cyber bully unleashes an online attack, the effects can be more devastating than in-person bullying. Even though most children say they are not affected by cyber bullies, the victimized child might already be in physical isolation.[75] Threats to that child's only safe refuge of online friends can result in poor grades, severe depression, physical ailments, and the risk of suicide.

Statistics show 50% of all children are threatened with some form of cyber bullying at some time. Half of them never tell a parent. All 50 U.S. states have laws in place protecting victims against bullying, and 48 states include cyber bullying and forms of electronic harassment.[76]

So, what do the bullies look like? Cyberbully411 has answers —

Characteristics of teens who admit to being a cyberbully or Internet harasser:
- *In general, boys and girls appear to be equally likely to harass others online. In the Youth Internet Safety Survey, boys were more likely than girls to harass others frequently (once a month or more often). The Growing up with Media survey found differently, with boys and girls equally likely to harass others a lot or once or twice.*
- *In general, harassers are more likely also to report being aggressive and to frequently break rules.*
- *Teens who harass others frequently (once a month or more often) also report depressed or withdrawn behavior twice as often as teens who don't harass others online.*
- *Youth who have difficulty with concentration and/or low academic achievement are more likely to perpetuate bullying.*

According to teens who have been harassed:
- *Their harasser tends to be older teens (like 13-17 years old instead of 10-12).*
- *About half of online harassers and bullies are male, about 30% are female, and about 20% aren't known to the teen who is being bullied*
- *About half of the time, the teen knows their harasser in the offline world. The rest of the time, the teen knows the harasser only in the online world. Sometimes, but not often, teens are harassed by people they don't know online or offline before the incident.* [77]

Some aspects of cyber bullying are not what they appear to be. Cyberbully411 demystifies a few of our common assumptions:

Myths:
- *Most harassment occurs on social networking sites.*
- *30% of young people who have been harassed say it happened on a social networking site. But, 40% say it happened through Instant Messaging, and 29% say it happened while playing a game online. It's important to be aware of how you interact with others online, as harassment can occur in many different online places.*
- *Most youth are harassed at least once at some point when they are online.*
- *Rates vary depending on how Internet harassment is measured, but in most studies, most youth report not being targeted in the past year. For example, 91% of youth in the Youth Internet Safety Survey 2 and 76% of youth in the Growing up with Media survey reported not being harassed. Therefore online harassment is not necessarily "inevitable" or "normal teen behavior."*

Facts:
- *Internet harassment happens most frequently by peers. 63% of harassers are reportedly under the age of 18 years of age, as compared to 14% who are 18 years of age and older. 23% of targeted youth said they didn't know the age of their harasser.*
- *Everyone has a responsibility to reduce Internet harassment.*
- *Internet harassment is neither "normal" nor "okay." It can be extremely hurtful. There are healthier ways to share thoughts and*

feelings. If you see someone harassing others, do what you can to try stopping it. Let the harasser know that you're not okay with what they're doing. Because the Internet is a public space, we are all responsible for what happens online, and we all have the ability to make a difference. [78]

In this process, the keyword is "public." Harmful dark secrets are neutralized fast with the light of public disclosure. As we are likely to intervene or at least report a low-grade assault at a mall, we can also minimize cyberbullying by intervening and/or reporting it. In every case, we must first detect it.

Bushwhacker (a.k.a. Assailant, Robber)

"Awareness" and "safety" are nearly inseparable terms. They go together as well as peanut butter and jelly, as a bagel and cream cheese. In theory, our best level of safety is always achieved with heightened awareness. If we are continuously aware of our environment, including the people in it, the probability of being attacked is generally very low. Life's everyday challenge is this — in the real world, our level of awareness is generally low.

Ambush is the key to a successful in-person attack. If Villain can catch us by surprise, then we can only hope for reaction to his actions. Thus, Villain will be faster, we will be slower. Fortunately, there are obvious signals of Villain's intentions. As with other varieties of crime, if we can detect a signal of oncoming bushwhackery, we can preempt it, *X-Pree* style. Here are some of Villain's techniques:

- **Isolation** — Bushwhacker will try to separate his intended victim from a crowd or from the safety of objects between him and his victim.
- **Position** — Getting behind his victim especially while walking, gives Bushwhacker a huge advantage. Getting in front of his victim while accomplices are behind his prey is another powerful play.
- **Charmer Role** — Smooth delivery of carefully selected comments to his victim is a very common and very successful strategy to get submission to Bushwhacker's sometimes deadly plan. "Wow, you know I've worked down the street for months and I've never seen you here!" is a line that might distract his female prey long enough

Extreme Preemption

to get within arm's reach.
- **Intimidation** — Yelling sudden loud commands is a strategy to stun his victim into submission, or at least distract to gain advantage.
- **Oscar-Winning Performance** — Rapid switching from his ugly-in-your-face menace to a smiley-let's-be-buddies softy, within seconds, is a popular prelude to his physical attack.
- **Pursuit** — In an urban setting, Bushwhacker might follow his victim by walking or driving to an optimal location for his attack, taking an abnormal route to stay with his target.
- **Eyes** — One sure signal of an oncoming attack is Bushwhacker's chin lowered and eyes staring coldly into his victim's. Or, he might unnaturally avoid making eye contact to move very close.
- **Stature** — Bushwhacker might lower his body and lean forward into an attack stance, or he might stretch higher than normal to appear formidable. Lowering his chin and advancing straight toward his victim is highly popular.
- **Grab** — Most obvious on this list is Bushwhacker's grab by hand or arm, a sure signal that good things are not coming next. Even a friendly version of the grab should be avoided. Submission to his grab is permission for the Control Villain to move on to his next play. Remember, 75% of rape victim's already know their attacker.
- **Alcohol and Drugs** — These can stimulate Bushwhacker to become offensive. That's all he might need to leap from planning bushwhackery to actually doing it.

As attacker, Cash Villain (who steals your personal property), or general arm's length troublemaker, Villain **always** broadcasts at least one signal that control and/or injury is coming next. His ambush is **always** accompanied by a strong signal ahead of time. You might not have a lot of time, but it's there for you — use it wisely.

Housebreaker (a.k.a. Burglar)

Our term "housebreaker" originated in the late 13th century as "a person who illegally enters a house in order to steal something."[79] There are some movies and TV commercials that depict Housebreaker as a stealthy, silent, even good-natured soul who only wants some of your jewelry.

Chapter 3 - Your Mission: Detect

Unfortunately, our wake-up call is that 1 out of every 3 Housebreaker visits turns violent, because Villain often finds people inside the house! He reasons that people who can identify him should be silenced. He concludes that people who can be raped should be raped — what better place than in a quiet, private home, with a handy bed! Housebreaker usually makes his move during the daytime (between 10 AM and 2 PM), and he attempts to enter through the front door.

Can we see Housebreaker coming? Absolutely, yes. Here are the pre-incident signals:
- Our biggest advantage is the planning that he does. It takes time; sometimes only a few minutes, but usually two days or more.
- Driving through a neighborhood slowly, with Looky Lou or rubbernecker behavior
- Driving slowly at night with headlights turned off
- Parking an unfamiliar car near his target, to observe who is home and when
- Strangers snooping in backyards, looking in windows

These are signs Housebreaker is at work:
- Arriving with unusual wheeled devices — shopping cart, stroller, hand truck, or dolly
- Van or box truck parked in the targeted home's driveway
- Operation of tools, such as a compressor or drill
- Stranger making a forced entry through a door or window
- Hurriedly stacking equipment or small appliances near the front door
- Running out of the house carrying stolen property (sound system, TV, camera, computer)

Housebreakers want to gather as much personal property as quickly as possible. They don't want to get hurt in the process. They **always** conduct some planning ahead of the break-in.

Summary

Villain's breadcrumbs, his possible pre-incident habits, are not necessarily numerous. He might drop only a few, but you can detect them all. Consider what Villain needs to perform successfully in each category of crime. Then work backward to determine what hints he will leave while preparing to commit the crime. Detection is not a heady skill reserved solely for the world's elite intelligence specialists. You can live your life as a relaxed, yet prepared, Defender by looking and listening for Villain's signals.

If you can simply determine the steps Villain needs to take when he works his criminal slime into your life, you will know precisely what signals are detectable. You must know those signals and you must recognize them before he can work his injurious plan. New flavors of crime will surely become popular even before this book is released. However, Villain's inevitable vulnerability to observation will always fester to the point where you can detect his schemes. If you envision how he is able to hurt you, then see early traces of him, you are detecting him!

My hope for you right now is that you understand why true safety is not wishful thinking. It is not blind optimism. It is based on the reasonable action by you to *Train, Detect, and Preempt — FAST*. Whether your detection effort is directed at an invasive drone, illegal compilation of medical records, or the final planning by an active shooter, you can be certain that Villain is discoverable.

Just one more thing! This time we live in can be viewed as an age of social disunity. Accelerating technology gives us the ability to live in total physical isolation, while at the same time we're able to personally observe and intimately communicate with people throughout the world. Our successful detection of Villain requires knowledge of his lifestyle. If we can rekindle a social landscape that is truly unified, the preemptive detection of Villain's plans will then be shared by many citizens. Decades of "team-building" strategies which have been so lucrative in business now need to be avidly applied to our families, our communities, and our nation. Who will drive this essential reunification? Maybe you and I will.

Complete Topic Discussion 3,
then go to Chapter 4 — Your Mission: Preempt.

Topic Discussion 3 — *Detect*

Why is early detection of Villain nearly always possible?

Is hyper-vigilance healthy? Why or why not?

How will more "see something, say something" help our society?

Can a sociopath easily blend into a neighborhood? Why or why not?

Have you ever met someone who appears to be narcissistic? In what ways?

Have you ever observed someone who acts machiavellian? In what ways?

Are all terrorists psychopathic? Why or why not?

Topic Discussion 3 — Detect

In your own words, what is COVER as it relates to detection?

How can viewing Internet pornography support Slave Traders?

What qualities do the Child Slayer and the Rapist have in common?

How are the Control Villain and Intimate Demon similar and different?

What are 5 pre-incident indicators of the Bushwhacker which you can detect?

Notes:

Chapter 4 - Your Mission: Preempt

Safety Bubbles

Earlier in the book, I've often mentioned Villain's "plans." He always has some kind of strategy to work injury for his victims. His decision to carry out an attack might be shortly before the act itself, but he always has a plan. Similarly, we **always** need safety plans. They don't need to be complicated procedures which suck the enjoyment out of everyday life. Each safety plan for your present time and location needs to be doable by you, that's all. It requires your foresight to envision what Villain might do to you, coupled with your matching *X-Pree* defense. Here is a simple system to help you define safety plans and actions.

When you construct a precise safety plan, how do you build a specific array of defenses against an unknown Villain? Answer: By employing your Safety Bubbles. From another perspective, your environment might quickly transition from one that is exceptionally safe to one that is ultra dangerous. How do you actually respond to what is happening? Answer: By employing your Safety Bubbles.

Imagine that you're standing in the center of several concentric Bubbles which surround you. It appears that you're standing in the center of a giant onion! (If you're not an onion lover, my kindest thoughts are with you.) Envision Bubbles, not circles, because your defense needs to be ready in all directions — left, right, front, rear, above, and below. Each Bubble has a personal set radius. As we proceed further, be entirely honest when you determine the following:
- Distance from you to the edge of each Bubble
- Specific self-defense tools that you are truly capable of using within each Bubble
- How fast you are able to move within each Bubble

Chapter 4 - Your Mission: Preempt

Now, let's explore some details about your Safety Bubbles to see how they are useful.

Bubble 1 — This is your innermost, sacred space. Bubble 1 has an approximate radius of 5 feet, or a little more than arm's length. It is the critical zone where bare hand defenses, for example, need to be used. Applying the One-Second Law to this Bubble around you, stop here and determine what defenses you can honestly employ in this area. Your options will be few. Most likely, it is within Bubble 1 that your final defenses will be needed to preempt imminent injury.

Bubble 2 — We define Bubble 2 as the distance up to 10 feet. Time is always your closest ally. Outside the reach of your arms, you might have the ability to move so that a simple barrier comes between you and Villain, such as a large chair or a post. You might find a door to escape from the room you're in. Or, you might be in a vehicle. Possible defense tools increase in number within Bubble 2. They include your masterfully drawn gun or knife, objects you can throw at Villain, pepper spray, and the vehicle you're driving.

Bubble 3 — This one resides at about 20 feet. Within Bubble 3, your quick retreat to safety, dodging around other people to run away, or adopted tools are all viable defenses. For many Defenders, their One-Second Law will enable confident use of a concealed handgun within this Bubble (using the gun's sights).

Bubbles 4, 5, etc. — Additional Bubbles are not defined by distance, per se. They are defined by objects, structures, or processes. So, if we want to develop a safety plan for a restaurant, Bubble 4 might be the perimeter of the dining room, and Bubble 5 might be the outside walls of the restaurant building. If we want a safety plan for a conference center, Bubble 4 might be the walls of a large banquet hall, and Bubble 5 might be the limit of coverage by the facility's closed-circuit TV system. For a safety plan to be used at a residence, Bubble 4 could be outside walls or outside lighting around the home, and Bubble 5 could be a fence around the property. In a corporate cyber-security system, Safety Bubbles are the company's series of virtual firewalls.

Why are these distances the right ones? Is there some mystical delineation that dictates which are correct?

- First, the radii of Bubbles 1, 2, and 3 are guidelines based on real events. Available Internet videos depicting recent violent attacks are numerous. From what we have observed, each of the Safety Bubbles represents an important change in the proximity of Villain. Consequently, the opportunities for Villain to deliver injury increase as his distance from Innocent decreases. If Villain is able to move from Bubble 3 to Bubble 1, the probability of successfully injuring Innocent sharply increases.

- Second, the radii correspond to your individual ability to use various defense tools at their respective distances. For example, your defensive knife can work well for you up to 5 feet (Bubble 1), but at 20 feet from Villain (Bubble 3) its utility is radically diminished.

Keep in mind, you must construct your own personal Safety Bubble definitions. If your ability to draw a concealed handgun is not developed sufficiently to stop Villain who is charging from 20 feet, then for now include the handgun in your personal Bubble 4 with a radius of 30 feet or perhaps 40 feet. For each Safety Bubble, identify which defense tools work for you at that distance. Planning and study of your personal Safety Bubbles will enable you to make decisions about your self-defense with *SPEED*. Constructing your own Safety Bubbles is essential.

Your honest evaluation of the environment you're planning for, coupled with the realistic estimate of your detection and defense skills will pave the way for *X-Pree* solutions. If you try to cheat around the facts, that self-indulgence will give you a safety plan which is practically unattainable and dangerous. *Extreme Preemption* is founded on your confident self-reliance. Keep it real.

If you always prepare your coffee with one sugar and no cream, you probably don't find yourself frozen in a time-consuming quandary about how to fix a morning cup of java. Likewise, in the face of Villain's attack plan, crippling seconds of delay and indecision will fade away, because you will make your choices reflexively when employing your pre-planned Safety Bubble defenses.

One-Second Law

In the enormous swampland of criminal activity, actions always trump reactions because of the inherent chronological sequence. Our challenges in preempting Villain's attack include the *FAST* defensive action by Innocent after the threat to safety is identified. We have already explored the need to *Train* for, then *Detect* every future breach of our Safety Bubbles that we can think of. What's next? Answer: *SPEED*.

You probably recall the **SAFE** memory aid in Chapter 1 — **S**peed **A**lways **F**oils '**E**m. Great! How *FAST* should we be? It is entirely possible for you to practice use of your self-defense tools to be able to get those tools into the fight with Villain in less than One Second.

Remember, Villain has no concern for your safety. He or she is not going to wait politely while you ready your defense, because ambushing you is a highly successful tactic. Your best preemptive solution includes your own *FAST* counter ambush.

Why is "One-Second" so important? Because, it is an attainable span of time for nearly every citizen. If you choose to live a sub-second self-defense life, my compliments to you. *SPEED* saves! Apply the One-Second Law to your readiness with every defense tool.

Preemption Basics

"Weapons HOT!" is the commanding officer's license to his troops to freely engage the enemy. In a firefight, that's the authorization for each trooper to take his adversary to room temperature as quickly as possible. In the civilian self-defense world, we need a little more lawful discretion, but the same passion and speed.

There are 100 scenarios coming up where self-defense is needed. All of these narratives are based on actual events. Some of the scenarios are so common and frequent in today's culture that they are nonspecific. If they depict circumstances which you have experienced but have not made public, please know that I do not ever have the right or desire to judge or critique your response to danger. Any details closely resembling your events which are not public, and which you have not personally shared with me, only appear here coincidentally.

Is there a list of corroborating sources for the scenarios? No. Some of these incidents are available in public records, others are not. Many of my students have come to me for training after they experienced injuries by Villains who have not been arrested or prosecuted. Due to legal and privacy constraints, I will never disclose the sources of these narratives.

There is a specific structure for the scenarios. Each one begins with a description of an unsafe encounter. It's followed by a "Common Solution" then an "*X-Pree* Solution," that is, a self-defense solution illustrating *Extreme Preemption*. Remember, there are an infinite number of possible unsafe scenarios in your real civilian world. This book includes only a sampling.

Before we get going, let's review three principles found in the narratives:
1. This scenario-based style of learning is not the be-all and end-all for your life. Some of these plots might closely resemble events you or someone you know has experienced. We give you *X-Pree* self-defense remedies as guidelines only, not absolute formulas. In your everyday life there is an unlimited range of possible circumstances. Your fast decision-making when facing a threat to your safety is always your most valuable means of staying safe. It's my hope that you will learn to make self-defense decisions more quickly after studying this content.
2. Every framework has boundaries. So does *X-Pree*. Use the ITOTR to determine if Villain has crossed your safety threshold. What's that? It is an imaginary line or boundary that defines your safety perimeter. It is your personal Safety Bubble 1 or 2, where you determined Villain is not allowed to work. If Villain charges inside this critical limit, then you have only one choice — stop him. If Villain's behavior justifies your use of force to protect yourself, then you must do one

thing: You must counter attack Villain. That's it. Your genuine self-defense when attacked is most often your own *X-Pree* counter attack.

3. If you are forced into a physical fight, your only goal must always be to win the fight. How do you really do that? Answer: Set the unshakable course in your mind to win the fight. Decide with every speck of conviction within you to prevail over your attacker. Not to spar or dance around. Prevail. Dominate with your own brutality directed at Villain. Remember, you did not start the conflict, and you can't quietly escape the conflict. You're stuck in the middle of it, and you need to get out as quickly as possible.

In the midst of trouble brought to you by Villain, be clear about this: Someone else has decided to treat you to a large portion of hurt. Now, you must simply decide to shove it all back in Villain's face, while you run over him on your way to safety. Fight until you can no longer fight. Your nuclear counter attack must win it. More than physical strength, skill, or any psychy thing, your uncluttered, unstoppable inner drive to get back to safety will most likely win the conflict in your favor.

**If he has chosen to disable you with a stone,
then you need to immediately strike with a boulder.
If he attempts to injure you with a boulder,
then you need to crush him with a mountain.**

These 100 scenarios coming up are not grouped per se, because it's important to study all of them. Most likely, you will find at least one scenario that closely matches an event which you or someone close to you has already experienced. Again, the primary goal here is to help you learn *X-Pree* for your future.

Each *X-Pree* solution is optimal, the very best we can offer you. If you already had an encounter with Villain in which your response fell far short of the *X-Pree* solution given here, then count it as priceless training. Your ability to read this book right now means that you lived through that event with Villain, and you're safe. No regrets. No wallowing in dismal hindsight. Instead, let's enjoy maximum gratitude that you are safe at this moment, and that you can look forward to improved safety in the future.

Extreme Preemption

If you're in the middle of a protracted bout with Villain right now, which involves a hurtful intimate relationship, hopefully you can employ an *X-Pree* solution to get out of your crisis soon.

X-Pree solutions have cross-over applicability. In other words, an *X-Pree* defense in an attempted street mugging might also work nicely in an encounter with an abusive family member. So, please read them all. Study the defensive concept in each one and make it your own. Your life and the lives of people close to you are sacred. You have the right and the responsibility to protect them.

Discussing violence, particularly your violent counter attack against Villain, is a repulsive activity for most civilized people. Your willingness to discover *X-Pree* safety solutions will certainly give you confidence to not only discuss unsafe encounters, but also embrace genuine solutions.

Our characters for the scenarios are:
- Sheza Villain — female criminal offender
- Heza Villain — male criminal offender
- Sheze Innocent — intended female victim
- Heze Innocent — intended male victim

Every scenario here is based on real-life circumstances. *X-Pree* solutions were not applied during these events when they occurred. Introducing you to *Extreme Preemption* and helping you learn its value is my goal in writing this book. At first glance, some *X-Pree* answers might seem unrealistic to accomplish. Know with certainty that every *X-Pree* solution here is not only humanly possible, but entirely possible for you right now.

Summary

Extreme Preemption is the driving principle in successful safety. As I stated at the beginning, "Self-reliance is the heart of present-day safety." What gives your safety plans their energy? *X-Pree*.

Volumes of historical and contemporary accounts illustrate the failure of delayed and/or weakened responses to dangerous human circumstances.

CHAPTER 4 - YOUR MISSION: PREEMPT

We must act decisively in the face of a threat to our safety. And, we must act quickly.

You are in great company if the thought of injuring another person is abhorrent to you. Whether your defense is an accurate report of cyber crime to law enforcement or a focused bare hand gouge to Villain's eyes, your resistance to acting defensively is common.

As a Defender, you will need to accept the reality that Villain doesn't think about you with an intent to protect. For whatever reason, he wants to take something from you or control you. In the absence of Villain's restraint in doing bad things to you or a person near you, someone must fill the gap. You.

In the next chapters, we have 100 scenarios where the three components of your *X-Pree* framework work together as *Extreme Preemption*.

> Complete Topic Discussion 4,
> then go to Chapter 5 — Scenarios 1 to 10.

Scenarios are formatted as follows:
  Scenario [number] — [Type of threat], [Location].
  For example, in Scenario 1 Villain rapes Innocent in her home.
  This scenario title is "Scenario 1 — Rape, Home."

Topic Discussion 4 — *Preempt*

What are the defense tools that work for you in Safety Bubble 1?

What are the defense tools that work for you in Safety Bubble 2?

What is your Safety Bubble 3 where you work or go to school?

Why do people hesitate in self-defense events?

Are you willing to injure another person in order to preempt injury to yourself or someone near you? Why?

Notes:

Topic Discussion 4

Chapter 5 - Scenarios 1 to 10

Scenario 1 — Rape, Home

That guy at work who doesn't really have many friends asks Sheze Innocent to go hiking. He acts a little odd, but his body is like something that even a CG special effects team would have trouble improving — he's just plain hot! She's known him at work for over six months, and he seems very nice. He doesn't share anything about himself with anyone, like where he lives, tidbits about his family and home town. He must be really shy.

Whenever someone at work gets upset with him, he stares at that person with a half-smile, saying nothing. No one can tell if he's angry inside, or what he feels. Maybe he has exceptional self-control.

He asks Innocent if she would like to go hiking. Her gut says, "Nah, a little creepy." But, after two weeks, he asks Innocent again. This time, before she can respond, he adds, "I'll bet someone as attractive as you probably wouldn't have time for a guy like me. My people skills are not very good, are they?" Feeling somewhat sorry for him, aroused by his build and vulnerability, and feeling obligated to answer in a positive way, Innocent agrees to go hiking with Villain. He asks her to not say anything at work about their hike, so there's no gossip about dating a co-worker in the same department. She assumes that request is part of his over-amped shyness.

On their date, Villain opens up to Innocent sharing some superficial details about his teen years in a small town that's 1,400 miles away. He talks about his current position as a volunteer firefighter, impressing her with a story about assisting another fireman making a rescue in a structure fire. Villain's contribution to that event was his brute force in helping the fireman get access. He monopolizes the conversation. Innocent is not able to squeeze in many remarks about herself. Villain isn't interested to hear about her life.

CHAPTER 5 - SCENARIOS 1 TO 10

They finish a morning hike, and both agree that they're starved. It happens that the drive back to Innocent's house is much shorter than a drive to any restaurant. As Innocent is making lunch, Villain becomes amorous, then aggressive, then forceful. Within four minutes Innocent is raped and threatened with death if she tells anyone.

Common Solution:
Devastated by the attack, Innocent silently cowers into fear-filled isolation. She believes she has no lawful recourse, because she invited Villain into her home, agreeing to make lunch. Fear of his stature and respected role at the local fire department entirely wipe out her desire to report the crime. She continues faithfully at her job, never seeking help from family, friends, or a counselor. After a month, Villain leaves the company and moves out of state. No one knows where he went.

Your *X-Pree* Solution:
Statistics vary slightly each year. However, 85 to 90% percent of college-age rape victims know their attacker.[80] Listen to that inner, non-hormonal voice that was screaming "Nah, a little creepy!" Villain's radical shortfall in sharing details about his personal life is a warning sign. His emotionless stare in the face of personal conflict is also an unnatural, blazing signal. His structuring the first date with you, designed with the utmost isolation, is another sign of big trouble.

Your Safety Bubble 2 is your limit on Villain's access to you. Schedule a lunch with him at work, creating a short, informal interview in a public place. Any honest man will share a little about himself. In this scenario, Villain has textbook narcissistic and sociopathic characteristics. It's very likely that he will hide details about himself in any setting. He has a lot to hide, including prior rapes. Remember COVER — Character OVER everything else. In this case Villain might look good, but his character flaws are numerous. You can easily head off danger in this early stage.

In this case, Safety Bubble 1 is Innocent's ability to ward off Villain in her home. Her readiness was zero. Her expectancy of trouble was zero, because she didn't believe the signals. She was entirely unprepared for Villain's attack. She did not train, nor did she detect, but you certainly can be ready.

Scenario 2 — Espionage, Corporate

Heze Innocent is a middle-age widower who's worked hard at computer programming his entire adult life. He now has a position as one of nine senior business analysts with a defense contractor. His west coast company builds aerospace weapon systems.

Innocent has a limited social life. His wife passed away three years ago, and he has recently begun to explore social media. One interesting young woman from Iowa has shown an interest in his hobby, renovating personal computers. They exchange messages twice during the day and several times in the evening. She is a midlevel programmer working diligently for advancement.

She asks Innocent if she can visit him for a weekend and he accepts. She's even more attractive in person than her online photos revealed. Innocent is smitten by her lovely affectionate candor. They enjoy a special weekend that is passionate in every way. At the airport they agree to phone each other frequently.

After a few days, Innocent's online friend phones him with an urgent request. Apparently her new work project is an exciting opportunity to get a promotion, although she is unable to sort out a critical algorithm. She asks to get his help. Without hesitating, he agrees to look at her work.

Common Solution:
Sheza Villain sends Innocent a bogus algorithm filled with predesigned flaws. He immediately sees some errors in the program and eagerly offers to fix them. Villain proposes another juicy weekend with Innocent, after she "gets this project straightened out at work." She gushes over his willingness to help, because it means so much to her and their future together.

Computers at his workplace are so fast, Innocent runs a test of the corrected algorithm at his company workstation. Unfortunately, the algorithm is infected with a sophisticated virus designed to steal company secrets. His company's cyber security team discovers the virus and is able to isolate and remove it. Innocent immediately loses his job and his security clearance. His career in the defense industry is over.

Chapter 5 - Scenarios 1 to 10

Sheza Villain does not live in the city where she claimed to have a home. Her phone, email, and social media profile have suddenly disappeared.

Your *X-Pree* Solution:
Establish a skilled cyber security team at your company. Train all employees to meticulously do the following:
- Never share a personal login or password with anyone.
- Never share trade secrets in any form with people who are not authorized to receive them.
- Never open or respond to an email from someone outside the company, unless the source is thoroughly vetted by security personnel.
- Always be on alert, watching for evidence of inside corporate espionage.
- Immediately report suspicious activity to your security department.

In this scenario, your Safety Bubble 1 is your workstation login. If you are an employee who works with sensitive information, treat all of your company's security mandates with the highest respect and attention to detail. Espionage continues to be a significant global challenge. Just one stolen employee ID and password can open the door to thousands or millions of dollars in stolen or corrupted corporate data and compromised personnel files.

Scenario 3 — Accidental Shooting, Inner City

This scenario involves three Innocents. They are young boys ages 9, 8, and the younger brother of the nine-year-old who is age 7. There is heavy gang activity in their neighborhood. Near the Innocents' street there is an abandoned lot with tall weeds. Innocents wander onto the lot, looking for anything interesting. Some cans, bottles, and broken furniture are their only treasures today. Between the cushions of a broken down sofa Innocent age 8 finds a rusted handgun. It's an old .38 caliber revolver.

All of the boys huddle in excitement. Their game of mock cops and robbers follows with Innocent, age 9, as self-appointed police officer. As the chasing between trash piles winds down into a rest period, 7 year-old Innocent picks up the handgun. He fiddles with the trigger because it moves a little. Then he grips the gun with both hands, pressing hard on the stuck trigger with his thumbs. He does not recognize the two live cartridges left in the gun. With a frightening blast one bullet enters his forehead.

Common Solution:
Innocents' families are heartbroken beyond their imagination. They have no idea what to do except bury the young boy, missing him and mourning their loss forever.

Your *X-Pree* Solution:
Depending on the focus of various advocacy groups, the number of reported accidental shootings in the U.S. by young children differs — from one per week to one per month. Our collective goal should be none, ever.

To combat this type of horrible event, the National Rifle Association began its Eddie Eagle GunSafe® Program in 1988. Even though Eddie Eagle has trained over 28 million children throughout all U.S. states, the program is still grossly underutilized. Unlike many other NRA courses, the Eddie Eagle curriculum is NOT a firearm safety course. It teaches four simple steps which pre-school through 4th grade children must follow. Eddie Eagle's video is a lively, entertaining eight minutes (for children under age 10). They are taught to take these life-saving steps when they merely **see** a firearm:
- STOP!
- Don't Touch
- Run Away
- Tell A Grown-up[81]

If your home has a firearm in it, beware of the "the forbidden fruit syndrome." Curiosity about firearms can quickly escalate to real trouble for exploring children. Likewise, it can quickly be dispelled with a talk about firearm safety at whatever age your child is old enough to understand. Include some evidence of the kinetic energy in just a single round from a small caliber gun. This can be demonstrated by shooting an apple or an orange. In every instance, securely lock up your firearms and ammunition when they are out of your reach. Your children's Safety Bubble 2 here is knowledge about firearms; their Safety Bubble 1 is acting safely within reach of any firearm.

Scenario 4 — Bushwhackery, Street

Heze Innocent is having a less than perfect day. His supervisor climbed on his back the instant he logged in this morning, slinging accusations based on the decline in department sales. Even though the guy is over 500 miles away, the furious tone in his emails makes Innocent feel defeated and small. Managing an inexperienced sales staff is challenging for the world's best sales chiefs. Dealing with his supervisor's tactless impatience is a double burden.

On his walk back to the train station, Innocent is so absorbed with the day's circumstances that he doesn't notice that an approaching street corner is void of pedestrians. It's the top of rush hour in a busy district of the city, but no one is around at this particular corner. At average height and build, Innocent's only regular exercise is his four-block walk between his office and the train station.

Innocent hugs the building, sputtering to himself about his boss. He turns the corner and runs face-to-face into a group of four teenage Villains. They quickly surround him and demand his wallet. One displays a folding knife, another has his hands inside the pouch of a hoodie. Teen number three presses up close behind Innocent.

Common Solution:
Freezing in terror, Innocent fishes for his wallet. As soon as the Villains have it in hand, one of them lands a blow to the side of Innocent's head from behind. He drops to the sidewalk, unconscious. When he awakens, his wallet and briefcase are gone, along with the Villains. Many instances of this scenario occur with severe beating and stabbing added to Innocent's injuries.

Your *X-Pree* Solution:
Avoid being late for your train. Allow an extra few minutes for changes you might need to make in your walk route. Whenever you approach a blind corner, always check first for any abnormal activity. Villains' presence obviously scared off other pedestrians. Always adjust your path to cross the street ahead of the corner, or at least take the corner with a wide berth,

watching for trouble around the other side. In doing so, you're maintaining the integrity of Safety Bubble 2.

If the Villains are successful in surrounding you, a handy wad of old credit cards, a few dollar bills, and several coins work well as a life-saving prop. In one orchestrated movement,
- Pull the whole collection out of your pocket.
- Drop everything on the sidewalk.
- Bend forward and scream.
- Using your briefcase as a ram, charge the least threatening Villain.
- Stomp his lower leg and foot, running him over as you race toward safety.

What appears to be a treasure of cash and credit cards will probably buy you 2 seconds to escape. If they pursue you, drop or throw your briefcase, scream, and fog the air behind you with pepper spray as you run.

Being prepared with your chump change and, if legal in your city, pepper spray at all times is mandatory. *Extreme Preemption* calls for a little prior planning and as much speed as you can bring to the fight. You don't need to be an Olympic runner. You need to stay on your feet and get away from your group of Villains, running to the closest safe location.

If you're a good runner and Villain pursues you, here's a creative solution: During the chase, abruptly turn back on him unleashing a violent counter attack. Your overconfident predator will be in momentary shock that he is now the prey, giving you a significant advantage. Disable him, then continue to run to safety. (Bare hand techniques are coming up.)

Scenario 5 — Abduction, Park

Sheze Innocent is ten years old. At the neighborhood park there is always a lot of activity. Innocent has played there after school since she was very young. She has memorized every swing, patch of dirt, and certainly every burr on the metal play set. Innocent is friends with all the neighbors who use the park for sitting, walking, or sweaty exercise. Today she notices something different. One man is new to the park. He has a little puppy on about eight feet of small rope. The man is sitting on a bench while his dog sniffs everything around them. Even though his puppy is happy rolling in the grass, the man looks sad.

Innocent approaches him and they talk for almost half an hour. The man says he lives alone because his wife left one day for no reason. Over the next week, Innocent happens to go to the park when the man is there too. They talk about all the different things they both do and people in their families, but he doesn't bring the puppy after a few days.

Innocent asks about the puppy, and the man says that his puppy is at his house. You guessed it! This man is a child slayer who is grooming Innocent for kidnapping then enslavement. One small puppy and his loneliness are his bait. After a few more days of visits, Innocent asks about the puppy and Villain invites her to take a quick trip to his house, in time for the puppy's dinner.

Common Solution:
Innocent hops in Villain's car. She is never seen again by her family. Villain borrowed the puppy from a neighbor who lives near a house where he does handyman work. He was in Innocent's neighborhood just long enough to kidnap a child. His current slave is now seventeen, and she's too difficult to manage. He will dispose of the older slave and move to a new town with Innocent.

Your *X-Pree* Solution:
Communicate with your children to know exactly what they're doing when not at home. Instruct them to never get into a vehicle without clear permission from you or their temporary guardian. No playground is exempt from Villain's twisted plans for ruining the lives of his child victims. Every

child who is not able to physically win a fight with an average adult should always be accompanied by another person who can.

Teach all children **UFLI**. Every child who feels threatened should immediately run to someone wearing a Uniform, a Family, a Lady, or Inside a business to find safety. Each one needs some tag, label, or bracelet with the best phone number to call a parent or guardian.

At the earliest possible age, teach every child to speak up if anyone touches a spot on the child's body normally covered by a bathing suit. Finally, all neighbors who use a neighborhood common area, park, or playground should be on high alert for strangers who suddenly show up. That's a good example of the community Safety Bubble 3 — the park's perimeter. You have the right and responsibility to question and/or report to law enforcement anyone who looks even slightly suspicious around children.

If you observe the taking of any child by any force,
1. Call law enforcement, then
2. Call 800-THE-LOST (800-843-5678); National Center for Missing & Exploited Children.[82]

Scenario 6 — Rape, Nightclub

Sheze Innocent visited the club with friends last Saturday, the one on 9th where they caught a glimpse of Mr. Wonderful. He's been on her mind for more than six grueling days! She's worked hard to finish the semester with good grades, but the vision of this guy has hounded her all week. He might be back this weekend. Her life is on hold until she tests the water with him.

Innocent wonders if he'll be there this Saturday. Her friends are busy with their own family plans. She convinces herself that it's worth the risk of going alone. Parking is restricted so she has to walk two blocks. Her four-inch heels tighten up those legs to super model quality. Coupled with her red cocktail dress, she's looking fine. Her car beeps as the doors lock and she's off on an adventure. It's only a two-block walk. No homeless men are in sight. Everything looks normal.

There were two fights at the club last month, though only one arrest was made. Innocent heard they brought in an additional bouncer. She feels safe. Finally, she's inside the club.

By 11:45 there is still no sign of Mr. Wonderful. Then Innocent spots three of his friends. They've been drinking a lot, but she assumes they can still function enough to tell her where Mr. W. is. Plus, they're unusually cute. They explain that he's working, a definite no-show for the night. She looks disappointed, but they comfort her and ask if one drink with them would help soothe the sting of her setback. Innocent had not been drinking, so she agrees. What can possibly go wrong with one cocktail? One of the three nice guys gets her drink.

At about 4:30 Sunday morning she wakes up in the back of her car still parked down the street. Both of her arms and elbows are bruised and scraped. Her shoes and underwear are gone. She had been drugged, then raped.

Common Solution:
Is this event Innocent's fault? No. She is still a harmless victim. Best case, Innocent can get medical help and rape counseling. Any report to police will bring her an array of questions she can't answer, because she remembers nothing after taking her drink. Was the sex consensual? She can't say for sure. Can she identify the three Villains? No, because she doesn't remember details. In reality, they are also college students and they don't know Mr. Wonderful at all. Innocent had observed him speaking to them, but they are not his friends.

In this scenario, Innocent abandoned all of her Safety Bubbles simultaneously.

Your *X-Pree* Solution:
Are you entirely captivated by a Mr. Wonderful? Wait until at least one friend is with you before interacting with him. Never take a drink that someone else touches. With nail polish called *Undercover Colors* [83] on one finger, you can identify a drug such as GHB (G-juice). It turns color if you dip it in a drink that is spiked with a date-rape drug. Your pursuit of any of these options will normally preempt the Villains' drug-assisted assault.

Among the greatest challenges associated with this crime is the absence of reporting by victims. If you or someone you know is an unfortunate victim, always make a police report and always get psych help. Embarrassing? Yes. But, how many other women will be raped if Villains are not stopped?

Scenario 7 — Mass Murder, School

Heze Innocent is a high school science teacher. Today's quiet drone of activity is interrupted with commotion down the hall. All the students are stunned as everyone in the room hears loud firecrackers going off in a slow sequence. Several seconds of jaw-dropping disbelief are followed by the chaos of students outside Innocent's room running past his door. Before anyone reacts defensively Villain, age seventeen, enters the classroom and fatally shoots Innocent with three rounds from a handgun. Then, other students in the room are randomly murdered.

Common Solution:
Many of the school's staff and students wait for law enforcement to arrive. After a few minutes, Villain is dead, and another heartbroken community mourns the loss of its children for years.

Diligent work by government and non-government professionals is being conducted to reduce the number of mass murders in schools. Our U.S. Department of Homeland Security has gobs of beneficial resources on the subject.[84] Much of the info focuses on how to react to the mass murderer.

As in many venues, the school environment is a challenging one in which to safely accomplish the popular "Run, Hide, Fight" paradigm. Acoustics in school halls and the chaos of fearful crowds make it hard to select the best direction to run. Also, open classrooms are intentionally designed as poor places to hide. Finally, as gun-free zones with an emphasis on non-aggression, it is challenging to instantly rally a civilian school team of minors to fight the murderer.

Waiting in a school until the mass murderer shows up is as dangerous as waiting until Villain raises his sledge hammer and begins the downward strike toward your defenseless head. Delaying preparation until an attack is launched is the antithesis of preemption. It's entirely void of safety.

Chapter 5 - Scenarios 1 to 10

Your *X-Pree* Solution #1 — Far ahead of any murders on school grounds, you and other teachers notice Villain's signals. All teachers and staff members are trained in the most recent compilations of pre-incident indicators, so they know what to watch out for. Parents in the school district have already been invited to a meeting about mass murder precursors.

Villain's grades drop significantly. Even though he's been bullied for months, without warning, his disdain for being teased doesn't seem to matter anymore. His friendships dwindle, replaced by a lot of time by himself. Some students wonder if the morbid posts by someone new to a popular blog belong to Villain. His parents are notified, invited to a meeting with Villain's counselor, and encouraged to notify the school if any of the following occur:
- His behavior includes sudden outbursts.
- He has an intensely possessive attitude about guns, ammo, or knives.
- He writes journal entries or social media posts about seeking revenge.

Obviously, these measures need to be pursued with extraordinary care. This is the school's Safety Bubble 4.

Your *X-Pree* Solution #2 — Innocent's school faculty, staff and student body have rehearsed all of the following to preserve their Safety Bubble 3:
- Recognizing the actual sound of gunshots in the buildings (police coordinated with the school to demonstrate with blank cartridges)
- Immediately reporting any oversize/overweight backpack or bag brought onto school grounds
- Performing a carefully designed "Secure-in-Place Plan," triggered by a distinct alarm or actual gunshots
- Running away to safety if caught outside the buildings
- Locking and darkening all classrooms
- Reinforcing door locks by jamming pencils, pens, folded paper between door and floor (or door jamb)
- Barricading doors with heavy objects
- Quickly turning off all electronic devices
- Using two-inch thick book(s) as a shield to stop an average handgun bullet

- Identifying classroom objects which qualify as "cover" to stop a bullet, versus "concealment" objects to only hide behind
- Hiding silently out of sight in the darkened room until released by a law enforcement officer
- Accessing the first aid kit with trauma supplies and the flashlight in the classroom
- Using pads and tourniquets for gunshot wounds
- Deploying a rope ladder stored in the classroom if it's above the first floor
- Responding to law enforcement by leaving the buildings, walking fast with hands raised and fingers spread apart

Your *X-Pree* Solution #3 — Due to school policies and/or statutes, some of the following *X-Pree* solutions may not be viable for you right now. Please urge your school district officials and legislators to allow school faculty and staff members the training, possession, and use of self-defense tools to preserve Safety Bubbles 2 and 1:

- Concealed handgun
- Non-lethal handgun cartridges with lower velocity, non-penetrating bullets
- Defense tools such as cane, high-intensity flashlight, knife, kubotan, pepper spray, and tactical pen
- Adopted defense tools such as: attache, backpack, book, broom, chair, fire extinguisher, knickknack, mug, desk organizer, stack of paper, handful of pens or pencils, picture, potted plant, plate, paper punch, scissors, stapler, table, wall plaque, and waste basket.

Obviously, some of these defense tools are less-than-lethal force against a mass murderer. They can sufficiently disrupt Villain's attack long enough for one or more Innocents to restrain or incapacitate him.

Advances in training over the last few years have resulted in fast, aggressive counter offensive action by skilled law enforcement teams when they reach the mass murderer's school site. Likewise, modernized self-defense training of adults who work in education will boost the *Extreme Preemption* of mass murders at schools.

Some school districts are currently assembling trained response teams of teachers and staff. For example, over 71% of Ohio counties currently have districts where such teams are able to respond with defensive firearms.[85]

In addition to all of the above, the presence of a trained School Resource Officer (SRO), preferably one who is armed, is an exceptional asset to define an additional Safety Bubble. It would work as a new #4 in this case, bringing the total to five. Your SRO can be arranged through many police departments.

Scenario 8 — Carjacking, Mall

On the way to work, Sheze Innocent stops at the mall. She makes a quick purchase and runs back to her car, which is parked between two other vehicles. She unlocks it, gets in, and puts her key into the ignition switch. Two men run up from behind. Villain #1 pounds hard on the body of her car, moving to the passenger side window as a distraction. Villain #2 quickly gets to her driver window, and displays a knife while he opens her door.

Common Solution:
This is a popular carjacking strategy. Innocent is fundamentally defenseless. She unknowingly and immediately allowed Villain into her Safety Bubble 1. In many of these incidents, Villains simply leave with the car. In other cases, less fortunate victims are often kidnapped, raped, and murdered.

Your *X-Pree* Solution:
To preempt this type of event your parking garage safety should always be this:
- Scan the area where you are about to park; if something doesn't feel right, leave immediately.
- Remember where you park; use the building's alpha/numeric parking sectors or the building's features as memory aids.

- Make sure that one arm and hand are completely free — always.
- Exit your car and lock it quickly.
- Before getting into your car check around, under, and inside it for anomalies; if something doesn't look right, go back inside and call for help or ask someone to walk with you to the vehicle.
- Re-enter the car quickly.
- After re-entering, first lock all doors and windows.
- Start your car and leave quickly.
- Texting, emails, phone calls, and other personal needs can occur later at another safe location.

If your event is similar to Innocent's, except you are safely locked inside, you can use the car itself as a defense tool. In this instance, ITOTR allows you to use force to defend yourself. Given Villain's display of a knife, crowbar, or bat, and the presence of two assailants, if your honest perception of the event will likely be a threat of severe bodily harm to you, then your moving car is the best defense tool. Drive away *FAST*, then call law enforcement.

Scenario 9 — Robbery, Parking Lot

Sheze Innocent leaves the bank and heads for her car. It's a large parking lot with a natural wooded area next to it. She had parked in the farthest corner because there were no other spots. As she beeps to get her car unlocked, Heza Villain springs out of nowhere on the driver side, and with a knife in his right hand he charges toward Innocent. She is licensed to carry a concealed handgun at all times.

Common Solution:
It's been awhile since she practiced her armed self-defense skills. Her gun is in a special concealment sleeve in the purse, but she fumbles to get to the pistol. Solidly within her Safety Bubble 1, Villain knocks Innocent on her rear and takes the purse with her gun still in it, cutting her arm deep as he slashes the shoulder strap. She screams for help. Villain is gone in less than ten seconds. He escapes into the nearby woods.

Your *X-Pree* Solution:
You already have your hand on the concealed pistol inside your purse. You are within the ITOTR guidelines to use lethal force against Villain; there is no

time for an onsite psychoanalysis. You begin to fall backward, but reflexively drop into a squat. Then you rock backward into a supine shooting position which you've practiced hundreds of times. As you nearly flatten on the pavement, you draw your semi-auto pistol from the purse in less than one second. You scream, "Get back!" Villain still advances with his knife. Barely clearing your holster purse with the gun, you fire shots into his chest until he staggers backward dropping to the ground and/or surrendering. This entire event lasts less than five seconds.

Pre-thinking a possible scenario like this one months earlier, you are mentally prepared. In your home, you regularly practice the controlled fall into the supine position while simultaneously drawing your gun. At less than five feet from Villain, there is no opportunity to use the gun's sights. No worries. Your are proficient in the One-Second Law.

You have also prepared in advance to seek legal and psych counseling in the event you ever need to use deadly force. Your path beyond the event is challenging, but you are able to resume a healthy life.

Of course, your improved awareness in this scenario would allow you to get a glimpse of Villain at your Safety Bubble 3 — 20 feet way.

Scenario 10 — Burglary, Home

Her daughter's board game isn't even remotely a challenge, but the 5-year-old's excitement in winning against Mom is beyond memorable. Sheze Innocent is alone with the little girl in her upstairs bedroom. As her daughter is busy brushing her teeth before bedtime, Innocent hears muffled breaking glass downstairs.

Common Solution:
Innocent gathers her daughter and hides in her closet behind some hanging clothes. She is terrified, hoping for the best.

Your *X-Pree* Solution:
You have a well-equipped Safe Room (Safety Bubble 2)— a single location in your house where you can retreat and defend yourself. Where should it be?

- If your have small children or a disabled person, your Safe Room will be their bedroom. In an emergency, it's faster to run to them than vice versa.
- Limited access is best; one man-door with a hefty deadbolt and strike plate.
- One lockable window is also useful; it improves your ventilation and ability to communicate with law enforcement outside the house.

Safe Room contents can vary a lot. Here is a list of necessities:
- Agree on a code word that triggers family members into action if it's yelled.
- Cell Phone — Even one that is out of service will usually be able to call 9-1-1 in the U.S., if it is plugged into a charger or it has a charged battery. Do not call 9-1-1 as a test! If you need reassurance, call your first responder's business office to confirm.
- Cell Phone Charger which can be plugged into a home outlet or portable version
- Flashlight with extra batteries — do not burn candles in your Safe Room. They are a dangerous fire hazard, and they consume precious oxygen.
- Snap Lights — 4 to 6 of them, as backups for your flashlight
- Water — 1 bottle per person
- Breakfast Bars — 1 bar per person
- Self-Defense Tools — 1 handgun & ammo locked in childproof safe is best; any other defense tools are beneficial.
- Blankets — 1 per person
- Fire Extinguisher
- Rope Ladder — if your drop to the ground is more than 8 feet
- Ear protection for everyone — if you have a gun with you

In an actual emergency,
1. Get all house occupants into your Safe Room immediately.
2. Lock and barricade the door.
3. Turn off all lights.
4. Quietly call 9-1-1. Stay on the phone call.
5. Demand silence from everyone.
6. Stay where you are. Wait for police to arrive.

Unless you have received specific, in-depth training, never attempt to "clear the house." Law enforcement professionals are trained to perform that task. If they arrive and you're playing Stealth Commander in your house, officers won't be able to distinguish you from Villain. Consequently, they might choose to defend themselves against you!

Safe Rooms are not new to safety planning. Your *X-Pree* solution includes meticulous maintenance of your Safe Room contents by refreshing perishables, checking the operation of devices, and practicing drills using your code word to get everyone to race into the room, securing it *FAST*.

Complete Topic Discussion 5,
then go to Chapter 6 — Scenarios 11 to 20.

Topic Discussion 5 — Scenarios 1 to 10

In the rape Scenarios 1 and 6, what are alternative defenses that Innocents can exercise in the two events?

What actions by parents or guardians are necessary in Scenarios 3 and 5 to prevent these types of events?

If you are Innocent in Scenario 4, will you overcome your fear to use the *X-Pree* defense described? Why or why not?

If the teacher in Scenario 7 is armed with a handgun, what critical safety issues does he need to train for?

What are workable locations for a Safe Room where you live?

Notes:

Topic Discussion 5 - Scenarios 1 to 10

CHAPTER 6 - SCENARIOS 11 TO 20

Scenario 11 — Verbal Abuse, Home

> Villain bellows, "Where are my jeans?"
> Innocent politely answers, "Which ones?"
> Villain fires back, "Are you stupid or what? My favorite jeans?"
> She softly replies, "Right here, ok? You don't have to yell at me."
> Villain: "Really? How else can I get through to you, Moron?"

Not one of their neighbors has ever invited them for dinner. Villain has not committed to marry her, even though he promised they would marry very soon after he moved in with her. His name calling, demeaning remarks, and yelling appear to roll off her, but they cut her heart deeply. She uses her drive to work to cry through the pain. They have lived together more than four years.

Innocent continues to endure Villain's verbal abuse. She's afraid it might escalate to hitting someday, but she's stuck right now. Talking to someone else doesn't sound like a good plan. Her life with Villain is painful and uncertain. She hopes tomorrow will be better. Tonight she silently cries herself to sleep.

Common Solution:
Innocent does nothing to change her home life. Her duties at work are reduced because she becomes absent-minded. Her pay is reduced. In a rant, Villain belittles her with more name-calling when he hears about her cut in pay. No co-worker or family member offers to help her.

Your *X-Pree* Solution:
Don't be late with your in-depth look at his **COVER** — **C**haracter **OVER** Everything. Whatever degree of charm, charisma, or machismo he bestows

on you, take a close look at his character. Observe him at home, in public, and at work if possible. Let's face it, everyone is a little off. All of us are flawed to some degree. We all have baggage. However, be confident that whatever state his character is in today, the prospects of a complete metamorphosis (i.e., his miraculous character improvement) are very low.

If you're in one of these relationships, get out of it completely. Do it now. Most likely, your Safety Bubbles are all compromised. Your only real tie to Villain is your feeling of love toward him. It is unbalanced and unhealthy for you. Verbal abuse can be deadly. You have no guarantee that his anger will not escalate to your physical injury. You deserve more than a disrespectful, malicious animal as your partner. You can find at least one person on the planet who will honor you with genuine love.

**Your safe exit needs to be planned.
Get help now to piece together a strategy!**

If there is no direct help for you through the nearest law enforcement department, any working phone will connect you to a help center 24/7.[86] You are in a dangerous, abusive relationship. Today's victims of the Intimate Demon include both women and men. You are not alone.

Scenario 12 — Mass Murder, Church

Villain enters the church parking lot more than forty minutes after the Sunday service begins. He strolls to the entrance of the main building and a couple of greeters give him a warm welcome. Even though the congregation is especially friendly, none of the regular members connected with Villain when he visited this church three weeks earlier. It's a hot, humid day, and he's wearing a light zippered jacket.

As Villain enters the sanctuary, an usher seats him in the back row. Later in the service, during a minute of prayer he stands up, draws a handgun from his waist band, and he begins shooting people in the congregation.

Common Solution:
This large room is filled with Innocents. Most people turn toward the mass murderer in stunning disbelief. Then, some of them instinctively crouch

down. Other people reflexively stand up, frozen in fear. With so many targets, Villain has a great time in this morning's church shooting gallery.

In the security world there are "soft targets" and "hard targets." Every person, vehicle, building, or other thing that is vulnerable to attack is classed as a "soft target." You guessed it, those people and other property that are relatively protected are called "hard targets." In the U.S. there are over 250,000 houses of worship. They are all classic soft targets.

Houses of worship are designed to be inclusive. This all-embracing ideology is the heart of their mission and the core of their success in serving the communities where they are located. Even as you read this, the concept of "hardening" a house of worship is at best contradictory and, worst case, a poles-apart unthinkable act — at least to many church members. Progress is being made in this area of safety, but the world still has far to go in making our places of worship safer.

Your *X-Pree* Solution:
As with all mass murderers, Villain gives you signs of his intent. His earlier visit and today's late arrival are blazing warnings that his interest in the church might not be aligned with everyone else's. Also, his light zippered jacket is not the best choice for today's sizzling summer weather. You recognize these signals.

You have in place a well-trained volunteer staff to meet the threat. They know how to spot someone who is carrying a concealed weapon. They know some fundamental bare hand self-defense skills, and they're capable of restraining Villain if necessary.

Your church fellowship has learned to apply these Safety Bubbles on the church property:
- **Bubble 5** — Parking Lot volunteers are aware that they are the most alert, front-line guardians of the church. If there is any way to stop a threat in the parking area, that is perfect *X-Pree*.
- **Bubble 4** — Greeters immediately outside the building are the second line of defense. Their care in getting to know the church members and casual visitors not only helps the church grow, it is a priceless profiling tool to identify potential threats.

- **Bubble 3** — Your church's consistent bag-check procedure will leave Sheza Villain wondering if her handgun might be discovered in her large purse. She might pick an easier target.
- **Bubble 2** — Ushers inside the building are in an ideal position to do a discreet hands-on check for a gun or knife which is hidden under a shirt or jacket. Non-intrusive, supportive hugs are warm and smart safety measures.
- **Bubble 1** — Finally, the church membership itself can be encouraged to personally know and care for each other. Villain's cloaking efforts will not be successful.

In nearly every case, mass murderers check out their target site before they attack it. Picture a fellowship of people who really know and pay attention to each other. In that setting, Villain's distant indifference will stand out like moldy blue-green chicken on a table of homemade delicacies at the church picnic.

These are additional possible pre-incident indicators for the mass murderer:
- Outbursts of anger
- Increased use of alcohol or drugs
- Lapses in personal hygiene
- Radical mood swings and emotions
- Depression and suicidal thoughts
- Relationship problems at home and/or at work
- Loss of employment

If all of the above efforts in your Safety Bubbles to preempt Villain's attack fail, there are only two remaining *X-Pree* defenses:
1. Someone who is trained to preempt Villain's intended attack with a handgun must take action. This Defender must be able to place an accurate shot on a pie plate at 50 feet, using the gun's sights, in less than 2 seconds after the threat is identified. Members must also be trained to immediately crouch down after hearing some prearranged signal. Your church will not appreciate the accidental shooting of an Innocent who semi-consciously stands up. That disaster will severely limit the success of any armed defense.
2. Church members must agree ahead of time to counter attack Villain as a group and disable him using adopted defense tools (chairs,

books, etc.). Don't underestimate the effect of 15 two-pound Bibles being hurled at Villain's head.

Extracting or concealing congregants are not optimal choices in a single room that is packed with people. In a 2013 webinar, leaders from government and private organizations reached this consensus in support of preemption:

> "Houses of Worship should learn the signs of a potentially volatile situation that may develop into an active shooter situation and proactively seek ways to prevent an incident with internal resources, or additional external assistance." [87]

No matter what scope of safety your house of worship chooses to embrace, its collective defense must be decisive, preemptive, and extremely fast. Waiting until a mass murderer shows up and begins firing his gun inside a church building is not only unnecessary, it's fatal for an unknown number of people in attendance.

Scenario 13 — Bullying, School

Sheza Villain and two friends had been picking on Sheze Innocent for many weeks. Their particular school has a chronic challenge with violence, which mimics the continuous turf battle between three rival gangs. Urban shootings are at an all-time high in this large city.

Today is filled the same hurtful remarks as Innocent walks by Sheza Villain and her allies, but Innocent's older brother is not with her. Smelling her vulnerability like fresh meat, the bullying intensifies. As she starts up the steps to the rear entrance of the school building, Villain's tallest friend knocks the papers and books from under Innocent's arm.

Common Solution:
Innocent stoops to pick up her books and is shoved until she falls, laying in a heap of school materials with abrasions on her arms and legs.

Your *X-Pree* **Solution:**

Your sacred Safety Bubble 1 has been compromised. Ignoring the dropped books, you quickly wheel around and you're greeted with a bear hug by the big girl. She confidently picks you up, but you have kept your hands free. As hard and fast as possible, you place a pounding blow with your hammer fist on the top of her head, while you let out a defensive yell. This strike will cause at least a partial knock out. You maintain your balance while the tall girl falls. Lower your chin, raise your hands, and stare at Villain silently until she backs away. You gather your belongings and report the incident to school staff.

This might not be the end of violence for you. Your dominance in the event will either deter future bullying, or you will face other challengers. Your humble, non-threatening confidence is a wise attitude to maintain.

Scenario 14 — Robbery, Mall

Sheze Innocent is in a big hurry. Her doctor appointment ran long. After her one-hour commute back home it's almost 6 PM. There is barely enough time to make a quick stop to grab some makeup at the mall. She pulls into a prime parking space, jets inside, scurries down one escalator flight, finds her cosmetic consultant, checks out in a flash, and bolts out of the department store into the parking structure. Innocent looks around for her car, tries "beeping" her key fob to find it, but then she remembers it's parked one level above.

Extreme Preemption

As she approaches the stairs in a dim corner of the parking area Innocent notices the stairwell is barely lighted. She hesitates for a second and then goes ahead, counting on her continued run of good fortune. Looks like she'll get home right on time.

After passing through the doorway at the foot of the stairs, she feels a tremendous shove from behind, falling face down on the concrete floor. Her head impacts the bottom step. Villain cuts the strap of her purse, snatches it, then disappears through the doorway. Barely conscious from her hard fall, Innocent collects herself on the step, with skinned hands and forehead.

Common Solution:
Innocent calls for help. Mall security personnel respond and take her to their office where she helps them, along with a responding police officer, gather info for their reports. She never saw Villain's face or clothing. Paramedics arrive and check her for a possible concussion. Innocent takes the rest of the week off notifying her bank, credit card companies, visiting the motor vehicle department to get her new driver license, and her doctor to check further for signs of a concussion. Innocent's haste cost her a lot. In addition to everything else that was lost, she had some old photos which can't be replaced.

In theory, she was able to preserve her Safety Bubble 2 by not entering the darkened stairwell. Instead, unknowingly Innocent invited Villain straight into her Safety Bubble 1.

Your *X-Pree* Solution:
Always remember where you park — every time, every place. When you're hurried, be especially alert and aware of what's happening around you in all directions. If you approach a space that is poorly lighted, never enter it alone. One of Villain's favorite tactics is removing bulbs or disabling lights in a stairwell. If you must enter that space, move slowly, check around corners, have your high intensity flashlight in your hand. Your world will not end if you take an extra two minutes to reenter the store and ride the escalator up one floor.

Reduce the number of credit cards, cash, or checks in your purse. Best of all, try to not carry a purse. Ridiculous? Not really. Be a trend-setter!

Scenario 15 — Vishing, Home

There is a very sweet sounding voice of the telephone caller who asks,
"Is this Mr. Innocent?"
Innocent answers, "Yes, it is."
Sheza Villain continues, "This is Sheza with the Universal Free Directory. We would like to verify some information for your company listing. May I confirm the name of your business, please?"

Common Solution:
Innocent hangs on the call giving every stitch of info that the sweety pie asks for. Her listing offer is "free" for everyone who receives the "directory," but there is a charge for Innocent's business to "sustain" the listing.

Your *X-Pree* Solution:
Hang up immediately. This is one of many vishing techniques to manipulate you into either a paid listing or volunteering info to build a profile which will enable Villain hackers to steal personal and/or company financial secrets. If your number is a cell phone, make sure it is listed in the National Do Not Call Registry.[88]

Scenario 16 — Cyberbullying, Home

At breakfast, Innocent's mom asks, "I talked to Eddie's mother yesterday. She said they're having a big sixteenth birthday party for him, and you and your friends are all invited. Should I plan to give you a ride?"
Heze Innocent shoots back, "Not me. I'm not invited."
"Well, that's not what his mom said."
Innocent replies, "I'm not invited, and I don't want to talk about it. Ok?"

Common Solution:
Innocent's mother let's the issue go. Eddie's party date passes.

Your *X-Pree* Solution:
You are Innocent's mother and you don't let it go. You check back with Eddie's mom, and she confirms that Innocent was invited by text message. When you ask Innocent about it again later, he says he received the text

message. But on the next day, he received another message from Eddie saying, "Plans changed. Cannot invite u this time — Eddie."

This is an instance of bullying by a classmate at the middle school. Bully Heza Villain is savvy enough to get the message sent using a burner application which creates a temporary phone number in order to disguise the real phone number that originates the call or text message. Innocent's cyber Safety Bubble 1 has been popped.

Innocent has been good friends with Eddie for five years, but he's not a very popular young guy. At this age, acceptance and affirmation are very important. Teenagers have committed suicide in similar circumstances, when a series of bullying rejections caused extreme isolation.

Your respectful family closeness allows you to intrude into your children's business to whatever degree is required to protect them. Build trust, enabling them to discuss challenges and disappointments with you and other family members.

Scenario 17 — Attack, Golf Course

Heze Innocent finishes his golf game and walks toward the clubhouse. A young player approaches him red-faced, calling Innocent a variety of colorful names. Innocent puts his hand up with a gesture to stop, and the man hesitates, but he accuses Innocent of having an affair with his wife. There is a short exchange of words between the men. Innocent is relatively calm, backs up two steps, yet he can't talk the young man out of his tantrum. Since Innocent doesn't know the man or his wife, he unconsciously grins slightly at the absurdity of the notion. This infuriates the man even further, and he raises a golf club to strike Innocent.

Common Solution:
Innocent backs up and brings his bent arm up near his ear to block the blow. As the shaft of the club breaks on Innocent's arm, the head of the club flips down striking Innocent, leaving a substantial contusion on the side of his head.

Your *X-Pree* Solution:

You will have your hands already at shoulder height, gesturing him to stop. At the point the mistaken young man raises his golf club, you immediately step toward him to shorten the radius of his swing. Use your right hand and arm to deflect away his left arm, then instantly strike straight in using the edge of your left hand to his throat.

To preempt a blow like this one, your defensive strike needs to be at lightening speed. Straight in, then out again, at your maximum speed.

In the aftermath, everyone learns that the young man is very much mistaken and a little intoxicated. According to ITOTR, you are justified in your defense.

Scenario 18 — Phishing, Online

Innocent checks his email three times per day. He uses separate email addresses for his business, H.L. Imports, and his personal activity. In the normal course of business Innocent frequently uses electronic transfers. This morning he opens an email that looks something like this one:

> eCheck Notification
> To: HLImports
> Reply-To: eCheck Notification
> Contact us too receive your funds
>
> Your account has pending deposit for $3,650.00
>
> Please log on at >> Payment Link <<
>
> User Name: innocent@hlimports.com
> Password: FMKR343#$@#

Common Solution:
Innocent hurriedly goes to the "Payment Link" and logs on. There are fields of info on the next page that need to be confirmed, including Innocent's business checking account and routing numbers. Villain hackers already have acquired Innocent's birthdate, work and home phone numbers through social media. Their fraudulent system asks for a test transfer of $1 (debit) by Innocent to confirm all aspects of his account. Innocent makes the $1 transfer. Within two minutes Villain hackers mimic this transfer, but increase the amount to $3,650. In his haste Innocent allows the $3,650 withdrawal out of his account, instead of a deposit into it.

Your *X-Pree* Solution:
Delete the fraudulent email message above and any others which are not entirely familiar. No legitimate funds transfer will ever be conducted in this manner. Report Villain to the Internet Crime Complaint Center.[89]

Scenario 19 — Burglary, Home

It's about 10:00 AM on Thursday. No Innocents are in their suburban home. Everyone is at work or school. Villain's mid-size box truck backs into the driveway, and three men get out. They go to the front door and knock. From down the street neighbors can hear voices. After a few seconds of conversation, one of the men says, "Thanks, we'll be quick!"

Innocents' home is being burglarized. Three Villains have been watching the house for over two weeks. They know that the Innocents are not at home, and they fake a conversation with occupants in order to fool curious neighbors.

Common Solution:
Residents in your neighborhood don't know each other very well. Villains quietly force the front door open, and quickly take whatever property they can, load it into their truck, and drive away.

Your *X-Pree* Solution:
You are employing these daytime Safety Bubbles for your empty house:
- **Bubble 7** — Some version of a watch program in your neighborhood. It's not a formal Neighborhood Watch,[90] but a few

of the residents are at home most of the time and you have informed them about your weekday schedule. One of them notices an unknown car with two men sitting in it for several hours one day and reports the plate number to police, asking them to patrol the street.

- **Bubble 6** — Two inexpensive wireless "perimeter alarm" devices cover the front and rear yards. Any units that produce an obnoxious noise will work.
- **Bubble 5** — Exterior doors have the following:
    - They're mounted with 3" long hinge screws which extend into the doorway framing.
    - They do not have glass that can be broken, enabling Villain to reach inside doorknobs.
    - Each door has a heavy-duty strike plate on the latch side.
    - Each door has a deadbolt with a 1" throw.
- **Bubble 4** — Cellular-based home security system for your garage and home with sensors on all doors and windows, motion sensors for interior areas, and window stickers; if you can't afford a security system, acquire some window stickers to imitate having one.
- **Bubble 3** — Inventory of your personal property with photos each showing a visible tag with your driver license number and a simple log with model/serial numbers
- **Bubble 2** — Important documents, log and photos of personal property are off-site in a trusted person's home, buried vault, or safe deposit box.
- **Bubble 1** — All jewelry and firearms are stored in a fire-resistant safe rated for at least 60 minutes.

These layers of security will slow Villains down and, hopefully, discourage their attack on your home.

Scenario 20 — Abuse, Parking Lot

Innocent is about to unlock her car in the parking area near her apartment. Villain is a persistent ex-boyfriend who refuses to stay away. Today, he goes too far by grabbing her arm, pulling her away from her car. He is eight inches taller and much stronger than she. It's challenging to pin down a label for this Villain — perhaps "Bushwhacker Meets Narcissist."

Extreme Preemption

Common Solution:
Innocent submits to another angry lecture about her poor decision to leave him. He detains her for half an hour until she breaks down in tears. Fortunately, he gives up and does not injure her this time.

Your *X-Pree* Solution:
You are trained in *X-Pree* and already have one hand on the pepper spray unit in your purse. When you're clear of the cars, you soak his face and neck with the spray while quickly backing away from him, holding your breath. There is no guarantee that Villain's anger will not escalate to a more intense level of violence when he comes back. You call 911 and report the incident.

Caution: Your canister's overspray can be as painful to you if it contacts your skin or airway.

In the future you visually check all sides of your car before approaching it.

Complete Topic Discussion 6,
then go to Chapter 7 — Scenarios 21 to 30.

Topic Discussion 6

Does the verbal abuse in Scenario 11 satisfy the ITOTR guidelines to use force? Why or why not?

What are the arguments for and against allowing citizens to be armed in a house of worship?

What defense will work for Innocent if her arms are pinned in Scenario 13?

Why does the abuse in Scenario 20 satisfy the ITOTR guidelines to use pepper spray?

What are the Safety Bubbles in your present location?

Notes:

Topic Discussion 6 - Scenarios 11 to 20

Chapter 7 - Scenarios 21 to 30

Scenario 21 — Groping, Parking Lot

After an exhausting work week, Sheze Innocent goes out for a couple of drinks with friends. On her way back to the car, a man she just met, Heza Villain, grabs her by the arm and starts forcefully guiding her in a direction she doesn't intend to go. She tries to get free from his grip, but he's very strong, and very drunk.

Common Solution:
Innocent continues to struggle, without getting free. Against the fender of a car, he gropes her for a minute, chuckles at his victory, shoves her away, and walks off.

Your *X-Pree* Solution:

While walking at his side, you appear to submit to him for a second. You look down without moving your head, time your strike, then stomp his leg from the side, just above his ankle. Your strike is as hard as you can make it. If you hit your target, his ankle should literally collapse under his lower leg. You will be able to run to safety.

Villain might out weigh you by 100 pounds or more, but he will have no defense against your strong counter attack. His focus is on that powerful grip on your arm (up high), so you strike a different part of him (down low). Don't wildly flail your free hand. Instead, deliver a targeted strike to disable Villain. You won't be chased by any giant predator with one non-working ankle.

Scenario 22 — Cyberbullying, School

Sheza Villain and her cyber bully friends are hard at work. Innocent is in their sights and her school popularity must be destroyed. Ridiculous as it might sound, scenarios like this one are playing out across the world with huge numbers of casualties.

Here's how the attack is conducted: Innocent makes a friendly post on social media. Villain comments with some creative, but derogatory, nickname for Innocent. Villain's friends pile on with other comments and posts using the hurtful nickname. The whole thing escalates with other students using the new nickname in their posts, messages, and emails.

Villain's death blow is made with the use of a fake email account and a burner phone which appear to belong to Innocent. Villain impersonates Innocent using the devices to angrily lash back at people who are mocking her. Rabid snickering at lunch one day leads Innocent to a trail of the malicious communications which she never knew about.

Common Solution:
Innocent is heartbroken, feeling betrayed by her friends who were weak enough to believe and engage in the con.

Your *X-Pree* Solution:
There is a giant hole in Innocent's cyber Safety Bubble 1. You might be thinking about the old axiom "Sticks and stones will break my bones, but names will never hurt me!" In ancient times long forgotten (15 years ago) when school communication was primarily in person, all rotten nicknames could be dealt with promptly. Communication among students is different now. Extended waves of secrets and insults crash through our cyber world with the emotional damage of tsunamis.

For school age Innocent, her array of friends turning fiends is genuinely hurtful. She might not ever tell a parent in order to get help. All right then, where is the *X-Pree* solution here? It's with Innocent's peers. If you are school age and you observe this type of secret abuse, you have a responsibility to speak up about it to Innocent, an adult, or school counselor. Early exposure of Villain's twisted plan makes it ineffective.

Scenario 23 — Physical Abuse, Home

Even though her sprained wrist stopped hurting last week, the bruises on her forearms are too embarrassing to wear a summer top. Innocent stays home while other moms go on the field trip with the third grade class. She hasn't had a free day in many months. That trip to the petting zoo sounded wonderful. Maybe she'll go next time.

Her husband has been mildly beating Innocent for several years. She's read some stories about how counseling helped other couples, but that possibility seems impossible now. Her requests to Villain for professional help always spark an argument. He never wants to hear about her concerns. When he's drunk, and she repeats a request for help, the angry slapping is sure to follow.

They have two boys, ages 8 and 10. Innocent and her sons live in continuous fear of Villain. He barely provides for their needs. His beer budget is substantial; it seems to be his top priority.

Common Solution:
Innocent endures the physical abuse. As her two sons get older, she misses more and more opportunities to explore life with them. Her frustration with the limits on her life nurture a rage within Innocent. Arguments with Villain have become more fiery; strikes against her become harder. She has difficulty concealing the injuries. Some neighbors and relatives know about the situation, but no one says a word. She feels entirely trapped.

Your *X-Pree* Solution:
To preempt this, remember COVER — Character OVER everything. You can tell all you need to know about this Intimate Demon by his COVER. When you meet: Is he stable in a job? Does he treat you like a lady or only a hot

bundle to have sex with between beers? Does he rant about other people who have wronged him? Does he show you respect when you're in public? His character is your barometer to forecast your future with him. He will deal with life experiences, including you, from his core — his character. Don't be blindsided!

If you're immersed in this mess you only have one safe short term option, and two safe long term options. In the short term, leave the home now. It is the only course of action in which you will be safe. Yes, you can do it. Every U.S. state has some form of assistance for battered women, by themselves and with children.[91]

Waiting only increases the risk of more injuries to you and your children. Your injuries are increasing in severity. If you wait long enough, you might be killed. Waiting to protect your children does not protect them from anything. They see and hear the Villain in their home. They are afraid for you and for themselves. This fear is wreaking havoc in their lives and prepping them with a model of violence which they can take into their adult lives, breeding another generation of violence.

Leaving Villain can be difficult and dangerous. Get help from a battered women's center to construct a plan before you go to the shelter.[92]

In the long term, you only have three safe options:
1. Villain must get professional help while you are safe, before you move back.
2. He experiences a metamorphic change; yes, it can happen.[93]
3. Stay away forever.

Scenario 24 — Burglary, Home

This year, Innocents have planned a wonderful vacation that takes them out of town for ten days in December. They have escaped the winter cold to a dreamy tropical island.

Common Solution:
While Innocents are away mail, newspapers, leaves, and snow accumulate at the house. Their two daughters are busy with posts on social network sites

telling all about the family vacation before and while they are out of town. Innocents' home is burglarized. They lose valuable jewelry and many small appliances.

Your *X-Pree* Solution:
In addition to all of the *X-Pree* measures described in Scenario 19, you get the help of a trusted friend who stops by every other day to pick all mail and newspapers. He clears the walks and driveway of leaves and snow. Also, he drives and repositions the car in the driveway to make it look like Innocents have driven it. No photos are posted on the Internet until after the family returns home. Everything remains safe, because Villain never suspects that Innocents are away.

Scenario 25 — Bushwhackery, Street

Sheze Innocent is walking down a street after dark, finished with holiday shopping. Her hands hurt from carrying several shopping bags at one time. She is grabbed around the torso from behind and pulled back toward a narrow alley. She hears Villain breathing heavily in her ear.

Common Solution:
Innocent tries to yell for help, but Villain covers her mouth with his hand. Her strength diminishes fast as she struggles to get free. Only a miracle will save her from his sexual assault, unless he merely wants the gifts she purchased.

Your *X-Pree* Solution:
You immediately drop all of the shopping bags and focus on two simultaneous counter attacks:
1. Find one of Villain's fingers and literally bend it backward with the force to break it off. It won't actually come off.
2. At the same time, run backwards in place violently scraping down Villain's shins.

As with all other *X-Pree* solutions, your defense is brutal and fast. You struggle to stay on your feet until he let's go. Then, you run to safety.

Scenario 26 — Robbery / Knife, Street

Innocent is approached by two young men who demand his wallet. At about twenty feet away, they both display folding knives and pause, waiting for his response. Innocent stands there in disbelief for about two seconds. Villains repeat their demand.

Common Solution:
Innocent produces the wallet and tosses it to the Villains. They leave. In many scenarios like this one Innocent is fatally stabbed.

Your *X-Pree* Solution:
Knowing that these Cash Villains have entered your Safety Bubble 2, you are ready with a licensed concealed handgun. At the instant Villains display their knives, you display your gun and yell, "Get back!" They will probably turn and run away. You are very upset, but your threat has ended, so you do not draw your gun. You call police and report the event.

Since Professor Gary Kleck first published research in 1993 there is still a professional consensus that in a high percentage of cases (75% or more), the violent attacker is dissuaded from pursuing his attack when his victim shows evidence of being armed with a gun.[94]

Scenario 27 — Credit Card Fraud, Phone

With his young daughter's help Heze Innocent is trying to get dinner prepared. As a single parent and successful sales rep, he does a lot of driving. His quiet time at home is rare. He receives a cell phone call from a woman with an attractive sounding voice. She apologizes for calling him around dinner time, but insists that he needs to confirm some activity with one of his credit cards.

Common Solution:
Innocent asks for more details, and Sheza Villain explains that she is with a processing center, and a purchase was made in a city several hundred miles away for "$2,473.36 using your AJAX credit card." She asks him to confirm his credit card number, expiration date, and security code by reading that info from his card.

Villain is certainly working for a processing center. It's a center where fraudulent purchases are made. Anxious to finish dinner preparation Innocent volunteers his credit card info. She assures him that they will remove the purchase in the amount of $2,473.36. They end the call. Villain's fake processing center then makes a fraudulent online purchase. Merchandise is picked up at a store, and there is no way to trace Villain or her location.

Your *X-Pree* Solution:
This is a breach of your cyber Safety Bubble 1. Your defense is simple and easy:
- Ask the caller for a good phone number to call back, or
- Immediately hang up and call the phone number listed on your credit card statement to confirm the legitimacy of the issue. If fraudulent, make a report with your credit card company.

This scam is a good example of "vishing," using voice communication to gather personal information for criminal purposes. All credit card companies have purchase protection in some form. Your card company reps might call you about a phoney purchase, but they will never call you asking for card info. Internet thieves do that.

Scenario 28 — Robbery, Store

Sheze Innocent is the only night time clerk at a convenience store. At about 11:00 PM Villain enters the store in traditional Villain attire — worn out jeans, black hoodie, sunglasses. He walks up to the checkout counter, pulls out a handgun, and demands cash from the register. Let's not forget that he holds the gun sideways, as every contemporary urban vigilante is trained.

Common Solution:
Innocent has absolutely no defense, so she hands over the cash and Villain leaves. In many scenarios like this one, Innocent is shot.

Your *X-Pree* Solution:
You do nothing to comply with the Cash Villain's demands. Your store is equipped with 24/7 surveillance cameras which are running. Your checkout area has the following:

- Large 1" thick clear plexiglass wall facing the customer area
- Narrow pass-through in the plexiglass wall
- Steel door which securely locks from the inside
- Silent robbery alarm for police
- Separate ventilation system
- Remote locking system for the store's front doors

You politely inform Villain that he is being recorded, his gunshots will not get to you, police are on their way, and if he attempts to leave with any merchandise you will lock him in the store.

Are the security measures described above expensive? Balanced against potential robberies and death, they are a bargain. When we add the comfort of customers who know that the store clerks are not likely to be robbed, the expensive security system becomes a worthwhile investment.

With these devises in place, the clerk's Safety Bubbles 1, 2, and 3 are secure. Without them, real safety is achieved only by chance.

Scenario 29 — Confrontation, Street

Heze Innocent is walking his small dog early on Sunday morning, still a little groggy from a neighbor's party last night. He makes his way down the street with the leash in his left hand. He's stewing over comments made by a neighborhood loudmouth. As he tries to guide his fidgeting dog, Innocent catches a glimpse of another person.

Someone he's never seen before approaches and angrily makes comments about Innocent's t-shirt. As they pass, Villain reaches out with his left hand and grabs a handful of Innocent's shirt at his chest.

Common Solution:
At first, Innocent is stunned by the man's behavior. He grabs Villain's hand, yells back at him, and the two men struggle for some unknown amount of time. With his legs wrapped up by the dog leash, Innocent is barely able to stand up. Villain kicks at the dog, and this scenario quickly escalates to serious injury of Innocent and his dog.

Your *X-Pree* Solution:

1. You are observant enough to identify Villain's anger, not allowing him into your Safety Bubble 1 (5 ft.). Taking two steps to the side or placing your dog between you and Villain will get it done.
2. If your morning grog prevents Solution #1, Villain's left hand is occupied with your t-shirt and his perceived authority to grab it. His right hand might follow up with a punch; you don't know for sure. Pull him even closer, pull down on his hand with your left hand, and strike him fast and hard with the edge of your right hand to the side of his neck. This blow will either stun him or knock him out. Then, you run to safety.

Villain's attention is on his grip of your t-shirt and whatever remarks coming out of his mouth. Your attention is on delivering your fastest, hardest strike to his neck.

Scenario 30 — Robbery / Knife, Park

Sheze Innocent is resting in the park on her way home. It's nearly dark, but some lamps in the park give enough light to navigate the walkways. There are only a few joggers in sight, no one nearby. She jumps as a young man with a knife approaches from her left and plops down on her bench. Villain demands her purse and watch.

Common Solution:
Innocent hands over her purse and watch, taking her chances that she won't be hurt. She receives several critical stab wounds.

Your *X-Pree* Solution:
You already have your hand on your pepper spray inside the purse. When Villain grabs it, you abruptly stand up, let go of the purse while drawing and soaking his head with the spray. He is likely incapacitated long enough for you to escape to a safe location. Dial 911 for help, then assist police by making a detailed report.

Complete Topic Discussion 7,
then go to Chapter 8 — Scenarios 31 to 40.

Topic Discussion 7

Why do the ITOTR guidelines support the X-Pree defense in Scenario 21?

Do you have the courage to report cyber bullying as in Scenario 22?

According to ITOTR guidelines, why are you legally correct to not shoot the Cash Villains in Scenario 26?

Does your level of fitness allow you to make the strike in Scenario 29?

Why is a police report necessary in Scenario 30?

Notes:

Topic Discussion 7

Chapter 8 - Scenarios 31 to 40

Scenario 31 — Carjacking, Street

On his way to work, Heze Innocent stops at the light about one mile from his house. He is last in the lineup of cars waiting for the signal to turn green. One of the men in the car at his left quickly opens his passenger door and charges Innocent's driver door. Still sipping a cup of coffee, with his door unlocked, Innocent is taken by surprise. Villain easily overpowers Innocent, unbuckles his seatbelt, throws him out of the car, and drives off in it. Villain's partner drives off in different direction.

Common Solution:
Fortunately, Innocent is not run down by another car. He staggers to the curb and dials 911. When police arrive he gives a description of his car, but he can't remember the license plate number. His car is never recovered.

Your *X-Pree* Solution:
Your first action when entering a vehicle is to lock all doors and windows. Always allow enough room behind the car ahead of you by making sure you see where the wheels of that car touch the road. When moving or standing, stay continuously aware of what's happening around you. Keep tabs of all the vehicles around you, by type, color, etc.

At the first instant you identify a possible threat, drive away. Law enforcement will probably understand if you explain that driving over a curb, median, or on the empty sidewalk was your only escape route.

Even if Villain successfully opens the driver door, you can back up fast and drive away to safety. Losing a door is far better than losing your whole car or your life. Remember, your *Extreme Preemption* is heading off the assault before Villain acts out his plan.

CHAPTER 8 - SCENARIOS 31 TO 40

Scenario 32 — Robbery Error, ATM

Innocent's restaurant is doing well considering his short time in business. Customers are raving about the food in their online reviews. His servers are only exceeded in their skill by the excellence of his kitchen staff. Life is good for Innocent as he arrives at the bank to deposit the day's receipts.

His regular time for depositing is around 1 AM. Tonight, he's a little late because of a faithful customer's birthday party. Innocent pulls up to the ATM side of the building. No one is around as he gets out of the van to walk over to the drop box.

Villain approaches from behind the opposite corner of the building. He's wearing a hoodie with his hands tucked in the pouch. As Villain gets closer, Innocent is very tense.

Common Solution:
Innocent freaks out! Happiness about the day's victories distracted him from preparing his handgun for concealed carry to the bank. Villain picks up his pace as he gets within 15 feet of Innocent. Suddenly he starts to run, but away from Innocent! Villain grabs a cell phone in his pouch and declares, "I'm trying to get there, ok? I got off at the wrong station."

Innocent's heart rate levels off after a few minutes. Villain is a young man who is new to the city and simply trying to connect with a friend.

Your *X-Pree* Solution:
You freak out! Your handgun is in the holster where you have carried it for several years. Villain picks up his pace as he gets within 15 feet of you. You have your shooting hand on the concealed pistol. You do not draw the gun because abruptly he starts to run, but away from you! Villain grabs a cell phone in his pouch and declares, "I'm trying to get there, ok? I got off at the wrong station."

Your heart rate levels off after a few minutes. If you had hastily drawn your gun, there is a chance the young man would see you as a threat and defend himself appropriately.

As a trained Defender your code is restraint, coupled with acute attention to detail. *Extreme Preemption* in this scenario is the lightening fast decision to keep the gun holstered and fully concealed.

Scenario 33 — Confrontation, Parking Lot

Having someone in your face is never tasteful. Heze Innocent has a full cup of it today. He mistakenly takes the parking space that Villain was waiting for in the crowded grocery store parking lot. After he parks, Villain runs over and intercepts Innocent right after he gets out of his car. Literally in his face, Villain launches into a verbal attack. Innocent tries to explain that he made a mistake, he apologizes, he assures Villain it is not directed at him personally, and he points out that his two young children are in the car. Villain is unrelenting in his tantrum. He moves even closer to Innocent, poking a finger in his chest and stepping on one of his feet.

Common Solution:
Innocent keeps apologizing, while his children are terrified. Villain humiliates Innocent by squeezing him against his own car.

Your *X-Pree* Solution:

Timing is the key to your defense here. After sincerely apologizing the first time, in the instant that Villain touches you, explosively strike straight upward with your palm — into his chin or nose. Give a loud yell, "Get back!" Your children are already scared. Better to have them remember Dad defending himself, rather than Dad be beaten in front of them.

This effective strike will likely stun Villain or send him falling backward, possibly resulting in serious injury. ITOTR use-of-force rules are not crystal clear in this scenario. Your perception of the potential injury coming at you is the key here.

Our current litigious culture easily justifies a good self-defense liability insurance policy. At this writing USCCA's insurance plans support the legal use of any self-defense tool, including bare hands.[95]

Scenario 34 — Rape, Home

Sheze Innocent is at home Saturday morning with her young children, scrambling to finish laundry and some cleaning. Above the drone of the vacuum there is a loud knock at the front door. Innocent heads for the door because her sister said she might stop by today.

Common Solution:
Innocent opens the door and large-frame Villain charges into the house. He knocks her backward and she hits the floor hard. Two punches to her head leave her unconscious. Villain takes only four minutes to scour the home for cash and jewelry. He rapes Innocent, then leaves.

Your *X-Pree* Solution:
In this disastrous encounter, Innocent compromised her own Safety Bubbles 2 and 1 in order. Villain sees absolutely no value in the welfare of you or your children. He must be treated that way. Do we know a stranger's intent? No. So, the safe response is extreme caution.

Whenever possible, check your front door from a window in a different room — before going near the door. Any inexpensive live camera or a wide-angle door viewer that allows you to view your front door area is a priceless aid.

Knowing the best safety practices, you do not open the front door. Instead, you gather a defense tool, immediately back away from the door and ask who it is. Villain tells you a story about needing the phone for an emergency call. He does not leave when you ask him to do so. You gather your children and immediately race to your Safe Room — *FAST*. Call police from there. If Villain tries to force entry to your Safe Room, shoot to stop him.

Scenario 35 — Slavery, Apartment

Living with a single mom who works a lot is difficult for Sheze Innocent (age 16) and her younger sister. There is a management couple in the apartment complex who are friendly with everyone. They have more stories to tell than ants swarming a cookie, and they're always very nice to Innocent. One day the husband compliments her hair, asking if Innocent ever thinks about modeling. She giggles and says, "Me? No! Well, sometimes, maybe." He says that he knows a talent scout who is looking for young women to do TV commercials; the pay is huge, he says.

Our managers are "facilitators" who work with human traffickers to locate new victims. This "scout" he's talking about is a sex trafficker's recruiter, a good looking young man who knows how to push every young girl's emotional buttons.

Mr. Manager baits Innocent with, "This young gentleman is going to be in town next week. Maybe your Mom will let my wife introduce you to him!"

Common Solution:
Innocent hounds her mother to give permission to meet the "scout." After all, what harm could there possibly be in one meeting? Mrs. Manager reports back to Innocent and her mother the time and place for the interview.

Villain (recruiter) is not only cute, he charms both Innocent and her mother with stories about young girls who have starred in recent commercials. As his story unfolds, of course some of them use Villain's boss as their agent.

Two months later, Innocent is gone one afternoon. She willingly leaves with Villain, voluntarily succumbing to the promises of fame, wealth, and love from a big family. Her life actually turns out to be imprisonment, poverty, and abuse. Innocent never tells her mother the truth about her new life. She eventually stops contacting her mom. Our friendly apartment managers stay for a few more months, then they move on to a new city. There is no verifiable evidence of their commission of a crime.

Your *X-Pree* Solution:
Assist as much as you can with awareness about today's slave traders. There are scams in play which are well-funded and carefully strategized to pull in victims who voluntarily leave their families behind in pursuit of modeling and acting careers. Learn about the multi-billion dollar industry. Teenagers from families with great wealth are not immune to the lures of skilled pimps. Competent "finesse pimps" are mind-game artists who psychologically control their girls.

Your *X-Pree* solution here is immediate homework. Thoroughly use third-party verification of your contact at an ad agency. Insist that any discussions about modeling are between you and your daughter only. Unless you know the couple very well, limit the time your daughter is alone with resident managers. Sixteen is the prime age of the 20 million victims in today's worldwide human trafficking industry.

There is a small group of young celebrities who experience fantastic limelight success; so, the possibilities of fame and fortune are out there, but they are few in number. Alternatively, there are vast legitimate resources which can enable your child to focus on a solid education.

By the way, if you know someone who can't live without Internet pornography, be aware that he or she is actively supporting sex slave traders online. That hottie who tickles the senses for a few minutes per day might otherwise be living a life of regular physical torture, emotional beat downs, gang rapes, and isolation — during her short remaining life off-camera. Remember, it's going to be over about seven years after she's enslaved. No online tickle is worth a person's life.

Scenario 36 — Attack / Knife, Street

Heze Innocent is approached by a man wearing a hoodie who lowers his chin, charging with a knife from about thirty feet away.

Common Solution:
Innocent is armed with a handgun, but he's entirely unprepared. He attempts to draw his legally concealed gun, and he botches the process. Villain carves him up like a Halloween pumpkin. Innocent dies within two minutes at the scene. Villain steals his gun and runs away unhurt.

Your *X-Pree* Solution:
You have not only trained for the One-Second Law, but you are proficient with your concealed handgun using its sights at a longer distance. As you draw your gun you shout "Get back!" There is no physical room for you to retreat. Every element of your ITOTR guidelines supports your use of deadly force.

Villain continues to charge with his knife drawn. You aim at the center of his torso and fire until he no longer poses an imminent threat to you. Villain is now on the pavement crawling away. You move to a safe spot, call 911, request police and medical help, then wait for the first responders to arrive.

Timing is once again critical here. No civilized person should prefer to take another's life in self-defense. However, your hesitation will bring you injury or death in this scenario. *Extreme Preemption* calls for proficient gun handling skills and your acute attention to every micro-portion of this event.

Scenario 37 — Carjacking, Parking Lot

On a cold winter day Sheze Innocent is having trouble getting her keys out to unlock her car. Fumbling to remove her gloves, she can't find the correct key. Heza Villain, about age 23, appears behind her, grabs her and says, "I'll take those keys, thank you." He spins Innocent around. Villain's dark pupils are very large, even in the midday light. His lips are very dry. He mutters some other incoherent remarks. She backs up two steps, but he moves in. Frozen in fear, Innocent can't run because Villain is blocking her.

Common Solution:
Innocent struggles to put her keys between her fingers. She half-heartedly swipes at Villain hitting his shoulder, but on impact the keys cut the webbing between her fingers. Innocent runs away with bleeding fingers. Villain takes her purse and car.

Your *X-Pree* Solution:

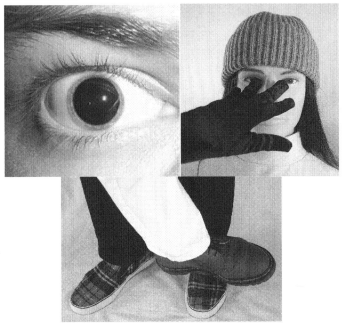

To hone your detection skills, you've done a few minutes of Internet searching about the signs of drug use. You know that cocaine, methamphetamine, heroin, and fentanyl cause mydriasis — extremely large pupils. Your Villain is high on a stimulant.

Opioid use is the leading cause of fatalities in America.[96] Some of the popular man-made drugs, such as fentanyl analogs (a.k.a. "designer drugs"), are powerful enough to cause massive, permanent brain damage or death with just one dose. While the actual use of synthetic stimulants is dangerous enough, the enterprises that move them are also perilous.

Heavy users need large amounts of cash to support their drug needs, resulting in our steady supply of Cash Villains. Drug traffickers need profitable networks of buyers and manufacturers to sustain their businesses. Rolled together, the global drug industry is a playground of control and a fountain of violence. Cash Villain is driven by his desperate need for your property, in this scenario your car. He has no desire to show consideration toward you, because the car is his efficient path to raise cash required to function in his world.

Your defenses against him must be energized. If he is loaded with a heavy drug, there is a good chance he won't feel physical pain. You *X-Pree* defense must somehow physically break him so that he cannot attack you.

As he spins you around, you take a step closer to him. Instantly, you notice his dilated pupils and dry mouth. With the speed of a slingshot, you extend your free hand jabbing your finger tips straight into Villain's eyes, causing them to water profusely. You stomp his instep then run to safety and call for help.

Scenario 38 — Carjacking Error, Parking Lot

On a cold winter day Sheze Innocent is having trouble getting her keys out to unlock her car. Fumbling to remove her gloves, she just can't find the correct key. Heza Villain, about age 23, appears behind her, grabs her and says something she can't understand. He spins Innocent around. Villain's face is soaked with sweat. Facing her, he mutters some incoherent remarks, making random hand motions. She is able to back up two steps, but he moves toward her. Innocent freezes in fear. She can't run because Villain is between her and safety.

Common Solution:
Innocent struggles to put her keys between her fingers. She half-heartedly swipes at Villain hitting his shoulder, but on impact the keys cut the webbing between her fingers. Innocent runs away with bleeding fingers. Villain leans against her car, emotionally distraught.

Your *X-Pree* Solution:
In this case, Villain is deaf. He is separated from an accompanying adult and incapacitated by fear. He has no intent except to get connected with another adult for his ride home. In a state of panic, he was trying to sign to Innocent that he needed help.

Your self-defense skills also include your ability to very quickly assess the threat in front of you. While there is no mandate for you to become a social scientist, there is tremendous opportunity for you to become reasonably proficient at reading someone's intent. In many instances, this is a legal requirement before you use defensive force against that person.

Once again, your awareness beyond Safety Bubble 1 is a priceless advantage. Quickly deciding to show restraint is your *X-Pree* solution here.

Scenario 39 — Robbery / Knife, Parking Lot

Heze Innocent left the hospital three weeks ago. His last post-op appointment is this morning, so he rushes out of the house without any defense tools except his walking cane. Today is a nearly perfect sunny day. It's just right for his long walk across the parking lot to the medical center.

From between two cars a young Villain leaps out at Innocent, displaying a hunter's knife as he demands Innocent's wallet. Innocent's recovery is progressing well, but he still cannot run. Villain gets closer, pointing the knife at Innocent's face.

Common Solution:
Innocent tries to back away as he gives up his wallet. His retreat is blocked by cars and his inability to run. He cringes as Villain stabs him.

Your *X-Pree* Solution:
You back away as you give up your wallet, throwing it on the ground as a distraction. Your retreat is blocked by cars and your inability to run. At the instant Villain continues to move toward you, with both hands gripping the shaft you ram the foot of the cane into Villain's solar plexus and quickly withdraw one step, as a fencing expert retreats to his en garde position.

Villain is now doubled over. Then, you either,

- Continue gripping the cane, and with both hands spread you smash it down on Villain's face.
- Or, swing your cane to impact Villain's head, neck, or knee.

Get to a safe location *FAST*, then call 911 to make a report. Walking canes are smart defense tools for millions of senior citizens.

Scenario 40 — Slavery, Church

Villain is sitting in the same church pew as he was earlier this morning. He moves close to an attractive young woman, exactly as he did at the 8:00 AM service. Here in his old college town, Innocent has ushered at the local church for over five years. He knows almost everyone in the congregation by name. He recognizes Villain from the earlier service that day.

Common Solution:
Innocent does nothing — assuming a no-harm-no-foul attitude.

Your *X-Pree* Solution:
You immediately make a note of Villain's description, and discreetly take a

photo of him with your phone. You have a log at the church where you keep records of people who behave out of the ordinary. You make contact with Villain, asking some friendly questions to get a read on his sincerity. He never returns to the church.

Church service is a prime setting for slave traders to make their first contact with possible victims. Houses of worship offer a relaxed, neutral ground for casually interviewing women who can be abducted. Making a note of Villain's behavior could seem meaningless now, but a prosecutor might later need to know details about his history of suspicious behavior.

Also, keep in mind, you are operating in the church's Safety Bubble 1; this is it's last line of defense.

Complete Topic Discussion 8,
then go to Chapter 9 — Scenarios 41 to 50.

Topic Discussion 8

What limits are there in legally using your car as a defense tool in Scenario 31?

In Scenario 33, is there an imminent threat of severe bodily harm? Is there a disparity of force? Is Innocent trapped?

In your everyday life, considering Scenario 35, what is your balance of vigilance and relaxation?

How much time do you need to distinguish between Innocent's attackers in Scenarios 37 and 38?

What are the personal considerations in profiling people at a house of worship? Are the considerations different in other venues? Why or why not?

Notes:

Topic Discussion 8

Chapter 9 - Scenarios 41 to 50

Scenario 41 — Molestigation, Gas Station

It's the hottest summer day Heze Innocent can remember. Everybody is complaining about the Midwest heat and humidity. Innocent and his attractive bride are two days into their honeymoon, driving their rented motorhome across several states. He stops for fuel at a gas station which is the only building in sight. Sheze Innocent is studying their map, when a mechanic in a greasy t-shirt startles her at the passenger window. He rests his folded arms on the window frame and leans in, trying to appear neighborly. As he gets close, it's impossible for her to miss the alcohol in his breath.

Common Solution:
Asking about the map on her thighs, he reaches in and runs his hand along her leg. Sheze Innocent is in shock with both anger and fear. Many questions instantly run through her head as she pulls away from Villain. What if he opens the door? What if he has a knife? Pulling away she calls out for her husband. Her Safety Bubble 1 is burst.

Your *X-Pree* Solution:

In the past Villain has probably been successful with his country-style molestigation.[97] You pull up your map to your chest and politely ask him to step back. He doesn't comply. As soon as Villain's hand approaches your thigh, you chop the front of his throat with the edge of your hand. Your strike is at the standard *X-Pree* speed. You call out for your husband, drive to a nearby safe location, and call highway patrol for help.

Your safety is dramatically enhanced when you stop for fuel in locations that are not isolated. In most instances, a little planning makes this possible.

Scenario 42 — Mass Murder, Mall

After reading a news story about a mass murderer killing shoppers, she ponders the question of jumping into an armed defense of strangers at the mall. In the article Innocent is reading, no one raised any kind of defense during the event. Many people were killed.

This morning Sheze Innocent is shopping at the regional mall in town. Everyone there is frantic today, grabbing bargains that can't be passed up. Innocent is burdened by three full bags of treasures and still on a mission to get two more items before heading home.

While walking through an atrium area, she hears yelling and shots being fired farther down the walkway, maybe in the food court. Innocent has defensive firearm training and is licensed to carry the concealed pistol in her purse. Her marksmanship is excellent and she is not shy about generally helping others in emergencies. Nearby, people start running chaotically in all directions.

Common Solution:
Innocent draws her handgun and slowly moves toward the gunfire. She moves out of the protection of cover (objects which stop bullets) slowly making her way along a series of store fronts. As she approaches the food court, a man behind her shouts, "Stop! Put your gun down!" Innocent freezes, standing in the open. Another man who has been shooting people in the food court peeks around the corner. He fires at Innocent.

Your *X-Pree* Solution:
Ok, let's back up a little. Nearby, people start running chaotically in all directions. You are motivated to help. Wonderful! You can do that while maximizing your own safety. Remember, a helper who is shot to pieces is no longer a good helper.

- Do not expose your concealed gun because you don't have answers to these questions: How many shooters? Where are the shooters, exactly? Is law enforcement on the way or already present?
- Do not totally expose yourself. Move fast from cover to cover. Storefronts and concessions have many excellent features that stop bullets.
- Maintain continuous awareness in all directions. If people approach you, from cover find out who they are — Security guards? Armed citizens? Law enforcement?
- Encourage anyone who passes by to call for help.
- If you CAREFULLY choose to engage the murderer, safely get as close as possible while maintaining your cover.
- Determine if the murderer is still killing people. If, yes...
- Do a fast, accurate check to see if your shots can be effective from your location.
- CAREFULLY make your next decision. You are about to take a life to save others, with your own life at risk. Are you honestly prepared?

If you are not a sworn law enforcement officer or hostage negotiator, DO NOT attempt to act like one!

Your life and many others can be lost if you attempt an armed defense for which you are not trained. Also, your imprisonment or bankruptcy caused by acting outside your ITOTR framework will be disastrous. On the other hand, your legally grounded and successful armed defense of other Innocents will be a highly commendable action. Know exactly what you're doing at all times! If you choose to retreat, wait for help in a safe location.

Scenario 43 — Road Rage, City

Heze Innocent is driving to work in a pricey sedan. Near an intersection where traffic is stopped, he gets bumped hard from behind. Looking in the rear-view mirror he observes the male driver making hand signals that he's apologetic, but he's laughing with a woman in his passenger seat. Then the driver bumps him again, still laughing with the female passenger. He motions to Innocent that they should pull into the parking lot. Villain gets out and pretends to not really care that he damaged Innocent's car.

Common Solution:
Innocent is upset at Villain's cavalier attitude and he points out that his bumper needs to be replaced. Villain acts offended by Innocent's tone of voice and he escalates the argument. Innocent is so easily provoked that he pushes Villain who falls, feigning injury to his head. He and his female accomplice call police to make a complaint. Later, he files a civil suit against Innocent. Villain had already done his homework, observing that Innocent lives in an upscale neighborhood. There are witnesses to Innocent's "assault" against Villain in the parking lot. Innocent will likely settle the suit with a juicy cash payment to Villain.

Your *X-Pree* Solution:
"Bumping" is a well-planned, highly successful Villain strategy with a few variations. However, you will not fall prey to bumping.
- Do not get out of your vehicle. In this scenario, you can easily trade insurance info with the other driver while sitting in your car.
- There is a different version of this scam where an accomplice in another vehicle other than Villain's (usually located in front of yours) will hop into your car and steal it while you're standing on the side of the road. Staying in your car prevents this ruse.
- Finally, your general level of anger and the temptation to shove Villain will be reduced if you're sitting in your car.

As always, your acute *SPEED* applies here with your fast, level-headed response to Villain's antics. De-escalating your own anger is the goal here. Don't be fooled!

Scenario 44 — Employee Termination, Office

Sheze Innocent is a Senior Business Analyst at her company. One of her subordinates has performed poorly in three consecutive quarters. Over the past two weeks, he had four days of unexplained absences. When asked about his behavior, Villain became boisterous and offensive. With her manager in agreement, Innocent decides that the hostile employee must be terminated.

Common Solution:
Innocent is upset about letting him go, so she meets with Villain mid-morning on Thursday, and tells him that Friday will be his last day. She wants to give him the opportunity to say goodbye to others and collect his personal items. In her heart, Innocent truly believes that is an appropriate, considerate thing to do. She feels sadness for her employee.

Villain's hostility is rekindled. He makes a loud raucous scene which agitates others who can overhear. He launches a long rant about the injustice of his termination. Innocent suggests that he should take some time to calm down, and he loudly charges through the maze of cubicles with a box under his arm, leaving the building in a rage.

Your *X-Pree* Solution:
As his manager, you have every right to know a legitimate reason why Villain was AWOL for four out of ten work days. His immature reaction is an excellent indicator of how his termination will be received. You arrange a short private meeting at the end of the work day. Someone who can handle potential security issues is nearby.

Respectfully explain to Villain that the decision was not an easy one, and that you believe he will profit from the change in his employment. Do not weaken or debate the decision. Be clear that his termination is complete and effective immediately. His access to all facilities must, by design, be cut off after the meeting.

Scenario 45 — Confrontation, Club

Newlywed Innocents are at a club in a neighboring city. They enjoy a few drinks and some dancing before leaving around midnight. One obnoxious patron who's been drinking too much tries to block their exit. When Heze Innocent explains that they are definitely leaving, mouthy Villain grabs a handful of the front of Innocent's shirt with his right hand. His grip is only moderate, as he tries to steady himself.

Common Solution:
Heze Innocent engages in some mutual grabbing and pushing with Villain, and the situation escalates to punching.

Your *X-Pree* Solution:

At the instant Villain grabs your shirt, you step closer to him, driving in with your right hand, clamping your fingers around the sides of his trachea with your right hand. You command Villain to get back and squeeze until he complies.

You execute this defense with *EXTREME SPEED*. It will only control Villain. It will not incapacitate him unless you crush the trachea, which can be fatal. Deadly force is not justified by Villain's actions in this scenario.

Scenario 46 — Low Fuel, City

That pesky fuel gauge on her car is never correct. Sheze Innocent struggles to estimate how long she can drive at 1/4 full. Sometimes she is not a good guesser. Five blocks from work, her car sputters and stops running. In this empty section of the industrial park, there are no other commuters around to help her.

Common Solution:
Innocent waits for a short time, then starts to walk toward her job location. In reality, scenarios like this one end with a wide variety of outcomes. Best

case is her late arrival at work, when five men compete for Innocent's rescuer award as they volunteer to take her for fuel and give a ride back to her car. Worst case is Innocent's rape and murder because she stopped in the wrong place.

Your *X-Pree* Solution:
- Completely fill your tank one time. Adding a healthy dose of discipline to always keep it full, you will not use any more fuel than when you drive around with the tank nearly empty.
- If your car is old and it starts to sputter with low fuel, safely swerve back-and-forth a couple of times to slosh the fuel in your tank. It can enable you to drive a little farther. This trick does not work in a newer car which has baffles in the tank.
- Avoid any route that takes you through an urban desert, even a small one. If you break down in a desolate part of town, stay in your car!
- Finally, your cell phone should be charged before starting your commute. Stash an inexpensive phone charger in the vehicle.

Scenario 47 — Mass Murder, Restaurant

Compared to other restaurants, Innocent's place is a popular one. In an upscale location with high income patrons, he runs a profitable venture. His menu is limited, but the entrees are elegant and healthful.

His world is turned sideways tonight when two men enter the restaurant, front and rear, and begin shooting the customers.

Common Solution:
Innocent, his staff, and the guests are stunned and frozen in disbelief. Many of them duck under tables and behind fixtures; some are murdered in the exact spots where they try to hide.

Your *X-Pree* Solution:
In your restaurant you have employed Safety Bubbles:
- **Bubble 4** — You have live video surveillance of all sides of your building which feeds to a monitor at the hostess station and the office.

- **Bubble 3** — Exterior doors are usually closed, and they can be remotely locked from the hostess station, the kitchen, or the office.
- **Bubble 2** — You have a verbal signal such as, "Threat!", which when called out sends the whole staff into defense mode. When this occurs: all lights are turned off, all employees immediately find cover, each employee has a high-intensity flashlight, at least one server and one kitchen staff member each arm themselves with a handgun.
- **Bubble 1** — If an attacker is still able to enter the restaurant, your employees know how to temporarily blind Villain with their defensive flashlights and then counter attack with handguns and adopted defense tools.

Restaurants are a treasure chest filled with adoptable self-defense tools — chairs, glasses, plates, silverware, bottles, hot food, pots, pans, knives, and more! Just think about this for a moment. There is no possible way a mass murderer can effectively operate his gun when a barrage of silverware or hot food is flying at him. Always launch your restaurant's ferocious defense with lightening speed to stop the shooting, preferably before it starts.

Scenario 48 — Abduction, Street

As she finishes the last three blocks of her morning speed walk, Sheze Innocent is thinking about a project at work. Today's morning sun begins to light her neighborhood. She celebrates the cool, fresh air listening to some saxophone jazz. There are no moving cars on the street, so she cuts across to walk with the normal flow of traffic. Several feet past a parked van two Villains dart out of the shadows and grab her from behind.

Common Solution:
Innocent tries to scream, but one of the abductors has his hand over her mouth. She struggles to break free, but within five seconds they have her in the van and drive away.

Your *X-Pree* Solution:
- Whenever possible, walk with a partner or a dog — even if you need to borrow one.
- Always walk toward oncoming vehicles, even when traffic is quiet.
- Always carry a fully charged phone.
- Operate with your awareness peaked.
- Carry a pepper spray canister in your hand or clip one to your waist band.
- Carry a concealed pistol or knife if it's legal in your jurisdiction.
- When you see a van or anything else that might offer a threat to your safety, avoid it by crossing the street, ducking into a doorway, or calling out to a bystander.

If all of the above don't adequately deter abductors, then you must soak them with pepper spray, or slice, stab, shoot, and break them until you can run to safety. Submission to get into the van is your blanket permission for them to do anything to you psychologically and physically that they desire.

Scenario 49 — Confrontation, Party

Heze Innocent shows up late at a friend's bachelor party. There's a lot of drinking and reminiscing going on. One of the guys' sister dated Innocent a few years earlier. This brother is not a criminal of any sort, but his beer has turned him a little Villainish. He harasses Innocent mildly about breaking off the relationship with his sister. When Innocent doesn't respond, Villain gets louder and more antagonistic. As the prospective groom tries to quiet Villain down, he shoves the groom hard and approaches Innocent.

Common Solution:
Innocent will likely push Villain away, or knock him down, as the violence escalates. In the thousands of scenarios like this one there is usually no winner; just a series of embarrassing moments of posturing followed by apologies the next day.

Your *X-Pree* Solution:

As Villain approaches, you will raise your hands telling him, "Get back." Villain will probably not comply, wanting to get in your face. As he gets within arm's reach, you plant your left hand on Villain's right shoulder (or behind his neck). Then, you pull him in as you drive your index and middle fingers of your right hand together inward and downward at the base of Villain's neck, in the front, just above the bone,[98] holding and adding pressure until he submits.

This defense requires practice. It will make Villain's breathing difficult. When he submits, you can politely direct him to sit down, without serious injury.

Scenario 50 — Bare Hand Attack, Parking Lot

As Sheze Innocent walks up to her car, Sheza Villain and an accomplice box Innocent between two cars. Villain is much taller and stronger than Innocent, and she demands Innocent's wallet and car keys. As Innocent reaches in her purse for her keys, Villain reaches for her throat to choke her with two hands.

Common Solution:
Innocent has no idea how to defend herself. Results from an assault like this one vary from critical injury to murder.

Your *X-Pree* Solution:

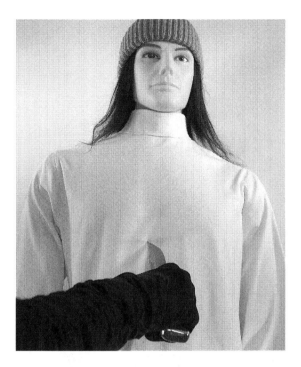

Instead of pulling your keys out, you pull out your concealed knife. Even though Villain is inside your Safety Bubble 1, she's occupied with your throat, holding her hands high. You instantly begin stabbing her solar plexus rapidly and repeatedly until she backs away from you or falls. What to do with Villain's accomplice? Direct her to "Get back!" Counter attack Villain's partner as needed.

Unlike movie and TV show incidents, your knife defense is a rapid-fire series of thrusts with ultra tight grip and full force when inserting and withdrawing your knife. Each stab wound is aimed and *FAST*.

Complete Topic Discussion 9,
then go to Chapter 10 — Scenarios 51 to 60.

Topic Discussion 9

How will you practice using your hand to chop Villain's trachea as in Scenario 41?

In Scenario 42, why does her ITOTR solidly support Innocent's decision to use deadly force?

If you were driving your dream car in Scenario 43, how would you remain cool after Villain ruined the bumper and then laughed about it?

What other defenses will work in Scenario 49?

In Scenario 50, what changes in circumstance would **not** support Innocent's decision to use a knife defense?

Notes:

Topic Discussion 9

Chapter 10 - Scenarios 51 to 60

Scenario 51 — Elder Abuse, Care Facility

It hurts to visit her dad in the nursing home. Heze Innocent can't seem to handle everyday tasks on his own, and his daughter is helping to raise her young grandson whose parents work full time.

Innocent is relatively healthy, but he's losing weight. His daughter notices bruises on his forearms. His attitude toward the staff is not as happy as it was several months ago.

His daughter is reading with Innocent, when a male nurse enters the room. Innocent is agitated and he moves to a spot farther away. As the nurse lowers his chin and gives Innocent a stern look, he makes eye contact with the nurse only for a moment.

Common Solution:
Innocent's daughter observes all of this and asks her father what's going on. He brushes off her concern, assuring her that everything is fine. Periodically, Innocent's bruising is refreshed until he enters hospice care.

Your *X-Pree* Solution:
Innocent is displaying classic signs of physical elder abuse at the care facility. As in cases of child abuse, many states are passing better legislation to protect elders. Avenues for reporting crimes against elders are increasing in number.[99] In this case, your father is experiencing not only physical injury, he is suffering the emotional trauma of anger and fear over his treatment.

You must act immediately!
- Get a clear description from your father about what is happening.
- Set up a meeting with the nursing home administrator, where you

outline your objections to Innocent's mistreatment. You request that the abusive nurse is terminated, and demand that he never comes near your father.
- Contact a legal firm that specializes in elder victimization.
- Contact local law enforcement and/or district attorney.
- Make a plan to move your father to another care facility.

Your inaction will facilitate more cases of abuse at the nursing home for many other seniors, with bad consequences for many other families. Without help, your father's quality of life will certainly decline.

Scenario 52 — Slavery, Junior High

Things at home are not good lately. Innocent's mom has a new boyfriend who drinks a lot. She and her mom barely talk anymore. Mom's attention is focused on her new man, and Innocent is now the part-time focus of the boyfriend's attention. He brushes up against her whenever possible.

Sheze Innocent drags out her time on school grounds to avoid going home. There are more students at the junior high school than last year, making after-school pickup nothing more than controlled chaos. Today Innocent is confused about whether or not Mom is picking her up. She decides to wait out of the way of all the traffic.

On a bench in the grass near the main parking lot a young man, maybe high school age, is writing on a pad while he has a happy phone conversation. Innocent overhears some comments about his new car which is due at the dealership in two weeks. He congratulates the person on the other end about scoring a big deal which "will take the whole family over the top."

Innocent is intrigued by the young man's nice candor. He invites her to take his bench, assuring her that he can write while standing up. She offers to share the bench, and they have a long friendly conversation. He explains that his family is large and everyone is exceptionally close.

This young Villain is a recruiter for local sex traffickers. School campuses are dreamland fruit stands for recruiters who manipulate young girls away from their homes.

Common Solution:
Innocent's mom never finds out about Villain and his grooming process which started with his not-so-chance meeting with Innocent after school. Three weeks of messages and phone calls eventually convince Innocent to move in with Villain's family.

Her role in the new family is actually one "wifey" in a large group of girls who are managed by their "bottom" — a female enforcer who schedules, trains, and if necessary tortures the girls within her domain. Innocent is now a prostitute under tight control.

Your *X-Pree* Solution:
As a rational contributing member of our society, you can now share this and other sex trafficking information with as many parents and teenagers as possible. Remember our discussion about the importance of "belonging" as a basic human need? In this scenario would Innocent leave a home where she experienced genuine safety and love?

Extreme Preemption is your *FAST* identification of Villain's breadcrumbs.

Scenario 53 — Attack / Knife, Gas Station

(Followup to Scenario 41) In response to Villain's bold molestigation, Sheze Innocent is successful in striking the front of Villain's throat, and he staggers back away from their motorhome. Hearing the commotion, her husband rushes over to find Villain trying to get up while pulling a folding knife from the waistband of his jeans.

Common Solution:
There is much yelling. Both Innocents scramble to get away in their motorhome. Villain cuts Heze Innocent as he tries to close the door of the motorhome. They drive away, but highway patrol officers stop the motorhome, detain the Innocents, and wade through a variety of conflicting stories about the incident.

Your *X-Pree* Solution:
As your new bride is calling for your help, you rush over to her door. Villain is on one knee, trying to stand. With an extremely hard hammer hand or

hand chop you break Villain's clavicle (a.k.a. collar bone). He is unable to use his folding knife with that hand. If you or your bride can safely take a photo of Villain on the ground, do it. Drive to a safe location very close by, call highway patrol, and give the officer a detailed description of the event.

Villain's injuries necessitate a police report. You should never leave this scene just hoping for the best. Testimonies can be easily distorted and worked against you.

Scenario 54 — Active Shooter, Office

Everyone is quietly enjoying a mass food coma after the quarterly department luncheon. Over 150 people attended. Lunch was catered, and at this moment is a huge damper on company productivity. Heze Innocent is back at his desk, struggling to stay focused.

He hears some voices down the hall that turn into shouts, then screams. Three loud explosions rattle everyone's stupor. Then there is more screaming. Innocent hears "Shotgun!" and knows there is an active shooter at work on his floor.

Common Solution:
All employees in his department have attended mandatory Active Shooter training. Still, many co-workers have no idea what to do. They are not at

their desks right now. Everyone is poised in confusion. During the next half hour many people are killed on two floors, until a special law enforcement team arrives and overcomes the shooter.

Your *X-Pree* Solution:
This murderer is not a vindictive former employee; he's a disgruntled customer. No one in Innocent's company has ever seen Villain before. There were no warning signs, at least they think so at first glance.

For this scenario, everyone must be Safety Bubble trained as follows:
- **Bubble 4** — To know what a shotgun looks like, how it can be carried, what it sounds like, and what response should be made to stop the murderer outside the building.
- **Bubble 3** — To signal for an immediate lockdown of the building. This includes not only exterior doors but also interior doors to limit Villain's access if he gets inside the building.
- **Bubble 2** — To use cover and any available barricades.
- **Bubble 1** — To use their own concealed handguns or adopted self-defense tools at close range.

Is it likely that a customer service rep or sales associate experienced an abrasive, hostile attitude from this customer? Of course. Is it likely that at least one employee saw Villain carrying the shotgun before he began shooting? Of course.

It is exceptionally challenging for such a large staff which is spread out on huge open floors to run or hide with success. In this scenario, your window to preempt the event is tiny. You probably have less than 5 seconds. Is *X-Pree* possible? Yes. Does it require precise training and planning ahead of time? Yes.

Let's look at bullet penetration. From a handgun, bullets go through
- about 1.5" of paper or wood and several layers of drywall which are oriented perpendicular to bullet path.
- about 4" of paper that is oriented parallel to the bullet path.
- [Rifle bullets penetrate more than the amounts listed above.]

In Bubble 2 the use of cover and barricades is critical. Scurrying into a storage room or bathroom is a brilliant start of your defense. Then, you must not only barricade the door, but also place solid objects between you and Villain in order to stop his bullets which can come in through walls.

Scenario 55 — Carjacking, Home Garage

Sheze Innocent is running late again. She hurries from the kitchen through the small laundry room into the garage. As soon as the overhead door is almost fully open, her eye catches a shadow on the garage floor.

Common Solution:
Innocent hesitates, moves to the side of her car, then looks under it. Villain wants to steal the car, and he has slithered under the opening door and moved very close to her. At this point Innocent's safety rapidly declines. He is already inside of her Safety Bubble 2, and she has few options.

Your *X-Pree* Solution:
Your safest procedure to enter the parked car in your garage is this one:
1. Turn off the perimeter alarm which includes your garage.
2. Open the man door to your garage.
3. By motion or manually turn on motion-sensitive lights in the garage.
4. You have installed two lights that are mounted low, illuminating the garage floor. It is on the same circuit as the garage overhead lights, all on a timer.
5. Thoroughly check around and under your car for Villain.
6. If you spot Villain, get back inside your house, lock the deadbolt on the door, and call police.
7. If there is no Villain, lock the man door, get in the car, lock the car doors, and open the garage door.
8. Start the car, exit the garage, and close the garage door. Your timer will turn all lights off.

This might sound like an enormous effort, but a large percentage of carjackings and attacks take place right in owners' garages.

Scenario 56 — Adultery, Anywhere

He appears to be her soul mate — Mr. Perfect in every possible way. His wooing of Innocent is a storybook masterpiece. She is radiant with the glow of his adoration which snowballs with every passing day. His 6:30 AM call is late today. Innocent is a little disappointed, but the phone rings at 7:30. Mr. Wonderful melts her again with assurance of his deep love. His call is late, he says, because of a delay in getting though airport security.

Villain announces that he has to go out of town two days earlier than he planned, arriving for his business meeting on Friday afternoon, not Monday afternoon. Innocent and her Romeo enjoy a few passionate days together in California before he leaves on his next business trip.

He mistakenly leaves behind a covered notepad with several past due bills and a foreclosure notice for property on the East coast. She discovers that he is married and has a family in Virginia.

Common Solution:
Innocent hangs on in the relationship, because of her emotional investment. Eventually Villain turns her life and his East-coast family's into rubble.

Your *X-Pree* Solution:
Villain is an artist in the field of deception. His competence in manipulating people rivals the brush skill of Michelangelo. But, your white knight is at his core still Villain. His score in the COVER department (Character OVER everything) is barely measurable, if not zero.

Your *Extreme Preemption* is to exit the relationship *FAST*. Hanging on and hanging in will get you more pain. Even if his heart appears to be with you, not his East-coast family, his relationship with you is still founded on a continental size lie. His treatment of you is not caused by any flaw in you. His choice to lie is machiavellian, narcissistic, or egoistic. Some mechanism in him has reduced his capacity for honest love. You have not caused it. You cannot fix it.

As soon as you can, change your door locks, phone number, bank, email address, social media pages, and even your work hours if possible. This is to limit Villain's future access to you.

Attention Ranchers: Your branding iron is not a legal self-defense tool in this scenario.

Scenario 57 — Bullying, School

Sheze Innocent is having a rough time with other girls at school. There are many Villains who don't accept her nationality. Innocent has a naturally quiet personality. Some members of the difficult group see her soft personality as a sign of weakness. They decide that it's time to test her. In the hallway during a break between classes one of the Villains stands behind her while another girl in the group pushes Innocent by the shoulders straight back. Villains set up for a game of to and fro designed to volley Innocent like a rag doll.

Common Solution:
Innocent is humiliated until she covers her face, cries, and gets knocked to the floor.

Your *X-Pree* Solution:
You know about the solar plexus or celiac plexus. It is a bundle of nerves located front and center on the torso just below the rib cage. When impacted, even lightly, the nerves react sharply to generate a temporary inability to inhale normally. We commonly call this "getting the wind knocked out."

You have already practiced to visually locate the solar plexus on people, matching the correct location with buttons, print on t-shirts, etc. As Villain approaches to give you a shove, you preempt it by lowering your chin, stepping into her reach, and striking straight into her sweet spot. You strike with the knuckles of your hand protruding slightly from a normal fist. She will at least double over, out of breath. One direct strike here, with moderate to strong force, can actually knock Villain unconscious. This is due to the intersection of many nerve fibers in the bundle.

With hands raised, you immediately turn toward and silently stare at Villain's partner encouraging her to leave you alone. If not, then you instantly bestow a brand new bare hand hurricane on the partner. Your own fear is your enemy here. Villain is weak, otherwise she would have come after you by herself. Dominate this event with your tornado-style counter attack.

Your strike must be practiced with a workable training dummy. It is critical to thoroughly understand all bare hand strikes which you plan to use.

Scenario 58 — Verbal Abuse, Office

Ten minutes ago Heze Innocent turned in a status report to his boss, Villain. In an instant, the manager comes unglued.

> Villain bellows: "I thought you had finished this thing four days ago!"
> Innocent: "I needed the data from our St. Louis office before completing it."
> Villain: "Whose fault is that?"
> Innocent: "No one's fault, per se."
> Villain: "Are you mocking me on this?"

Villain's people skills are consistently infantile. His solution for nearly every challenge is placing blame on one or more subordinates.

Common Solution:
Villain's verbal attack is unwarranted, as in all other previous instances. Innocent endures his remarks again.

Your *X-Pree* Solution:
Workplace verbal attacks might have been popular a generation ago. In today's business world there is too much liability and far too many negative effects on employees to allow for even a single instance of it.

If you ever receive a "piece of Villain's mind," your professional solution is not complicated:
- Offer no response — none. Immediately go silent. Adolescent yelling at least in the modern civilian world accomplishes nothing constructive. In this condition, Villain is incapable of adult reasoning. He might even be spurring you toward a physical confrontation. Those handy Miranda rights are useful here, "You have the right to remain silent. Anything you say, can and will be used against you..." When you have done nothing wrong, keep it that way.
- File a complaint with your company's human resources department. Could your job be in jeopardy? Yes, it could be. So could your safety and the safety of your coworkers if Villain's anger goes unchecked. Unmanaged verbal rage by someone at work is a solid indicator of the same violence at his home or elsewhere.

If your company gives you no support in putting reigns on Villain, find another job. *Extreme Preemption* is heading off the opportunity for Villain to continue injuring people by any variety of mean-spirited treatment.

Scenario 59 — Low Fuel, Rural

Sheze Innocent is excited to visit her sister. It's a long two days on the road, but a week with close family will be a healthy recharge for Innocent. In the afternoon on the first day she runs out of fuel in a remote area.

Common Solution:
Innocent barely pulls to the side of the road, before her car stops running. She calls 911 for help and waits two hours before a sheriff's deputy arrives with some gas.

Extreme Preemption

Your *X-Pree* Solution:
Your car will warn you that it's running out of fuel. It will hesitate or sputter. Pull off the roadway completely to avoid being rear-ended. Turn on your emergency flashers and keep windows only slightly open. Use your cell phone or tablet to determine your exact location. Call your roadside assistance number if you have a plan, or the nearest service station. Ask them to bring you some fuel. In the meantime, wait in your locked vehicle without using your phone or tablet — to conserve the batteries.

These are alternate *X-Pree* solutions for your anxiety about waiting by yourself in a remote area:
- Climb into the turret for the 50 caliber machine gun mounted on the roof of your vehicle and sit quietly.
- Inside the car, in the passenger seat, loudly sing songs from old musicals while excitedly moving your hands as the actors did.

Either of these tactics will probably ensure that local Villains don't bother you. If someone stops to sing along with you, choose a different defense.

Running your car on a full tank while paying close attention to your fuel gauge is a great strategy. Estimating how far you plan to drive will also nearly guarantee that you won't get stuck in the middle of nowhere.

Scenario 60 — Theft, Gas Station

Sheze Innocent finally makes it to a gas station in the next city. Busy people are everywhere at this station. Relieved that she is back in civilization, she finds a spot at one of the fuel islands and begins filling her car.

Common Solution:
Innocent is distracted by a young man two lanes away who asks her for directions to the small town she had lunch in earlier in the day. He has his notepad out, asking questions she cannot hear because he's too far away at the noisy station. While Innocent walks over to the cute young man and helps him, Villain pulls along side her car. He stops, takes the fuel nozzle from her car and fills his own. He replaces the nozzle back in her car, grabs her purse from the seat, jumps back into his own car and races away. Innocent is talking to a young man who is Villain's accomplice.

Don't laugh. This scenario has played out profitably on many occasions.

Your *X-Pree* Solution:
When you get out of your car to fill up, always lock the doors, and stay adjacent to your car. Theft of fuel, valuables, and the car itself can easily be prevented.

Complete Topic Discussion 10,
then go to Chapter 11 — Scenarios 61 to 70.

Topic Discussion 10

Considering Scenario 51, is it possible for families to pool their resources to provide excellent care for their elders?

How difficult is it to leave a relationship when you know that staying in it is bad for you? (Scenario 56)

What level of courage do you need to perform the *X-Pree* defense in Scenario 57?

In Scenario 58, what are your personal challenges in standing up to Villain?

Considering Scenario 59, how often do you sing in your car while moving your hands? Do you also simulate playing instruments?

Notes:

Topic Discussion 10

Chapter 11 - Scenarios 61 to 70

Scenario 61 — Confrontation, Parking Lot

This one is simple. Villain approaches Sheze Innocent, nose to nose as she gets out of her car. He is upset with her driving over the last two miles and positive that she needs his in-her-face training. He offers his opinion of her driving skills with only inches separating them — at very high volume.

Common Solution:
Innocent is embarrassed and afraid. She cowers as Villain wades through his demeaning lecture.

Your *X-Pree* Solution:
Among many good target areas on a man, the groin has become a true classic, especially among female Defenders. Villain is extremely overconfident. Here's what to do:
- Momentarily pretend to submit, then either
- Launch your knee into his groin with supersonic speed and force, or
- Palm strike upward to his face
- After Steps 2 or 3, bring your hand up under his genitals, dig your finger nails in, yank upward, while twisting your handful of jewels.
- Push him back, get in your car, lock all doors, and drive away.

In this scenario Villain has crossed Innocent's inner-most Safety Bubble 1. As always, accuracy, speed, and as much force as possible are your ingredients for success. Your half-baked effort will not work in this instance of *X-Pree*.

Scenario 62 — Elder Abuse, Home

For a senior who is in his late eighties, he takes good care of his house and yard. Heze Innocent is attended by a young nurse two days per week. She helps with physical therapy and some shopping.

They have become close friends, sharing family stories and views about everything from politics to recipes. Innocent's children live far away. His nurse's relatives are scattered as well. Both of them have no one nearby.

One day Innocent's nurse explains that her only brother needs a surgery, and he doesn't have the money to cover it. She is planning to give the brother about $40,000, all of her savings, but she's still short by nearly $15,000. Innocent offers to help, and the nurse emphatically refuses to accept his offer.

Common Solution:
Two weeks later, near the critical date for the brother's surgery, Innocent asks his nurse if her siblings are going to help with the $15,000 shortfall. Sadly, she admits that no one else can help. She really has nearly $40,000 in her account. Innocent insists on providing the funds, and he does so.

Innocent and his nurse grow even closer in their relationship. She expresses gratitude for his help by doing many things around the house. He invites her to work three days per week, she accepts, and within two years she inherits a substantial portion of his net worth. Although there is no proof, near the end of his life, the nurse is negligent with some of his medical needs.

Prematurely, Innocent dies as a happy man, and his nurse is also happy. She has no brother who needed surgery, and no siblings. Her bank account really did have $39,970 in it, money from previous scams perpetrated against elders. Nurse Villain quickly leaves town for a new location, and a new victim.

Your *X-Pree* Solution:
Care of senior citizens is a large responsibility which many family members don't want to accept. In this case, your children need to be aware of your actual needs, rather than giving them empty assurance that you are always "fine." Any in-home care providers need to be properly vetted, with references thoroughly checked.

If you are a child of a senior, you can find the generosity to give loving care and genuine comfort to your parents as they glide through their last season. Even if their care of you has fallen short of your present estimate of what they might have done in your childhood, that's all they knew how to give you.

Extreme Preemption in this case is realized with family members all moving beyond what is comfortable and convenient at the moment, to a level of inclusiveness where the elder knows that he or she belongs. Is it difficult? Sometimes. Is it worth the effort? Always.

Scenario 63 — Child Slaying, Home

As an athletic teenager, Heze Innocent is active in all school sports with his sights on a college scholarship in two years. His math teacher is an attractive young woman in her mid-twenties who takes special interest in him. Innocent struggles with math and she offers to help whenever possible.

Innocent's parents have a large home with a guest house that they lease. Our math teacher happily moves in as a tenant in August. Innocent's parents are ecstatic that she can help him with his weakest subject. They get close to her as a member of their family.

In April, Innocent's grades plummet for no apparent reason. He falls behind in his performance in baseball, and he confides in his older brother. Teacher Villain has been having frequent sex with Innocent for over five months. Eventually the lid comes off her continuing statutory rape of the minor.

Common Solution:
At first, his parents are convinced that Innocent is lying, or at least exaggerating the details. Villain is questioned and even when law enforcement intervenes she elicits support from Innocent's family in the legal proceedings which follow.

Your *X-Pree* Solution:
As a parent engaged in "the talk" with your minor child, let's not forget a clear followup discussion about child slayers. These criminals prey on both

girls and boys. In today's culture, their own genders are not a barrier to sexual abuse that defies one's normal imagination. Their methods of grooming the victims are varied, subtle, barely detectable, and in some cases hardly believable.

Your *X-Pree* counter attack is this:
- Powerful education for you and your children about child slayers' and narcissists' methods
- Your aggressive personal campaign with fellow parents to see that these Villains are uncovered and arrested

Scenario 64 — Bushwhackery, Home

Innocent's increasing responsibilities at work make his days on the job uncomfortable. While his supervisor helps with genuine encouragement and sincere compliments whenever possible, Innocent's growing pains seem to be calling out for more of both. He knows all of this is stretching him in a healthy direction. However, this version of corporate boot camp has filled his mind and stretched him thin.

Tonight, he designs a short truce with himself. One very old movie classic and a decadent thick-crust pizza are his only action items tonight. Two gongs of the doorbell jolt Innocent from the mellow relaxation he's enjoying. Assuming that his pizza has arrived a little early, he grabs some cash and staggers to the door.

Common Solution:
Innocent opens the door without thinking. He is confused by the appearance of the two men on his porch, and there is no pizza. They are here to burglarize his home. Innocent is shoved back onto the floor, pummeled into unconsciousness and tied up. He miraculously survives the housebreakers' attack. His home is emptied of personal valuables. His Safety Bubbles 3, 2, and 1 never had a chance when he literally invited these Bushwhackers to crush them.

Your *X-Pree* Solution:
As you veg out in front of your movie, you are in what's known as Condition White — a state of unawareness that is one short step from obliviolence. In

many other settings you might then move to Condition Yellow, in which you will get dressed to leave your house and get in your car, with a general awareness of what's happening around you. As you drive onto a major highway your Condition Orange will take over, when your alertness is peeked. Finally, if a car up ahead loses a wheel, you will be in Condition Red when the alarm of an event causes you to respond defensively.

In this scenario, your *X-Pree* prime solution is simply to peek out a wide-angle door viewer or a side window, determine that Villains are on your porch, turn out your lights, and refuse to open the door. In a distant second place solution, with your whole body weight you can slam the door against Villains, lock it, and call police. Your third choice in *Extreme Preemption* is to take two steps back, firing at attacking Villains with your handgun which you have in your pocket or concealed behind your back.

What is most challenging in this scenario is the rapid escalation of your awareness and your actions. You must move from Condition White to Orange or Red in an instant. For many people, this is not easy. By approaching the front door in Condition Yellow, your transition to Condition Red is more manageable. But, your best solution is to always observe visitors from a spot other than through your front door — while continuously seeking to preserve your Safety Bubbles. That's *X-Pree*. You snuff out the flame of danger before it burns through you as a wildfire.

Scenario 65 — Bushwhackery, Park

Sheze Innocent is out for walk early on Saturday morning. This area of the park is quiet. No one is nearby. After a few seconds Sheza Villain comes down the trail walking straight toward Innocent with her head lowered, steeped in a cold stare. When she makes eye contact with Innocent her pace quickens, closing within twenty feet. Innocent turns around and runs in the opposite direction, but Villain pursues her.

Common Solution:
Innocent runs as fast as she can, but she's quickly caught and beaten.

Your *X-Pree* Solution:
Our current culture shows no signs of guaranteed safety for a solitary

walker. You should always walk or jog with a partner (human or canine). Just as Innocent does, you turn and run in the opposite direction for a few seconds. Villain feels confident about her ability to complete the assault. Then, you turn around, charge into Villain, bring your foot up high and stomp downward on Villain's instep, knee cap, and/or shin.

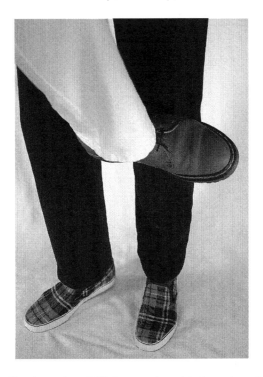

This defense is effective when Villain attacks with bare hands or other hand-held attack tool. One excellent target is the knee cap (patella). It is extremely painful when it's dislodged, giving you an excellent disabling action. However, it is very small; so, your sudden counter attack must be meticulously practiced.

Scenario 66 — Sexual Harassment, Office

Everything at her company is good. Sheze Innocent is appreciated as she moves up the corporate ranks quickly. One of the managers invites her to the annual "Company Recharge," an annual retreat which is one month away. Innocent is a stunningly attractive married woman who is exceptionally responsible. She is a skilled and efficient worker who is well-

Extreme Preemption

liked by employees above and below her in the corporate food chain.

As the weekend gets closer, the manager (Villain) who invited her announces that a special session of the retreat will be in a different location, near the main session. Innocent inquires about how many people are attending the special session. Villain replies, "Two other couples. I mean teams. Did I say couples? I'm sorry."

Over the next few days, Villain tests Innocent about hooking up with him by floating many hackneyed suggestive comments. His psuedo-witty banter makes Innocent feel intensely uncomfortable.

Common Solution:
Absolutely paranoid that her job might be at risk, Innocent endures Villain's slime. She takes a sick day ahead of the retreat and stays home over the weekend. When she returns to her job the next week, co-workers and other managers express disappointment that she did not attend the event.

Your *X-Pree* Solution:
Sexual abuse in the workplace is a deadly quagmire for both women and men. Your *Extreme Preemption* here is your clear refusal to plunge into it. Let's take a blunt look at this problem. Is this a sermon about office morality? No, this is an honest look at office reality. There are two ponds:

Pond #1 —
- Dress professionally, without emphasis on cleavage or a bulging package.
- Screen your employer, and subsequently your supervisors, to assess where their attention resides. If their interest is limited to your body, move on. Be honest. You know this in about thirty seconds after your introduction.
- Allow an accurate message to spread that you don't have sex with people at work. You're not heartless or rude, you're professional.
- Work hard learning as much as you can and earn promotions by your integrity-laced success.
- There is nothing to hide, nothing to fear.
- You are well-liked and respected.

Pond #2 —
- Dress to show off your finely tuned body.
- Wade through the army of gawkers at work, returning flirtations with the good-looking ones.
- Keep everyone curious about how easy it is to sleep with you.
- Try to work hard, but you're distracted and conflicted by the promotional favors that may or may not come your way.
- Harbor many secrets that someday might result in a disaster for you.
- You have many admirers, but you're hated and rejected by others.

You can't swim in both ponds at the same time. After you give Villain a license to exercise his verbal sexual abuse, he might easily convince himself that he must satisfy his "uncontrollable desire" to rape you. Finding yourself on the receiving end of an unrestrained private physical attack is bad, possibly fatal.

Many good people suffer from the common theme in this narrative. As our industries continue to demand high productivity with the sustained risk of layoff, few employees can afford to casually leave their jobs. Even if your organization is small, help establish a system for reporting sexual harassment. Begin with education for all employees.

Scenario 67 — Attack, Park

While walking her small dog in the community's common area, Innocent passes a bench where a woman is sleeping. She notices the needle of a syringe reflecting a spot of late afternoon light. On her way back home, the woman is sitting up. Sheza Villain stares at Innocent and her dog as they pass by. Villain asks for money, Innocent says nothing and continues walking. Weighing only 110 pounds with a shy personality, Innocent is not at all intimidating.

Villain approaches Innocent quickly and demands money. Villain has one hand inside her sweater pocket.

Common Solution:
Innocent dodges Villain's approach, and turns her walk into a run. In spite of

her dog's protective bark, Innocent is now wrestling Villain who is trying to steal her small daypack.

Your *X-Pree* Solution:

More and more Defenders are acquiring Tactical Pens. Didn't I vow to avoid getting **Tactical**? Ok, ok. Only twice... maybe. This pen is an ultra-strong writing implement usually made of high-impact aluminum with a sharp point on one end. It can be slipped into a wide variety of hiding places, such as most pockets, strap of a day pack, portfolio, or planner.

Employing the Tactical Pen is simple:
1. Get a very tight grip.
2. Stab Villain in her standard targets — eyes, neck, shoulder, breast, solar plexus, thigh, or groin.

Is your ITOTR in play here? Yes, it is. If your honest estimate of Villain is a genuine, serious threat, you have the right to use a forceful counter attack.

Scenario 68 — Mass Murder, Office

Heze Innocent is winding down from an intense day at the office, along with the rest of the sales staff. Hundreds of calls came to their center this week. All of a sudden, they hear the active shooter alarm. There are no sounds of gun shots, so everyone assumes that Villain is on another floor.

Chapter 11 - Scenarios 61 to 70

Common Solution:
Innocent and his co-workers are familiar with popular defense theories,[100] yet they have not defined any details or procedures for their immediate area. Some people dash into a stairwell to leave. Others stand in place, frozen in fear.

Your *X-Pree* Solution:
Your company has taken a huge step forward in implementing a specific alarm sound for the mass murderer. Villain can be in an assortment of locations, no one knows where. Running is not your best choice, because you can easily run straight toward Villain.

Right now, *X-Pree* calls for "Shelter in Place" or "Secure in Place." This means you must find a safe temporary refuge in your present location. Immediately accomplish the following:

1. Find a room in which you can Shelter in Place; preferably it has no windows, one door, and plenty of objects to barricade the door.
2. Direct everyone to quickly adopt a defense tool, flashlight, and bottle of water, then get in the room.
3. Insist that everyone inside the room turns off all cell phones.
4. Lock the door and jam pencils, pens, and paper at the edges to prevent opening.
5. Engage everyone to pile furniture, cabinets, and boxes against the door and walls that the shooter might send bullets.
6. Turn off all lights, quiet everyone, and wait for law enforcement to release you.
7. Confirm by phone through 911 dispatch that law enforcement is outside the room before dismantling the barricade.

Your stay in the safe room might last for hours. Silence is mandatory. Personal hygiene will probably be compromised for everyone inside. Some diplomatic fear management will be necessary.

If your *X-Pree* solution is not currently in place, meet with managers and other employees to construct an intelligent plan. If you are allowed to possess a handgun for your defense, bravo!

Extreme Preemption

Scenario 69 — Bushwhackery, Parking Lot

On this beautiful weekday evening Sheze Innocent is leaving her condo to make the short walk to her vehicle in the carport area. Innocent is thinking about her first exam of the semester when Sheze Villain pops out from around the corner of the building, claiming to sell cookies. After hearing a short sales pitch from the young girl, Innocent agrees to buy one box, and she reaches into her purse. Suddenly Villain's older sister appears from behind the same corner raising a short club to strike. She lunges toward Innocent.

Common Solution:
Innocent freezes in fear. Together the two Villains control the outcome, injuring and robbing Innocent.

Your *X-Pree* Solution:

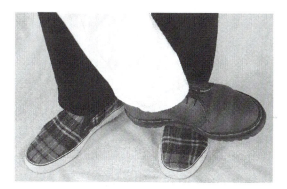

You immediately toss your purse down near the younger cookie sales imposter. As the older Villain gets within arms reach you lunge into her, blocking her strike with your arm, and stomping her instep. Your foot should come down using a moderate side step with as much of your weight and speed as possible.

This foot strike will possibly tear Villain's ligament and/or fracture a bone (metatarsal). In any case, the pain will be significant for Villain, giving you enough time to follow up with hand strikes and then escape. You will not be able to defend yourself this way with thin-soled shoes. Think safety!

CHAPTER 11 - SCENARIOS 61 TO 70

Scenario 70 — Sextortion, Online

Heze Innocent's high school grades are slipping. Spending many hours engaged in social media has taken up much of the time he normally spends on his homework. One girl is especially playful. Interacting with her is amusing and entertaining. His family life and social values are strong. However, one night Innocent foolishly undressed for her to music in front of the webcam on his computer. At the time, he didn't think it was anything but harmless fun. He was certain that his actions were entirely private between the two of them.

Sheza Villain secretly recorded the event by remote access to his webcam. She messaged him saying that he must pay $1,000 or she will post the video on YouTube. It's now a week later. She sends the video to Innocent, proving she has it.

Common Solution:
Innocent is in supreme shock. He doesn't know what to do. He's afraid that his reputation with family, friends, and his church might be completely destroyed. He believes his only choice is to somehow get the money.

Your *X-Pree* Solution:
Internet crime is steadily increasing. With advanced webcams enabling HD online video chats, there is an increase in criminal options for Internet Thieves all over the world. Sexting (sending naked photos by message) has opened the door to "sextortion," a variant of ordinary extortion or blackmail.

Your best defenses against this crime are,
- Stay fully dressed when you're in front of your computer.
- Cover your webcam when it is not being directly used.
- Avoid falling prey to these scams by simply acting wisely.

If you have blundered and you're being extorted,
- Never pay the money that is demanded. This will only lead to more future payments.
- Disclose to family members that you have been targeted. Your disclosure can often deflate the power of the threats Villain is

making against you.
- Contact your social media company, advising them of the incident. In many cases Villain has broken at least one law and can be pursued by a law enforcement agency.
- Report the event to law enforcement and the FBI's Internet Crime Compliant Center.
- Change your email, social media IDs, website domains, and cell phone number.

Genuine privacy in our current world culture is extremely rare — if not impossible to maintain. For your safety, if you behave online as you would with respectable people in person, you radically reduce the possibility of trouble.

Complete Topic Discussion 11,
then go to Chapter 11 — Scenarios 71 to 80.

Topic Discussion 11

In Scenarios 62 an 63 discuss the balance between background checks and scrutiny versus personal acceptance and healthy relationships?

In Scenario 64 describe Innocent's required level of handgun skill to defend himself at his front door?

Does Innocent's ITOTR support her force-filled counter attack in Scenario 65? Why or why not?

Does your company have a fully detailed mass murder defense plan? (Scenario 68)

How do parents balance teen privacy with teen protection against online extortion? (Scenario 70)

Notes:

Topic Discussion 11

Chapter 12 - Scenarios 71 to 80

Scenario 71 — Child Abuse, Grocery Store

There is no peace at the grocery store this Saturday morning as Sheza Villain slaps her ten-year-old daughter in the face. Villain's slap is hard enough to knock the girl against her cart. Everyone nearby retreats a safe distance away, embarrassed for the child who is trying to suppress her sobs. No one says a single word.

Common Solution:
Innocent is in the same aisle with her cart. She's agitated but feels that the situation is not her business. Two weeks earlier, Innocent observed the same behavior by this mother.

Your *X-Pree* Solution:
Everyone knows that disciplining children is important and challenging. Minors who are free to run wild often develop lifelong habits which are damaging to everyone else in their lives. Likewise, minors who are abused at home often develop a renewed array of damaging lifelong habits. Violence at home is all they know; it becomes the standard with their young families.

Parental responsibility includes knowledge of the restraint which is necessary to guide a child, without injury to the child. Open hand strikes to the face are excessive. They can fracture developing bones. In this scenario, public humiliation is equally as painful for the young girl as the slaps. Signs of child abuse in public are a solid indication of more extensive abuse at home.

This morning, Innocent is wrong by remaining silent. You have a responsibility to inform any adult that laws throughout the U.S. protect every child against abusive treatment, and that you will not hesitate to report such incidents to law enforcement. Your intensity in the delivery of that message is your decision, of course. What would be your response if you observed a thirty year-old man striking an adult woman in the face? Hopefully, you would have the courage to intervene or at least report the incident. Likewise, report this type of child abuse to law enforcement immediately!

Child abuse victims who never receive help often inflict more injury on individuals and communities where they live as adults. You are not alone in your hesitation to defend an abuse victim. Is the thought of making a complaint intimidating to you? Imagine the level of intimidation the abused child is experiencing.

Very few citizens are willing to report violent incidents. You can be the one who cares enough to make a difference. Report it now!

Scenario 72 — Child Slaying, Junior High

He has been enjoying a buffet of minors to prey upon for more than six years. Villain's repertoire of refined skills in his manipulation of the children work as smoothly as instruments in a philharmonic orchestra. He pompously views the three grades in his junior high school as requisite movements of his twisted sexual symphony. Villain's popularity among music students is stellar. His instruction as the district's music teacher is exceptional. His sexual crimes against his students are unthinkable.

One of his intended victims, Sheze Innocent, abandons her friends at school. She asks her parents for permission to get private piano lessons from her music teacher. He has assured her that potential success in music is only limited by her desire to learn.

Innocent is an adorable, precocious teenager in every way. She shuns interest from the boys in her school while continuing to distance herself from girlfriends as well. At a community event, one of the other parents asks Innocent's mom if her daughter has somehow offended Innocent. Best-friend messaging has dwindled to almost nothing.

As time passes, Innocent shows less interest in family events. Her devotion to piano playing is strong, but her desire to be with her teacher is stronger. At first, Innocent's mother is deeply concerned.

Common Solution:
Innocent's mother later assumes this is all part of an adolescent phase her daughter is experiencing. Her concern fades away.

Villain successfully moves his relationship so far that he and Innocent enjoy a loving session of kissing and touching during her piano lessons. He is so smooth in the portrayal of lewd behavior that Innocent believes it is part of a true musician's lifestyle — a version of artistry. He is "so nice and sweet" that young girls progress through his perverted playground, then move on in their lives while carrying the secrets with them. After all, they wanted the affection too, and they rationalize away Villain's crime spree.

Eventually Villain's empire as a child slayer falls apart because a parent asks police detectives to investigate. Young women testify against their former teacher. Families are riddled with pain.

Your *X-Pree* Solution:
As a parent, when your radar tells you something is not right,
- Listen to the message.
- Immediately report the crime.
- Immediately get help for your whole family.

Sex crimes against children are currently epidemic in scope. Minors must be taught what is heathy and legal, versus what is unhealthy and illegal. This education must be earnestly supported by parents, schools, and local law enforcement in every community. If there is no open program to teach this subject, you can start one!

Scenario 73 — Abduction, Park

Heze Innocent is finishing a run along his favorite trail. As he comes up over a small hill, he observes Heza Villain carrying a young girl, gripping around her waist. She is flailing away at her attacker and screaming, but he is relentless in taking her. Villain is headed for a car which is parked close by.

Common Solution:
Innocent yells at Villain, and struggles to use his phone to get a picture of him. Villain only hurries more to get away. In seconds, he successfully leaves with the girl.

Your *X-Pree* Solution:
Is this a frustrated father scooping up his rebellious daughter to take her home, or is it a genuine kidnapping? Abduction is a terrifying, often deadly experience. These counter attacks, from behind, will incapacitate the predator:
1. Figure out what's going on by calling out to the victim. Listen carefully to the response. If it sounds like a father/daughter issue, still get a license plate number and call law enforcement. If not,
2. Quickly come up behind Villain and land a hard stomp to back of his leg, just below the knee (top of the calf). This hard, fast strike will likely strain or rupture ligaments and tendons, disabling Villain's leg.
3. Or, stomp the back of Villain's heel. One very vulnerable tendon on the human body is the Achilles (calcaneal tendon); a torn Achilles tendon disables that leg.
4. Or, quickly approach Villain from behind and strike upward with the heel of your open palm to the base of his skull (occipital bone). Strike #3 can cause a mild to severe concussion.

These strikes must be practiced. Your intervention as a third party in the event increases your need to be *FAST* and precise in your counter attack. You must also be sure that your ITOTR criteria support the use of force in defending this stranger. Otherwise, there is no guarantee that your assistance will be successful, or even legal. In every instance, you should immediately report this type of incident to law enforcement via your 911 call. Take photos if possible.

Scenario 74 — Negligent Gun Storage, Home

Safe gun storage is not Heze Innocent's highest priority. He has firearms and ammo stashed throughout his house. His sister and her family come over for dinner on this Saturday night. One of the young boys, age 8, goes exploring in the hall closet to find a board game. Instead, he finds a shotgun inside the closet next to the door. Excited about his discovery, he brings the gun back to the family room where everyone is gathered around the table. Unfamiliar with basic gun safety, the young boy waves the gun around dangerously.

Common Solution:
Many scenarios like this result in an accidental shooting of the minor.

Your *X-Pree* Solution:
Lock up your guns and ammo! There are a lot of inexpensive solutions for safe firearm locking and storage:
- Convert a closet to a gun storage locker by adding a deadbolt to the door.
- Build a shallow gun locker behind a door. Secure it with a padlock or two.
- Add a padlock to the storage area under a window seat or in a cabinet.
- Encourage all of your relatives to get minor children trained in basic firearm safety.

Check your state's laws concerning firearm storage. Unspeakable devastation has occurred when a parent loses a child to accidental discharge of a firearm, then additionally faces a criminal conviction for unsafe storage of the gun.

Scenario 75 — Auto Fire, Highway

Sheze Innocent and her daughter have spent their best time ever, touring the western states for two weeks. They are both glad to be returning home. As Innocent cruises along a major highway a young couple in a pickup come up to her side and start waving frantically. They point to the road under

Chapter 12 - Scenarios 71 to 80

Innocent's car with expressions of terror as if a tyrannosaurus is under her. After a few seconds of confusion, Innocent recognizes the young man mouthing "F-I-R-E."

Common Solution:
Innocent quickly pulls over to the side of the road. She and her daughter bolt out of the car. It burns quickly, like an oversized can filled with newspaper and fuel.

Your *X-Pree* Solution:
Some steps you can take to lower your risk of auto fire:
- Watch out for rapid changes in fuel level or engine temperature.
- Get a complete inspection after any minor accident.
- Keep grease and oil from building up on your engine and transmission.
- Replace all cracked or leaking hoses and lines.
- Keep electrical connections tight and clean.
- Keep the battery liquid levels normal, and clean the terminals.
- Tighten caps for fuel and oil securely.
- Never carry a container of fuel inside the passenger compartment.
- Always carry a fire extinguisher and a smoke detector in the passenger compartment.
- Keep the vehicle free of debris and trash.
- Never park over any combustibles that touch the hot parts under the vehicle.
- Always look out for any signs of vandalism.

If you discover a fire in the vehicle while driving:
1. Immediately signal and pull off the road completely, onto dirt if possible.
2. Turn off the engine.
3. Get out of the vehicle. If you can't exit by door, kick out a window to get out.
4. If necessary, use your fire extinguisher to break windows and get everyone out.
5. Move away at least 75 feet. Your vehicle will burn extremely fast. Usually, there is no time to save the contents.

EXTREME PREEMPTION

Scenario 76 — Bushwhackery, Home

Worn out from a long, difficult work day, Sheze Innocent walks up to her back door. As she inserts the key into the door lock, her body jolts with surprise. Heza Villain has sneaked up close behind her. He grabs her around the waist with his left arm and covers her mouth with his right hand.

Common Solution:
Innocent tries to yell out, struggling with her bushwhacker. He quickly overpowers her and moves his attack inside her house. She has mistakenly given up all of her Safety Bubbles without any defense. In this common solution, there is never a good outcome.

Your *X-Pree* Solution:

With the singular goal to get safely inside your house and lock the door, you must disable Villain. Your keys are attached to a Kubotan. Villain has given you five delicious spots to concentrate your ferocious counter attack. They are juicy ones:
1. With your back still toward Villain, you reflexively crouch a little, tightly grip the shaft of the Kubotan, and drive the pointed tip of the Kubotan into Villain's thigh or groin.
2. Open your mouth so that one of his fingers slips inside. Bite hard to tear his flesh. No worries, a doctor can give you a shot later.
3. Select one of his fingers (on his left hand) with your left hand. Grab

it and bend it backwards to break it off. This is not playtime!
4. Stomp his shins and insteps.
5. As he backs away slightly, drive your Kubotan into his throat, face, or eyes with rapid-fire strikes.

Any screaming you can do during your *Extreme Preemption* also helps. When he shows signs of retreating slightly, race into your house, lock yourself inside, then call police.

Your *X-Pree* plan is to perform #1 through #4 at the same time, in about 3 seconds maximum, then follow up with #5. You will not attempt #1 and wait for a response. You will not try fancy spinning footwork. Those are wonderful scripts for make-believe movies. *X-Pree* is designed to save your life *FAST*.

Your counter attack will be vicious, merciless, and at maximum *SPEED*. Remember, your failure to complete a decisive turn-around in this scenario is Villain's license to rob, rape, and murder you in your own home!

High-intensity speed is more important than nuclear power in your strikes. In this scenario, Villain has personally invited you to disable him. He will be busy reacting to the pain you deliver while you race to safety inside your house.

Scenario 77 — Grab & Grope, Club

Sheze Innocent is clubbing with friends. At one of the happy hour bars Heza Villain has his eye on her for about fifteen minutes and offers her a drink. Innocent politely declines and he is offended. Later, on her way to the restroom Villain grabs her around the waist, face-to-face, and he lifts her up high with a big grin. He let's her slide down so that he's holding her up by her buttocks — giving them pulsating squeezes.

Common Solution:
Innocent doesn't want to make a scene, but she struggles to get free. Other men help her, and a scuffle follows. Some minor injuries occur. Villain is escorted from the bar.

Your *X-Pree* Solution:

When Villain lifts you, his hands and arms are occupied. Slam your cupped hands against Villain's ears as hard as possible. This defense will either disorient him or rupture his eardrums.

Is this response by Innocent too severe? Grabbing and lifting a stranger inside a busy club can result in serious injury. Villain's self-issued license to do so is an indicator that he feels comfortable violating Innocent's safety in any circumstance. What level of respect will he show toward the next attractive woman he spots? Is there any guarantee that you will not be thrown down and severely injured? *Extreme Preemption* is your answer.

Scenario 78 — Slavery, College

For over a month in the new semester Sheze Innocent takes the same route to her car after the last class. At 8:30 PM it's dark near the commons, so she hurries to the lighted parking structure. Another student often walks past her in the other direction at the same time every Tuesday. Tonight he asks her to meet him for a hot drink off campus. She accepts and they meet about a half-mile away.

Innocent is shy. She's finishing her degree in finance, looking forward to her career in accounting. When Villain describes his adventures — rock climbing, parasailing, and body surfing — she craves to share some of the same excitement. They set up a date to meet for weekend fun. Innocent can hardly wait.

At the last minute, Villain calls and says that two other couples will be parasailing with them on the lake. He explains that he has car trouble and asks if his friends may stop by and pick her up.

Common Solution:
She agrees, but only the two young men show up to give her a ride. Innocent's body is found near a country road one week later. Her hands are duct taped together. Villain is a slave trade recruiter. It's likely that Innocent did not respond well to "seasoning," the process of breaking down her will to resist belonging to her pimp. His final reprimand was murder.

Your *X-Pree* Solution:
In your lifetime you might never be confronted by a slave trader. There is just one problem with only one encounter; it can be fatal. Your search for Mr. Wonderful might be delayed by your *X-Pree* solution, but these are the steps to stay safer:
- Do some sort of screening (by friends or relatives) before you agree to date any stranger in a private place. Yes, Villain was still a stranger even though she saw him many times in passing. It was a strategy to encourage Innocent to let her guard down.
- Never agree to be picked up by strangers when you're alone.
- Practice a simple technique to escape restraint of your wrists. If your wrists are taped together, align your forearms so they are tight together. To break free, raise your hands above your head then drive your elbows down and out to the sides of your torso. Your wrists will end up right in front of you, with your hands ripped free of the duct tape.
- Carry, on-body, a concealed defense tool with which you are proficient.
- Always report suspicious activity. You might see something that saves someone else's life.

Scenario 79 — Attack, Wheelchair

Among all possible ADA[101] locations at the mall, Innocent chooses the longest ramp; it is steep and barely compliant. He has a short distance to the department store, and his new wheelchair drives like a small racer. There are only a few shoppers around this evening, but he feels safe. Long past the ramp and around the last corner, before the straight-away to the store, young Villain jumps out and charges Innocent while issuing a string of profanities.

Common Solution:
Heze Innocent is thrown off guard. He puts up his hands in a fearful defensive huddle. Villain quickly overpowers him, robs Innocent of all valuable personal property, and beats his head and neck.

Your *X-Pree* Solution:
At the first sight of Villain, you quickly engage him:
1. Roll to a level, open spot and stop, shouting "Get back!"
2. As Villain gets close, pull him toward you with one hand, taking him off balance.
3. Pummel his head and neck with jackhammer strikes.
4. Stay on him with your counter attack until he relaxes.
5. Let him retreat or fall to the sidewalk, then drive to safety.
6. Immediately call police to report the event.

Practice is especially important with this *X-Pree* solution. Find a partner to assist you with the experience of pulling your predator into striking range, throwing him off balance. Use a training dummy to deliver practice strikes at full speed. It is critical to never pause, checking for the effectiveness of your strikes. When Villain relaxes, throw him off and race to safety.

Scenario 80 — Attack, Parking Lot

Heza Villain is extremely drunk. He is lonely and looking for love tonight. On his best days Villain's social skills are barely above neanderthal. Right now, he's simply a social clod who was uninvited from the restaurant's happy hour three blocks away.

Innocent is on her way into the hospital to start her shift. Villain stumbles across the parking lot toward her. As she walks toward the entrance, he can't resist her petite frame. She's two cars over, so he sprints up behind her curling his left arm around her neck from behind. His attempt at a cunning hookup line comes across as a disgusting smelling slur of words which Innocent can't understand.

Common Solution:
Innocent reacts to his grip around her neck by arching backward. She remains off balance while Villain swoons over his attractive prize. Fortunately, some co-workers observe what's happening. As they start to walk toward Innocent, Villain slowly releases his grip and Innocent runs into the hospital.

Your *X-Pree* Solution:
Again, your best solution is to observe Villain outside of your Safety Bubble 3 (moe than 20 feet). This gives you time to elude him. Simply get back in your car if he breaches your Safety Bubble 2 (10 feet). After he enters your Safety Bubble 1 (5 feet), you have few self-defense options outside your car. However, he's probably slow in his reaction time, giving you opportunities for a *FAST* bare hand defense:
1. Reach up with both hands, grabbing Villain's left arm.
2. Crunch forward, throwing your hips backward.
3. Drive several fierce elbow strikes into his torso.
4. Step backward and to Villain's left side, while pushing his arm forward.
5. Break free of his grip.
6. Smash his lower leg from the side, above his ankle, or
7. Stomp the back of the same leg from the rear, just below his knee.
8. Run to safety and report the attack.

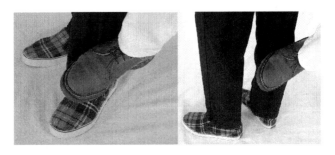

Complete Topic Discussion 12,
then go to Chapter 13 — Scenarios 81 to 90.

Topic Discussion 12

Are you motivated and willing to report the child abuse in Scenario 71? Why or why not?

Whom will you contact to report Villain in Scenario 72?

Would you intervene in Scenario 73? Why or why not?

What common defenses will work for Innocent in Scenarios 73, 76, and 80?

How can you practice the *X-Pree* in Scenario 80?

Notes:

Topic Discussion 12

Chapter 13 - Scenarios 81 to 90

Scenario 81 — Rape, Anywhere

Villain has her pinned. His weight on top of Innocent is nearly suffocating. She struggles to push him off, but it's not possible. His foul breath is like a hot blast of rotten eggs mixed with sweat. Villain has both of her wrists pinned as he pulls her skirt high enough for the rape.

Common Solution:
Innocent quickly becomes exhausted. Villain finishes his attack and leaves her lying there as nothing more than a defeated pool of emotion.

Your *X-Pree* Solution:

With lightening speed, you counter attack:
1. Find some way to reach his face with one hand — by force or temporary faked submission.
2. Simultaneously, (A) drive your thumb into his eye socket on the inside, next to his nose, as far as possible, while you (B) reach behind his head with your other hand to pull his head toward you.
3. Squeeze outward to crush the globe of his eye. Yes, it's messy.
4. Squirm backwards, pushing with your legs, or
5. Bend one of your knees to bring your foot closer to your butt, then blast him off you by pushing with your foot, rolling to your side.
6. Run to safety and report the attack.

This defense is effective when you are literally face-to-face with the rapist. It will abruptly end his assault on you. He will not be able to see, while experiencing significant pain. Is this defense justified? Remember the current statistic — 1 sexual assault every 98 seconds, with only 3 convictions for every 500 incidents. If the price of a fun-filled rape is increased to equal the permanent loss of Villain's eye, perhaps we will see a statistical change.

Scenario 82 — Attack, Laundry Room

Saturday morning laundry is rarely any fun, especially in a shared laundry room. Sheze Innocent starts early today at 6:00 AM. Most of the other tenants in her project are still in bed. Her plan is looking good. Innocent has the wash and dry cycles synchronized precisely with her weekly apartment cleaning.

As she bolts through the laundry room doorway, a guest is there to greet her. Villain has pulled clothes from a dryer apparently in search of a some new outfits. Innocent asks, "What are you doing?" Villain responds by grabbing her shirt collar.

Common Solution:
Innocent reacts by grabbing his hands, trying to break free. Villain throws her across the room, fracturing her arm as she impacts one of the washers. Many conclusions in this scenario end with a kick to her head or a knife cut to her throat.

Your *X-Pree* Solution:
In the instant that Villain reaches to grab your collar:
1. Step toward him.
2. Without looking, stomp his instep as hard as possible.
3. Walking forward, with one hand, pull down on his hands to make room for your strikes.
4. With your other hand, you rapid fire a palm strike to his chin, then hand chop to the side of his neck or throat.
5. Do not engage in a tug-of-war while Villain is holding your collar!
6. Continue to move through him, striking, as you run to safety.
7. When you are sure of your safety, call police and then your apartment manager.

As always, *Extreme Preemption* is your explosive charge into Villain to disable him without hesitation, without checking to see the results of your strikes. You will know your strikes are successful when Villain falls or retreats.

In the self-defense marketplace there are many techniques being taught to defend yourself in this scenario. Most of these elaborate approaches need to be practiced intensely. This *X-Pree* solution is effective in a wide variety of situations and it's easy to learn.[102]

Scenario 83 — Bushwhackery, Alley

There is strict gun control in Innocent's large city. Heze Innocent is not able to obtain a permit to carry a concealed handgun. On his walk home from the subway station, he's blocked from leaving a narrow alley between buildings. Villain pulls a short baseball bat from under his long coat. He starts yelling obscenities at Innocent as he charges toward him.

Common Solution:
Innocent turns and tries to run away. Villain catches him and critically beats Innocent for entering the wrong neighborhood.

Your *X-Pree* Solution:
Your defense is an all-out blitz to counter attack Villain:
1. From the instant you identify his bat, you blast directly toward him, to shorten the radius of Villain's swing. This radically reduces the velocity and power of his strike with the bat.
2. Drive into and through Villain as you stomp his instep, palm strike his chin, and hand chop his clavicle or neck with the edge of your hand.
3. Then, you literally run over him. *Extreme Preemption* is your no-

hesitation, all-powerful, lightening-speed drive through Villain as you escape past him.

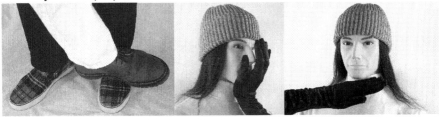

Scenario 84 — Elder Abuse, Home

Happy memories of childhood adventures race in Innocent's mind as she watches her grandma sleep. Spending many summer vacations together, her grandparents traveled with Innocent and her older brother to see some of America's best scenery.

Grandpa has been gone for more than a year. Innocent's mother and stepfather invited Grandma to live with them, and it's not working well. In the beginning everyone in the family assumed there would be an adjustment period. Recently there are more and more signs that her grandma is extremely unhappy. She jumps at any loud noise. She spends very little time with her friends. Her light work in the garden lasts only a few minutes each day. She stays in her bedroom most of the time.

Common Solution:
Innocent is uncomfortable with the situation, but she has no idea what to do. Life goes on unchanged. After Grandma eventually dies, Innocent is plagued with guilt.

Your *X-Pree* Solution:
Nearly 75% of today's elder victimization occurs in their own homes by family members, friends, or neighbors. In this scenario Grandma is emotionally abused.[103] Being yelled at can result in her fear of loud noises. Other forms of verbal abuse can ruin her sense of self-worth. Overbearing control can be accomplished by limiting her access to friends. These are injuries to her dignity and her basic desire to live. Aging is certainly a natural process. Aging in continuous fear is entirely unnatural.

If you have a senior in your family who is receiving care by your relatives, do your homework. Learn about the demands of in-home care and share the info with your whole family. Your *X-Pree* solution includes the following:
- Spread the responsibility of care to other relatives, by inviting them to occasionally bring in meals or take Grandma for an outing. Their observations of her well-being will also help.
- Pay attention to her medical needs — prescriptions and doctor appointments.
- Start a dialog with a support center to learn as much as possible.
- Be prepared to report the abuse. This is a heavy, difficult decision. However, getting the right help for everyone will benefit everyone.
- Remember, everyone needs to belong somewhere. It's basic emotional health.

If you are an elder who wants to maintain your healthy lifestyle:
- Exercise and get all of your necessary medical care.
- Maintain your own monetary accounts.
- Keep your own cell phone with you.
- Stay active with a social, community, or faith-based group.
- Open your own mail.
- Continually read and study topics that are interesting to you.
- If you want to be independent, do as many things independently as you can!

Scenario 85 — Phishing, Online

Her everyday barrage of incoming emails is sometimes overwhelming. Sixty, seventy, or eighty worthless emails per day! Sheze Innocent has become jaded toward the whole medium. Today's batch includes an alert from her bank. It also refers to an account which is the same type that Innocent owns. Content in the email says, "We have frozen your account, pending verification of necessary information" — it's followed by a directive to click the highlighted link.

Common Solution:
Innocent clicks on the link and responds to the questions. Her personal information is now compromised, stolen by an Internet Thief.

Your *X-Pree* Solution:
Emails from the following imposters can flood you on a daily basis: shipping companies, credit card companies, overseas investors, Internal Revenue Service, vendors, refugees, and sources of any "Free Gift." You get the idea. Internet thieves are at this moment impersonating all of these entities and many more.

Here's your *Extreme Preemption* — delete them. That's all. Write down the source email address, then delete the garbage and make a quick report to IC3.[104] Any legitimate entity that desperately needs to communicate with you will always do it in writing (by postal mail), perhaps with a followup phone call.

Scenario 86 — Terrorism, Market

When the village produce market opens Heze Innocent is first in line. His restaurant customers will be dazzled by the seafood entrees, garnishes, and dessert specialties he is able to prepare. All of the fruit is peaked out this week. It's a smorgasbord of culinary ingredients that won't last long. Every narrow aisle is packed with buyers.

Standing near Innocent is a young man who has not picked out any produce or meat. He is quite still, staring down the street. In the next instant, his suicide bomb vest explodes.

Common Solution:
Emergency teams pick up the pieces, and merchants eventually get back to business.

Your *X-Pree* Solution:
Suicide bombers are much easier to locate after they blow themselves up. Those large charred spots on the ground are magnificent markers.

Your challenge in detecting a bomber before detonation is the very short ignition time. Our Villain who strikes with his hand gives us a window to counter attack before the strike lands on us. Our suicide bomber's total time in attacking is only a fraction of a second.

Extreme Preemption

Extreme Preemption is based on the common actions of the suicide bomber or builder of an IED (Improvised Explosive Device) before arriving at the site of the murders. Based on past bombings he might,
- Reduce his belongings at home to some minimum amount
- Limit his social contacts
- Get his personal accounts / agreements in final order
- Carry fraudulent identification
- If traveling by common carrier to site of the attack —
  - Carry unusually sparse luggage
  - Sit near a wing of the airplane, where fuel is located

Remember the eight common behaviors prior to a Terror Villain's attack:[105]
1. Financing Examples — movement of large amounts of Villain's cash by deposit or withdrawal from one or more accounts; online solicitations for funds
2. Surveillance Examples — Villain's visits to the attack site multiple times at different hours; parked vehicles adjacent to a target for long periods
3. Elicitation Examples — gathering info from site personnel about the target by phone or email; befriending employees at a local eatery
4. Security Probe Examples — gathering info about security at the site to construct a schedule for guards; setting off false alarms as a test of the systems
5. Supplies Examples — accumulation of bomb-making materials, such as unusually large quantities of common household chemicals; purchase of nails, screws, and ball bearings for no actual project
6. Suspicious Presence Examples — out of place appearance by his candor and/or clothing; loitering in a populated area for no reason
7. Dry Run Examples — close attention to a written list while briskly walking through a target area; repeatedly checking his watch while following a handwritten map
8. Deployment Examples — unusual actions immediately before an attack, such as a vehicle which is out of place; Villain walking against the flow of people in a crowded area

Above all, someone who is ready to blow himself gives these warning signs:
- Especially nervous, restless, or agitated behavior
- Aggressive attitude while traveling by car, bus, train, or airplane

- Refusal to accommodate changes in seating, walking/driving route, or destination

Your contribution in the war against Terror Villains is your vigilance in continuously assessing people and property around you. Anything which is odd, abnormal, or irregular could be Villain's betrayal of his cloaking efforts. Remember, if you see something, say something. If you intend to say something, do it immediately!

Scenario 87 — Vishing, Home

As Innocent is sitting down to his favorite home-cooked meal, his cell phone rings. So sweet and sincere is the voice of the telemarketer that Innocent thinks for a moment that it's a family member. Sheza Villain represents an environmental contractor. She explains that they will be in his area next week. One of the solar company's estimators can perform a free assessment of their electrical system.

Common Solution:
Innocent is polite while Villain navigates through her sales pitch answering his objections with answers which are already scripted.

Your *X-Pree* Solution:
Hang up! No responses. No courtesy. Hang up. Then, when you have a few minutes, make sure your number is included in the U.S. National Do Not Call Registry.[106] If Villain calls again, she will probably insist that it's "not a sales call, just an opportunity for a free evaluation." Hang up. Then file a complaint with the Registry.

Villain might actually be working for a solar company. She might also be an identity thief who his trying to incrementally build a profile about you. Beware! Simply hang up!

Scenario 88 — Bushwhackery, Sidewalk

Sheze Innocent is walking down the sidewalk near her apartment. Heza Villain approaches from the rear and punches her in the side of her head. She is unconscious before hitting the concrete hard, face down.

Common Solution:
There is no common solution for this one that avoids serious injury. It's a popular urban game called "Knockout." Villain's goal is to render the victim unconscious with one punch to the temple.

Your *X-Pree* Solution:
Fearless awareness is your defense here. You are not afraid to be constantly aware of what's happening around you. If someone approaches, you will lower your chin and make silent, direct eye contact. This sends a clear signal that you are not afraid.

Many people still don't believe in making eye contact. They somehow conclude that avoiding eye contact will mysteriously reduce your provocation of Villain. This is an outdated and dangerous pseudo defense. In the case of "Knockout," Villain is relying on your inattention to land his critical strike. Your fearless personal attention might entirely dissuade him from trying to injure you. If he persists in his effort to hurt you, then launch your alternative *X-Pree* defenses.

Obviously, your careful selection of personal defense tools and your training in their use are crucial. Trying to sort out a defense strategy when Bushwhacker is inside your Safety Bubble 1 is not a healthy plan.

Scenario 89 — Credit Card Skimming, Gas Station

This morning is quiet at the gas station. Only one other car is at a pump on the other side of the station. Sheze Innocent happily fills her tank, swipes her card at the island, and leaves for work.

Common Solution:
Villain has secretly installed an unauthorized card reader at the pump. As Innocent swipes her card, Villain gathers a record of her credit card information. Innocent's card ID can then be used directly or sold to other Villains.

Your *X-Pree* Solution:
Before swiping your credit card on any device, look all around it for signs of tampering — scratches where cabinet pieces meet, a broken seal, gouges

or pry marks on the lock. If you see anything that looks suspicious then pay with cash inside the gas station, or fill up somewhere else.

Scenario 90 — Knife Attack, Anywhere

For some reason Heza Villain is fanatically driven to intimidate Innocent with a knife. He's as determined as a hungry puppy that wants his dinner. He approaches from the front. Villain's knife is in his right hand in front of Heze Innocent's body, pointed slightly upward.

Common Solution:
Innocent raises his hands in submission. This scenario has played out thousands of times in locations all over the world. Sometimes the cash that Villain demands satisfies him enough to break off the attack and leave. On countless other occasions, Villain completes his robbery and also fatally stabs or slashes his victim.

Your *X-Pree* Solution:
If your only defense tools are bare hands, raise them slightly higher than Villain's:
Either,
1. Swat to the outside with your left hand, moving his knife away from your center.
2. Launch your rapid-fire chops to Villain's head, neck, and collarbone.

Or,
1. Grab Villain's right wrist with your left hand.
2. Push against the knife blade with your right forearm, forcing it out of his grip.
3. Launch your rapid-fire chops to Villain's head, neck, and collarbone.

As in every *Extreme Preemption*, practice for speed and accuracy in your movements. If you use a training partner, your practice can be conducted with any short stick or large plastic spoon, instead of a sharp knife.

Complete Topic Discussion 13,
then go to Chapter 14 — Scenarios 91 to 100.

Topic Discussion 13

In Scenario 81 are you ready to destroy Villain's eye to prevent his rape? Why or why not?

What speed is necessary in *X-Pree* for Scenarios 82 and 83?

How will you discuss the abuse in Scenario 84 with other family members?

What is the common *X-Pree* thread in Scenarios 85 and 87?

Are you confident that you can make direct eye contact with Villain as in Scenario 88?

Notes:

Topic Discussion 13

Chapter 14 - Scenarios 91 to 100

Scenario 91 — Attack / Handgun, Anywhere

Imagine Scenario 90 with Villain pointing a handgun at you. In this condition, your general awareness has probably been less than perfect. Once again, the primary enemy in this incident is your fear.

Your *X-Pree* Solution:
Guns are awfully loud and powerful, but they don't send bullets in curved patterns. If you are out of the line-of-fire, you're safe at least for that moment. Villain is close to you with a gun pointed at your face, chest, or the back of your head:
1. Raise your hands to about the level of the gun, faking submission. Your award-winning performance will be valuable here.
2. Now, at the same time, move to one side with a short step while you slap the gun in the opposite direction. Remember, bullets don't follow curved paths, they move in a straight line. If you get away from that line, any fired bullets will miss you.
3. As soon as you are clear, move in with your counter attack to his face and neck. We have already explored a variety of bare hand defenses. Pick two or three and counter attack!

Your supreme *SPEED* is the key to *X-Pree* success here. Also, your focus on disabling Villain must take precedence over your fight to control the handgun. Villain's attention will be on his gun. Your attention must be directed elsewhere. In this case, your mind will be zeroed in on immediate injury to his body — *FAST*.

Never practice this defense with a working handgun, no matter how sure you are that it's unloaded! Many inexpensive training guns or water pistols are available to purchase. Or, just crudely carve one from wood.

Scenario 92 — 911 Call

Since 1968, the number series 9-1-1 has been the universal emergency phone number in the USA. Some areas don't yet have this emergency service, and some existing 911 call centers still don't have the ability to locate the caller by GPS coordinates. Is there a right way to make a 911 call? Yes![107]

Common Solution:
Many people connect with the 911 operator and launch into a hysterical, incoherent discourse. Granted, it is extremely difficult to speak intelligibly to an operator when you're in the middle of a crisis, especially a violent one. When portions of seconds matter, a fragmented 911 call is dangerous.

Your *X-Pree* Solution:
Above all other priorities, your location is the first detail to offer the 911 operator. There are instances when your billing address is the only info displayed at the office of the 911 operator.
1. Clarify your location immediately.
2. Speak as clearly, if not as slowly, as possible during the call.
3. Let the operator direct the conversation by asking you appropriate questions. Keep your answers as concise as possible.

To teach your child how to call 9-1-1, help him/her learn these steps:
1. Know the keypad buttons.
2. Say first name, last name, and your home address (or location).
3. Describe the emergency — fire, unconscious person, burglar, etc.
4. Identify if someone is breathing or not.
5. Never dial 9-1-1 for any reason other than an immediate emergency.

Every 911 call that is mistakenly placed depletes first responder resources which can otherwise be directed to a genuine emergency. Any 911 call dialed as a prank subjects the caller to possible arrest and criminal prosecution.

Scenario 93 — Burglary, Toolshed

One of his immaculate spaces is Innocent's small tool shed. His six-foot by eight-foot sanctuary resembles a pristine display of handyman treasures. Every implement and hand tool has a designated place. Every square inch of the shed is exquisite.

Common Solution:
Innocent locates his shed near the house, because it's a handy place. He keeps fuel and paint thinner in it to avoid storing flammable liquids in his garage. There are no special locks on the shed.

While Innocent is away on vacation, Villain shows up and gains easy access to the shed and every tool he needs to break into Innocent's house.

Another disaster can occur when a fire outside the home, such as a grass fire, penetrates the shed quickly igniting the contents which in turn spread fire to the house.

Your *X-Pree* Solution:
- Always locate your tool shed away from valuable structures.
- Always install at least one secure padlock to slow Villain's access.
- Never keep flammable liquids in a small space. Fuel and paint thinner need a mixture of air and vapor to burn (explode). It's far more likely to attain that perfect mixture in a small space, as in a tool shed or empty fuel container.

Scenario 94 — Credit Card Skimming, Store

Heze Innocent races to the checkout stand with a ream of paper, felt pens, and file folders. His financial info is due at the accountant's office in the morning, and he has over an hour of printing to complete tonight.

Sheza Villain gives him a slow, friendly smile as she scan's his items. She asks him to run his credit card through the reader. There are a few seconds of processing time. Then she asks to see his card, and she scans it a second time in another reader behind the check stand.

Common Solution:
Innocent was set up for a fraudulent purchase using his card. He thinks nothing about it until he receives his credit card statement with one or more unknown charges on it.

Your *X-Pree* Solution:
When checking out at a store there is never a need to scan a credit card with two different readers. If you are asked to comply with this scam, immediately persist in asking why it's necessary. Complete your purchase with one scan, or leave your products and walk out of the store (with no scan). Immediately report the incident to the FBI's Internet Crime Complaint Center.[108]

Scenario 95 — Snakebite, Garden

For nearly six months Sheze Innocent has not seen a single poisonous snake on her property. Previous years have brought many close calls with aggressive snakes, but none so far this year. As Innocent carefully lifts a large pot to empty the dirt out of it, the eighteen-inch snake under the flower pot becomes agitated. She backs up slightly, but the snake bites the edge of her hand.

Common Solution:
Innocent dashes to her house. She calls 911, and then wraps her wrist tightly with an old belt. She frantically drives to a nearby fire station for medical treatment.

Your *X-Pree* Solution:
Avoidance is always your best defense for a poisonous snakebite. Use extreme caution while moving any object where your slithery attacker might be hiding. When you keep the object between you and the snake while you uncover it, your ability to observe what's under or behind that object is dramatically increased.

These are guidelines to follow if a snakebite occurs:
1. Don't panic! Breathe smoothly.
2. Move away from the snake to immediate safety.
3. If possible, snap a photo of the snake, but don't waste any time.
4. Call 911 — Get instructions for formal medical care as soon as possible.
5. Remain as motionless as you can while waiting for medical help.
6. Don't cut or disturb the bite area, to avoid spreading the venom.
7. Use a firm wrap near the bite, between the bite and your heart. Don't cut off circulation to the bitten limb with an ultra-tight tourniquet.
8. Don't allow a partner to suck on the bite area.
9. If possible, apply a suction pump to the bite marks, but don't waste time.
10. Keep the bite area lower than your heart.
11. Allow some minor bleeding; it will flush out a little venom.
12. Apply a clean, absorbent bandage to the bite area.
13. Don't spread the venom that oozes out.

You guessed it! Your *X-Pree* solution here is *SPEED*, to administer simple first-aid *FAST*, then get professional medical care *FAST*. Remember, some snakebites are radically more toxic than others, leaving you little time to get help.

Scenario 96 — Robbery, Vacation

Saving up for her dream vacation was easy. Sheze Innocent has wanted to get to this tropical island for five years. One six-hour flight tomorrow and then her next stop is the warm sandy beach!

Common Solution:
Blinged out with stunning jewelry, Innocent walks into the baggage claim area at the small island airport. Her trendy clothing makes an emphatic statement. She's ready to party for ten days! Some local Villains also notice. Innocent is robbed within two days, after taking a short taxi ride to do some shopping.

Your *X-Pree* Solution:
Celebrating your dream vacation must include radical blending with the local population. Your inclination to show off that flab-free body needs to take a back seat to looking at least a little bit like someone native to the area. Wearing that pristine off-white sunhat, magenta tights, and your flowered plum top is certainly a fashion triumph. But, you could also wear a sandwich board labeled "ROB ME FIRST."

These foreign travel tips will improve your safety:
- Do your homework to examine the hotel's location, security staff, room security, and local area crime rates.
- Confirm that the hotel has a front desk staff on duty 24/7.
- Learn to say, "I need help" and "Call police" in the native language.
- Pay attention to customs and dress that might be offensive or illegal.
- Use traveler's checks and credit cards; as little cash as possible.
- Leave all expensive jewelry locked up at home.
- Stay in a room that is not above the seventh floor. Fire trucks with ladders can't reach higher if they need to get you out of the hotel.
- Be certain that your name and room number are not shared with anyone, especially in the lobby.
- Learn to operate the phone system immediately.
- Carry local emergency numbers and a map with you at all times.

In every circumstance, your awareness of people around you should be keen. Balanced attention to detail is critical. Paranoia is not necessary — it's your vacation!

Scenario 97 — Vehicle Attack, Vacation

Heze Innocent and his family are strolling through the cafe district in a big city. Their comical banter is suddenly disrupted by loud voices down the street. Within a couple of seconds, the yelling turns into screams. Other tourists begin running chaotically in all directions.

Moving fast and erratically, a vehicle mows down pedestrians as it races toward Innocent's family.

Common Solution:
Many human targets stand still in shock, until the vehicle slams into them. Others try to run away. Some are hit by the car, some are hurt from falls. Injury and death are extensive.

Your *X-Pree* Solution:
Keen awareness on any street is your highest priority. You direct your family to walk along a route that's protected from vehicles by fences, trees, low barricades, or elevated sidewalks. When you cross a street, move quickly. Frequently pick out escape routes which, if necessary, allow you to run to spots where a car cannot drive.

Is this a buzz-killer for your family fun? No! There is still plenty of headroom for lively amusement while you silently protect the people you love. Villain's attacking vehicle traveling at just 20 MPH covers a distance of about 90 feet in only 3 seconds. There is no time for delayed responses to his deadly aggression.

Have you experienced a lapse in your attention to detail, leaving you in the path of the attacking car or truck? Then run for your lives. Run perpendicular to the direction of the attacker. Get behind anything which the car can't drive beyond. This is another use of cover where the projectile is not a bullet weighing less than one ounce; it's a 4,000 pound vehicle.

If you're allowed to legally carry a concealed handgun in that location, make your target the operator of the vehicle — while you move! It doesn't drive by itself. Stop the driver and you'll stop the attack. Keep in mind, your bullet through the windshield of an oncoming car will deflect slightly downward when it passes through the glass, because of the angle of the windshield.

Shooting at the attacking vehicle's tires, engine block, or gas tank are exciting movie stunts which have zero value during your real event. Likewise, standing in the middle of the street taking careful aim as a classic western gunslinger is extraordinarily macho and vividly majestic. It's also your ticket to the roadkill ward. Instead, be smart and *FAST*.

Chapter 14 - Scenarios 91 to 100

Scenario 98 — Drugs, Teenage Overnight

Innocents' daughter is articulate and spunky. Her mix of friends in high school is not large, though she seems extremely close to her current friends. This morning she asks to spend Friday night at Janet's house. It will be the third sleepover this month.

Heze Innocent drops his daughter off at Janet's house. She insists on walking to the front door by herself. Janet's father waves to Innocent as he backs down the driveway.

On Saturday, Innocents' daughter is late in calling to be picked up. When she gets home at 11:30 AM, she immediately goes to bed and sleeps most of the afternoon. Her clothes smell smokey.

Common Solution:
Innocents assume their daughter has been up late, talking into early morning hours. Her smokey clothing gets this explanation, "We roasted marshmallows last night!" Their daughter's grades drop sharply. All at once she cuts off her friendship with Janet completely.

Later she admits that Janet's father supplied them with marijuana and they smoked it during every overnight stay for three months.

Your *X-Pree* Solution:
There are a variety of respectful spy techniques that you can use to assess the trustworthiness of the other teenager's home. Take time and care to select where your son or daughter can stay while away.
1. Run a simple online profile of the friend's parents. Assume nothing.
2. Ask other parents if they know the family, and what they know about them.
3. Drive by the friend's home to get a feel for the family's lifestyle.
4. Get agreement about what activities will occur and not occur when she's there.
5. Make sure she has a cell phone to call you anytime while she's away.
6. When she gets home, joyfully declare, "Hey, tell me all about it!" If the info you receive raises your suspicions, act accordingly — more research, or worst case, a complaint with police.

7. Take time and maximum care to select where your son or daughter can stay while away from home. Did I mention that one already? If you missed it, go back to #1.

One abusive event for a teenager can produce decades of painful healing, if there is healing at all. Is your teenager's life your business? It certainly is. Do you have a right to snoop, dig, pry, interfere, and intervene for his or her safety? If not you, then who else will?

Scenario 99 — Trespassing, Rural Property

Innocent has been troubled by a group of teenagers hanging out at his front gate. Life in the backcountry is normally quiet and uneventful. With very few criminal incidents in the area, sheriff's deputies don't patrol in Innocent's neighborhood. His frustration is peaked because the teens frequently smoke in locations where they're surrounded by dry brush.

Common Solution:
Innocent walks down to his gate in a rage. He has a heated yelling match with the trespassers. They attack him near his gate, leaving him to die from severe head trauma.

Your *X-Pree* Solution:
Trespassing is not a capital crime. In most jurisdictions, it is a misdemeanor. In this case, the teenagers might be merely guilty of unlawful entry. Your anger about the disrespect which people show toward you or your property must not escalate to beating or shooting them without justification.

Your *Extreme Preemption* in this case is the rapid control of your emotions. If you have not previously informed teenage Villain that he is not invited to enter your property, then do that immediately. After that, if you intend to tell Villain to leave your property again, carry at least one self-defense tool. Drive to him in a vehicle and don't get out of it.

Remember your teenage years, when maximum distance from adults was a high priority. Today, the global adolescent quest for freedom is still in play. Your complacence, gullible tolerance, or uncontrolled rage are all unwise choices. Your mature communication without antagonization is the superior tactic. *Extreme Preemption* is your *FAST* counter action to snuff out the danger — never to escalate it.

Scenario 100 — Attack Error, City Street

Heze Innocent is crossing a busy street in the middle of the workday. There is a lot of congestion at this intersection. Struggling with a heavy bundle under his arm, Innocent hears someone honk. He quickly recognizes a friend in his car. Innocent raises his free hand to give a quick wave. It doesn't look quite right to bystanders, because Innocent's free hand is palsied.

Common Solution:
Two gang members in a nearby car interpret Innocent's wave as an insulting sign used by an inner city rival gang. Passenger Villain immediately jumps out of the car, runs to Innocent, and beats him unconscious on the sidewalk. Many people watch the beating. No one assists Innocent.

Your *X-Pree* Solution:
Self-defense rights and responsibilities include people near you. Our ITOTR rules allow us to defend ourselves and others who are in need. Obviously, you are not required to defend a stranger. Yet, this scenario burdens all of us with the healthy question, "As a bystander, what should I do?"

When are we obligated to assist? With a solid working knowledge of effective self-defense skills, when are we responsible for victims who are innocent and also helpless? Do we hesitate to intervene in an attack because we're afraid of injury? Are we afraid of legal problems? Are we waiting for police to arrive?

Police might not arrive as quickly as we want them. Many people are not aware that the ruling in Warren v. District of Columbia, 1981, states:
> *"District of Columbia appears to follow the well-established rule that official police personnel and the government employing them are not generally liable to victims of criminal acts for failure to provide adequate police protection. …This uniformly accepted rule rests upon the fundamental principle of American law that a government and its agents are under no general duty to provide public services, such as police protection, to any particular individual citizen."* [109]

EXTREME PREEMPTION

No clergyman, trainer, attorney, legislator, or law enforcement officer can dictate your response to a person in need. Any degree of genuine help you give will probably lessen someone's degree of injury. Be honest about your ability to assist and your commitment to preempt an attack on someone else. Your decision to act defensively in the face of a criminal act is solely your business.

*Complete Topic Discussion 14,
then go to Concluding Remarks.*

Topic Discussion 14

How does a reduction in fear help your *X-Pree* defense in Scenario 91?

Does 911 service work in your region? If so, can the call center locate your cell phone?

What aspects of your teenage behavior will you disallow for your children? (Scenario 98)

How would you approach and converse with the trespassers in Scenario 99?

Would you intervene to help the victim in Scenario 100? Why or why not?

Notes:

Topic Discussion 14

Concluding Remarks

From the beginning of my term as a self-defense instructor, occasionally a student asks, "Ok, really, how often do these things actually happen? Honestly, what's the likelihood of something bad happening to us?" My answer is always the same — "It doesn't matter what the likelihood is." In my family we have two relatives who were sexually assaulted. It's a difficult path to genuinely heal from that type of injury. Some victims never heal. For each of my relatives, there was only one attack. For them, as well as millions of other victims, one attack is one too many.

Our current world culture is blazing hot with local and global threats. Political correctness sometimes clouds our otherwise clear decision-making ability. We mistakenly brood over actions which we would otherwise take in a heartbeat. This book contains your path out of that tragic indecision.

Between these covers you have an array of the most learnable, valuable safety strategies that are possible for civilians. Your ITOTR is a valid framework in which you can decide the legal use of force. Bare hands and many other defense tools are available to you right now. There is no legitimate reason for you to continue living a fear-filled, stress-filled life — absolutely none.

Study this content. Apply it to your life today, without delay. I have researched the best defenses. All of them are attainable by you. Get started now. In one hundred scenarios I've shown you that your mind is the weapon which will defend you. Your conviction to be safe can rarely be shattered by any force outside of you. Defense tools that you choose will probably be different from the ones chosen by other people who are close to you. Investigate new defense tool options as they become available. Boost your own personal safety by making choices which give you the ultimate readiness.

Concluding Remarks

Defenders live as you do. In most cases, they aren't veteran martial artists. They train for as many possible threats as their resources allow. They select defense tools with which they can become proficient; then, they spend time practicing to improve. They have confidence in their self-defense skills, while honestly recognizing their personal limitations. Pursuit of these steps is your next course of action.

Over time, a Defender's attitude might change from highly motivated in preserving safety to a more halfhearted approach. Irregular fitness exercises and a general lackadaisical approach to self-defense training can become the new mediocre baseline. He or she might get sloppy with home security, breaking fundamental safety rules.

However, as you grow beyond the bare essentials of safety into a lifestyle of healthy awareness and readiness, you will discover that a lukewarm attitude about your security is undesirable. Honing even a few self-defense skills and general practices will give you a level of peace that you will never want to compromise.

Most of us really don't need a private security force. We just need protection from Villain's antics, either from our fear that they might occur or from actual encounters with them. For many people the stress of what might happen is as injurious to them as the actual episodes. But, you now have the knowledge to smash your enemy head-on by crushing the threat in your mind first, then in person if necessary. Obliviolence has no chance in your future. Waiting for police or a military Spec Ops team to arrive is no longer your only option.

Nearly all of the bare-hand techniques outlined here are savage and heartless, perhaps undesirable for you to employ. Your foundation in these methods is simple. Mercifully sparring or playing with Villain who outweighs and out-powers you is a sure path to your injury or death. My mission is to help you live more calmly as an educated Defender — not as a bloodthirsty aggressor, and definitely not as a powerless victim.

Together, the scenarios here show applications of both high-energy counter attacks and highly controlled restraint. Your mission is to find the safe, moral, and legal blend of defenses which work in your personal life. In this book, you have the info to accomplish that mission.

If you live your entire life without ever being confronted by a threat, that is especially wonderful! It's everyone's desire and prayer. My hope for you is this: If one exception spills into your life, one encounter with Villain, you will be ready to end the threat to your safety with *Extreme Preemption*, because you are motivated to *Train, Detect, and Preempt — FAST*.

How do we know that *X-Pree* works? After ten years of intense study, it is the best self-defense framework I can give you. Centuries of wrestling with the question "How do we stay safe?" have given us myriad worthwhile answers and an equal number of airy pontifications. Our civilized responses to safety threats have taken on countless forms — everything from fortified rock castles to nearly impenetrable digital firewalls. *X-Pree's* worth, for you, is not guaranteed. It is yours by choice. Over the next several years, it will be tested and proven valuable for an unknown number of people. Perhaps you will be one of them.

If you employ *Extreme Preemption* in your life, or you have a comment about *X-Pree* or this book, I want to hear from you. Please email me: Contact@OldJulianPress.com.

Thank you for the privilege of sharing *X-Pree*.

Always stay safe.

P. E. Schultz

About Defenders

Defenders: Citizens who are willing and able to preempt Villain's plans. They are, at all times and in every circumstance, the Defenders of Innocents while respecting and protecting the rule of law.

Train, Detect, Preempt

Their shield represents the Divine presence (top wings) which gives every Defender a complete (seven rivets) defense. This protection resonates in each Defender's mind and body (two stars), enabling vigilance (falcon) and the expertise to use force (sword) if necessary in carefully and legally defending himself, herself, or nearby Innocents by *Extreme Preemption*.
They *Train, Detect, and Preempt — FAST.*

Their mission is simple:
Defend Innocents

"My Defense is of God,
Who saves the upright in heart."

Psalm 7:10

About the Author

Peter E. Schultz is an author, lecturer, and certified instructor specializing in close quarters self-defense.

He spent most of his youth in the woods near his family's home. Those days in the quiet countryside are distinctly contrasted with the nearly frenetic pace of our current urban culture. He began teaching in 2003, continuing to acquire many instructor credentials and certifications throughout his successful career.

His mission is simple: "To improve your safety by self-defense education." He aims to downplay long recitations of tragic criminal attacks on civilians. These accounts are certainly crystal clear views of real crime. However, left by themselves, depressing narratives can drive away students who are desperately seeking useful answers.

Instead, Peter brings refreshing creativity, innovation, and lighthearted insight to his books as well as his classroom training. In both fiction and non-fiction, his readers find a healthy balance of life-saving instruction in safety and personal protection, coupled with lively entertainment and wit. Using combinations of colorful metaphors and straight talk, he offers a buffet of practical solutions which are effective in everyday life. See his course listings online at I Can Defend.

Many decades of entrepreneurial business experience and passionate people watching bring his readers vivid arrays of real life observations. Interpersonal relationships are the core of every work. Winning popularity at an astonishing pace, his books, lectures, and courses offer inspiring learning experiences to a wide audience.

Visit Old Julian Press.com

Endnotes

[1] Western Michigan University Archives, "MLK at Western," wmich.edu/sites/default/files/attachments/MLK.pdf.

[2] preemption, *Webster's Dictionary* (Springfield: G. & C. Merriam, 1856).

[3] By permission. From *Merriam-Webster's Collegiate® Dictionary*, 11th Edition ©2017 by Merriam-Webster, Inc. merriam-webster.com (accessed: 27 July 2017).

[4] preempt. Thesaurus.com. *Roget's 21st Century Thesaurus*, Third Edition. Philip Lief Group 2009, thesaurus.com/browse/preempt (accessed: 27 July 2017).

[5] Exod. 22:2-3 NKJV.

[6] Nancy Kollmann, *Crime and Punishment in Early Modern Russia* (New York: Cambridge University Press, 2012), 62.

[7] William Taft IV, "The Legal Basis for Preemption," Memorandum to Council on Foreign Relations, November 18, 2002, 525.

[8] John Kennedy, *Radio and Television Report to the American People on the Soviet Arms Buildup in Cuba*, October 22, 1962, Transcript JFKWHA-142-001, John F. Kennedy Presidential Library and Museum, jfklibrary.org/Asset-Viewer/sUVmChsB0moLfrBcaHaSg.aspx (accessed: 27 July 2017).

[9] Louis Rene Beres, "No Nuclear Weapons in Syria? Go Thank Israel," Israel Defense, April 27, 2017, israeldefense.co.il/en/node/29389 (accessed: 27 July 2017).

[10] The White House, *The National Security Strategy of the United States of America*, September 17, 2002, Washington, DC., 15, state.gov/documents/organization/63562.pdf (accessed: 27 July 2017).

[11] Government Offices of Sweden, *Prevent, Preempt and Protect — The Swedish Counter Terrorism Strategy*, Skr. 2014/15:146, August 27, 2015, Stockholm, Sweden, 8, 6, government.se/legal-documents/2015/09/skr.-201415146 (accessed: 27 July 2017).

[12] Les Picker, "Where Are ISIS's Foreign Fighters Coming From?", National Bureau of Economic Research, WP22190, June 2016, nber.org/digest/jun16/w22190.html (accessed: 27 July 2017).

[13] Assembly Bill No. 1014 (Session, California 2014), leginfo.legislature.ca.gov/faces/billNavClient.xhtml?bill_id=201320140AB1014 (accessed: 27 July 2017).

[14] U.S. law does not require this injury. Some obscure court decision might exist which states otherwise. If you find one, let us know.

[15] U.S. Federal Bureau of Investigation, "Uniform Crime Reporting," ucr.fbi.gov (accessed: 27 July 2017).

[16] John Dean "Jeff" Cooper (1920-2006) introduced "Safety Color Codes" in civilian

ENDNOTES

training.

[17] The Self Defense Company, *The Self Defense Training System*, myselfdefensetraining.com (accessed: 27 July 2017).

[18] Michael Martin, *Concealed Carry and Home Defense Fundamentals* (USCCA, 2015), 194-199.

[19] NRA, training.nra.org (accessed: 27 July 2017).

[20] USCCA, usconcealedcarry.com/training (accessed: 27 July 2017).

[21] Concealed Carry University, concealedcarryuniversity.org (accessed: 27 July 2017).

[22] I.C.E. Training, icestore.us (accessed: 27 July 2017).

[23] Katherine W. Schweit. *Active Shooter Incidents in the United States in 2014 and 2015*, Federal Bureau of Investigation (Washington: U.S. Department of Justice, 2016), fbi.gov/file-repository/activeshooterincidentsus_2014-2015.pdf (accessed: 15 August 2017).

[24] J. Pete Blair and Katherine W. Schweit, *A Study of Active Shooter Incidents in the United States Between 2000 and 2013*, Texas State University and Federal Bureau of Investigation (Washington: U.S. Department of Justice, 2014), 11, fbi.gov/file-repository/active-shooter-study-2000-2013-1-1.pdf (accessed: 15 August 2017).

[25] The Self Defense Company, *The Self Defense Training System*, Module 8, myselfdefensetraining.com (accessed: 27 July 2017).

[26] Patrick Van Horne and Jason Riley, *Left of Bang* (New York: Black Irish Entertainment LLC, 2014).

[27] Gavin de Becker, *The Gift of Fear And Other Survival Signals That Protect Us From Violence* (New York: Dell Publishing, 1997).

[28] U.S. Department of Justice, "National Sources of Law Enforcement Employment Data," bjs.gov/content/pub/pdf/nsleed.pdf (updated: 4 October 2016).

[29] Department of Homeland Security, "Creation of the Department of Homeland Security," dhs.gov/creation-department-homeland-security, 24 September 2015.

[30] DHS, "IF YOU SEE SOMETHING, SAY SOMETHING™," dhs.gov/see-something-say-something (accessed: 27 July 2017).

[31] *Sweden, Prevent, Preempt and Protect*, 17.

[32] *Sweden, Prevent, Preempt and Protect*, 5.

[33] Andrew Silke, *Research on Terrorism: Trends, Achievements & Failures* (New York: Frank Cass, 2004), 70.

[34] Wendy Patrick, *Red Flags: Frenemies, Underminers, and Ruthless People* (New York: St. Martin's Press, 2015), 16.

[35] Andrew Silke, *Terrorism: All That Matters* (London: Hoddler & Stoughton, 2014), 31.

[36] Randy Borum, *Psychology of Terrorism* (Tampa: University of South Florida, 2004), 5.

[37] John A. Horgan, et al., *Across the Universe? A Comparative Analysis of Violent Behavior and Radicalization Across Three Offender Types with Implications for Criminal Justice Training and Education*, June 2016, 24, ncjrs.gov/pdffiles1/nij/grants/249937.pdf (accessed: 20 September 2017).

[38] Frances Perraudin, "David Cameron: extremist ideology is 'struggle of our generation'," The Guardian, July 20, 2015, theguardian.com/politics/2015/jul/20/extremist-ideology-struggle-generation-david-cameron (accessed: 27 July 2017).

[39] Borum, *Psychology of Terrorism*, 17.

[40] Matthew Weaver, "Expert on Cameron strategy: 'People are drawn to terrorism more because of identity issues than ideology'," The Guardian, July 20, 2015. businessinsider.com/expert-on-cameron-strategy-people-are-drawn-to-terrorism-more-because-of-identity-issues-than-ideology-2015-7 (accessed: 27 July 2017).

[41] Borum, *Psychology of Terrorism*, 3.

[42] Silke, *Terrorism*, 64.

[43] Borum, *Psychology of Terrorism*, 67-68.

[44] Interneurons are components of the human nervous system.

[45] National Institute of Justice, "What Can We Learn From the Similarities and Differences Between Lone Wolf Terrorists and Mass Murderers?", January 3, 2017, nij.gov/topics/crime/terrorism/Pages/lone-wolf-terrorists-and-mass-murderers.aspx (accessed: 15 August 2017).

[46] A.H. Maslow: Hierarchy of Needs

[47] Polaris Project, polarisproject.org (accessed: 27 July 2017).

[48] Polaris Project, "Recognize the Signs," polarisproject.org/recognize-signs (accessed: 27 July 2017).

[49] Polaris Project, *The Typology of Modern Slavery,* polarisproject.org/typology-report (accessed: 27 July 2017).

[50] A.C. Carpenter, and J. Gates, *The Nature and Extent of Gang Involvement in Sex Trafficking in San Diego County* (San Diego, CA: University of San Diego and Point Loma Nazarene University, 2016), 109, ncjrs.gov/pdffiles1/nij/grants/249857.pdf (accessed: 15 August 2017).

[51] Borum, *Psychology of Terrorism*, 39.

[52] Martha Crenshaw, "The psychology of terrorism: an agenda for the 21st century," Political Psychology, 21, June 2, 2000.

[53] Picker, "ISIS's Foreign Fighters."

[54] Doug Wyllie, "8 Pre-Attack Indicators of Terrorist Activity," PoliceOne.com, (accessed: 27 July 2017).

[55] SecureTransit.org, "See Something? (What To Look For)," securetransit.org/see-something-2, (accessed: 27 July 2017).

[56] Brent Smith, Kelly Damphousse, Paxton Roberts, *Pre-Incident Indicators of Terrorist Incidents: The Identification of Behavioral, Geographic, and Temporal Patterns of Preparatory Conduct*, Doc 214217, May 2006, Abstract, 2 (updated data).

[57] FBI, "Active Shooter Resources," fbi.gov/about/partnerships/office-of-partner-engagement/active-shooter-resources (accessed: 27 July 2017).

[58] U.S. Congress, Investigative Assistance for Violent Crimes Act of 2012, H.R.2076, January 14, 2013, congress.gov/bill/112th-congress/house-bill/2076/text (accessed: 27 July 2017).

[59] Cyn Shepard, "Dylan Klebold's Journal," A Columbine Site, acolumbinesite.com/

dylan/writing/journal/journal4.html (accessed: 15 August 2017).

[60] Shepard, "Eric Harris' Webpages," A Columbine Site, acolumbinesite.com/ericpage.html, (accessed: 15 August 2017).

[61] See Police Executive Research Forum, *The Police Response to Active Shooter Incidents* (Washington D.C.: PERF, 2014) 9.

[62] PERF, Police Response, 9.

[63] Rape, Abuse & Incest National Network, RAINN, "Victims of Sexual Violence: Statistics," rainn.org/statistics/victims-sexual-violence (accessed: 15 August 2017).

[64] RAINN, "Criminal Justice System: Statistics," rainn.org/statistics/criminal-justice-system (accessed: 15 August 2017).

[65] U.S. Department of Justice, "Female Victims of Sexual Violence," 1994-2010, bjs.gov/content/pub/pdf/fvsv9410.pdf (updated: 31 May 2016).

[66] NIJ, "Intimate Partner Violence," nij.gov/topics/crime/intimate-partner-violence/Pages/welcome.aspx (accessed: 27 July 2017).

[67] National Coalition Against Domestic Violence (NCADV), "What Is Intimate Partner Abuse?", ncadv.org/files/Domestic%20Violence%20and%20Physical%20Abuse%20NCADV.pdf (accessed: 27 July 2017).

[68] CDC, Violence Prevention, "The National Intimate Partner and Sexual Violence Survey," http://www.cdc.gov/violenceprevention/nisvs/index.html (updated: 10 March 2015).

[69] Petrosky E, Blair JM, Betz CJ, Fowler KA, Jack SP, Lyons BH. "Racial and Ethnic Differences in Homicides of Adult Women and the Role of Intimate Partner Violence — United States, 2003–2014". MMWR Morb Mortal Wkly Rep 2017; 66:741–746. DOI: dx.doi.org/10.15585/mmwr.mm6628a1, (accessed: 15 August 2017).

[70] Patrick, *Red Flags*, 11.

[71] The National Domestic Violence Hotline, "Abuse Defined," thehotline.org/is-this-abuse/abuse-defined (accessed: 15 August 2017).

[72] U.S. Department of Justice, Office on Violence Against Women, "What is Domestic Violence?", justice.gov/ovw/domestic-violence (updated: 16 June 2017).

[73] Lawrence Robinson, Joanna Saisan, and Jeanne Segal, "Elder Abuse and Neglect," Helpguide.org, helpguide.org/articles/abuse/elder-abuse-and-neglect.htm#types, (updated: April 2017).

[74] Federal Bureau of Investigation, "Business E-Mail Compromise: The 3.1 Billion Dollar Scam," Alert Number I-061416-PSA, June 14, 2016, ic3.gov/media/2016/160614.aspx.

[75] Center for Innovative Public Health Research, "Who's Targeted?", cyberbully411.com/whos-targeted (accessed: 27 July 2017).

[76] Sameer Hinduja and Justin Patchin, "Bullying Laws Across America," Cyberbullying Research Center, cyberbullying.org/bullying-laws (updated: June 2017).

[77] Center, "Who Are Cyberbullies?", cyberbully411.com/who-cyberbullies (accessed: 27 July 2017).

[78] Center, "Myths and Facts," cyberbully411.com/myths-and-facts (accessed: 27 July

2017).

[79] *Cambridge Dictionary.* Cambridge University Press, dictionary.cambridge.org/us/dictionary/english/housebreaker (accessed: 27 July 2017).

[80] NIJ, "Most Victims Know Their Attacker," nij.gov/topics/crime/rape-sexual-violence/campus/pages/know-attacker.aspx (accessed: 27 July 2017).

[81] National Rifle Association of America, *Eddie Eagle GunSafe® Program*, eddieeagle.nra.org (accessed: 27 July 2017).

[82] National Center for Missing & Exploited Children, "If Your Child Is Missing," missingkids.com/MissingChild (accessed: 27 July 2017).

[83] Undercover Colors, undercovercolors.com (accessed: 15 August 2017).

[84] DHS, "Active Shooter Preparedness," dhs.gov/active-shooter-preparedness (updated: 12 May, 2017).

[85] Will Garbe, "Guns in schools: Mad River Schools trains 32 staff to shoot intruders", Dayton Daily News, 9 August 2017, daytondailynews.com/news/local/guns-schools-mad-river-schools-trains-staff-shoot-intruders (accessed: 17 August 2017).

[86] Hotline, "Get Help Today," thehotline.org/help/ (accessed 27 July 2017).

[87] U.S. Department of Homeland Security, *Guide for Developing High Quality Emergency Plans for Houses of Worship*, rems.ed.gov/docs/EOPGuide_HOW_Webinar.pdf (25 July 2013), 33. Complete document: fema.gov/media-library/assets/documents/33007?id=7649 (updated: 1 May 2014).

[88] Federal Trade Commission, "National Do Not Call Registry," consumer.ftc.gov/articles/0108-national-do-not-call-registry (updated: March 2017).

[89] FBI, "Internet Crime Complaint Center" (IC3), ic3.gov/default.aspx (accessed: 27 July 2017).

[90] National Crime Prevention Council, "Neighborhood Watch," ncpc.org/topics/home-and-neighborhood-safety/neighborhood-watch (accessed: 27 July 2017).

[91] Hotline, thehotline.org/help (accessed: 15 August 2017).

[92] HelpGuide.org, helpguide.org/articles/abuse/help-for-abused-and-battered-women.htm (updated: April 2017).

[93] Hotline, "Is Change Possible In An Abuser?," thehotline.org/2013/09/is-change-possible-in-an-abuser/ (accessed: 27 July 2017).

[94] Gary Kleck and Marc Gertz, *Armed Resistance to Crime: The Prevalence and Nature of Self-Defense with a Gun*, Journal of Criminal Law and Criminology Vol. 86 No1 Fall (1995), 185, scholarlycommons.law.northwestern.edu/cgi/viewcontent.cgi?article=6853&context=jclc (accessed: 27 July 2017).

[95] USCCA, usconcealedcarry.com (accessed: 27 July 2017).

[96] International Overdose Awareness Day — August 31, 2017. MMWR Morb Mortal Wkly Rep 2017;66:897. DOI:dx.doi.org/10.15585/mmwr.mm634a1 (accessed: 27 October 2017).

[97] "Molestigation" is low-grade molestation to test the willingness of a potential victim.

ENDNOTES

[98] Surpasternal (Jugular) Notch is the soft area above the Manubrium Sterni, which is the small bone above the sternum.

[99] Call your local law enforcement department, or search "report elder abuse" to find help in your region.

[100] DHS, "Active Shooter Pocket Card," dhs.gov/sites/default/files/publications/active_shooter_pocket_card_508.pdf (accessed: 27 July 2017).

[101] ADA.gov, "Information and Technical Assistance on the American Disabilities Act," ada.gov (accessed: 27 July 2017).

[102] SDTS, myselfdefensetraining.com (accessed: 27 July 2017).

[103] National Center on Elder Abuse, "Statistics/Data," ncea.acl.gov/whatwedo/research/statistics.html#18 (accessed 27 July 2017).

[104] IC3, ic3.gov (accessed 27 July 2017).

[105] Doug Wyllie, "8 pre-attack indicators of terrorist activity," PoliceOne.com, policeone.com/terrorism/articles/3421116-8-pre-attack-indicators-of-terrorist-activity, March 11, 2011.

[106] National Do Not Call Registry, donotcall.gov (accessed: 27 July 2017).

[107] In the United Kingdom, dial 9-9-9. In Australia, dial 0-0-0.

[108] IC3, ic3.gov (accessed 27 July 2017).

[109] Warren v. District of Columbia, District of Columbia Court of Appeals, December 21, 1981.

Made in the USA
San Bernardino, CA
16 February 2019